IMAGES
of America

PENDLETON COUNTY

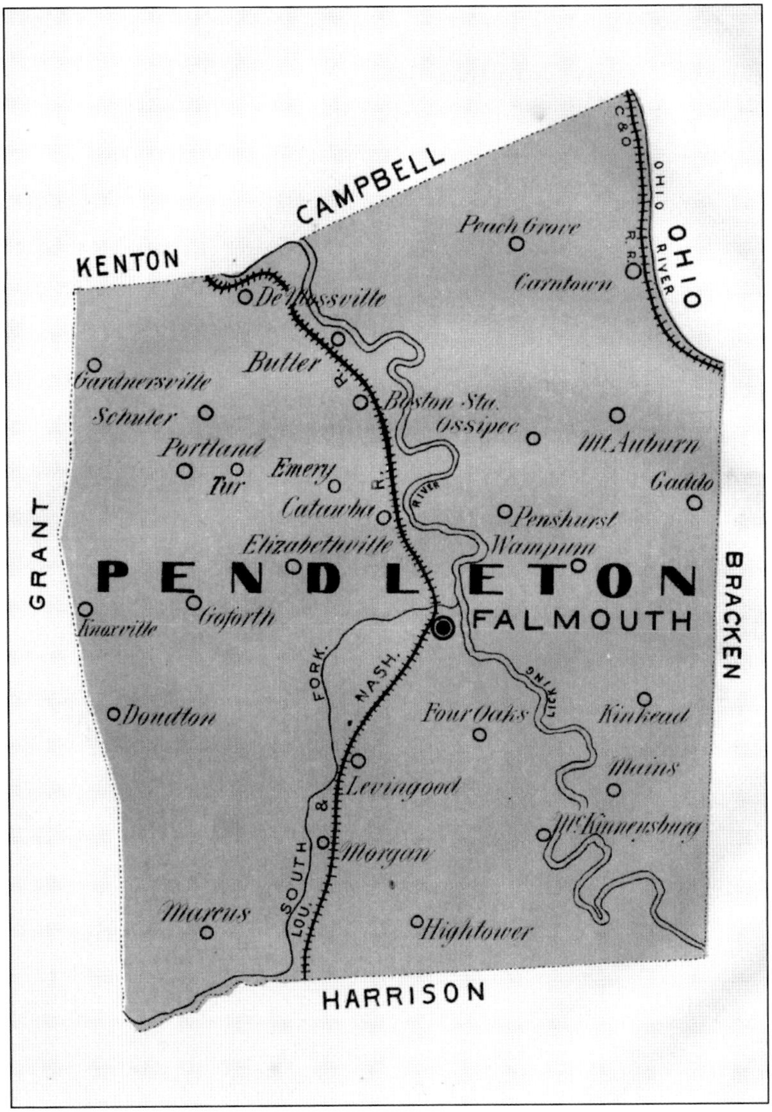

This map shows Pendleton County's many towns and small communities. Falmouth is the county seat, located at the fork of the Main and South Fork Licking Rivers. Butler, the next largest town, is in the northern part of the county. Pendleton County is bordered by the Ohio River and five other counties. (Courtesy of the Pendleton County Historical and Genealogical Society.)

On the Cover: This early 20th-century photograph shows a group of unidentified loggers and guests posed around a large log within a portable sawmill. It was common to use this type of saw for raising a building near the logging site, especially on hills or in areas where it would be difficult to haul the logs out and the lumber back.

IMAGES
of America

PENDLETON COUNTY

Penny Tuemler Conrad

ARCADIA
PUBLISHING

ISBN 978-0-7385-8621-2

Published by Arcadia Publishing
Charleston, South Carolina

Printed in the United States of America

Library of Congress Control Number: 2010922402

For all general information, please contact Arcadia Publishing:
Telephone 843-853-2070
Fax 843-853-0044
E-mail sales@arcadiapublishing.com
For customer service and orders:
Toll-Free 1-888-313-2665

Visit us on the Internet at www.arcadiapublishing.com

This book is dedicated to my mother, who has instilled in me a love of history; to my sister, Hope, who asked, "Why don't you publish a pictorial history book?"; and to my husband, Russ, who continues to support me as I try new things.

Contents

ACKNOWLEDGMENTS

Until one begins a study of local history, it is hard to realize how much there is yet to learn. This project was indeed a time of learning for me. Thanks to all who said yes to my call for photographs and information about the community. Thanks to the Pendleton County Historical and Genealogical Society for their assistance and support. A special thanks to Teresa Johnston for her tireless assistance. Thanks to my family, who gave of their time when I needed some, their energy as mine ran out, and their encouragement as time passed, allowing me to complete this endeavor. Thanks to Amy Perryman, my editor, for her patience and strong support.

Unless otherwise noted, all photographs are from the author's collection.

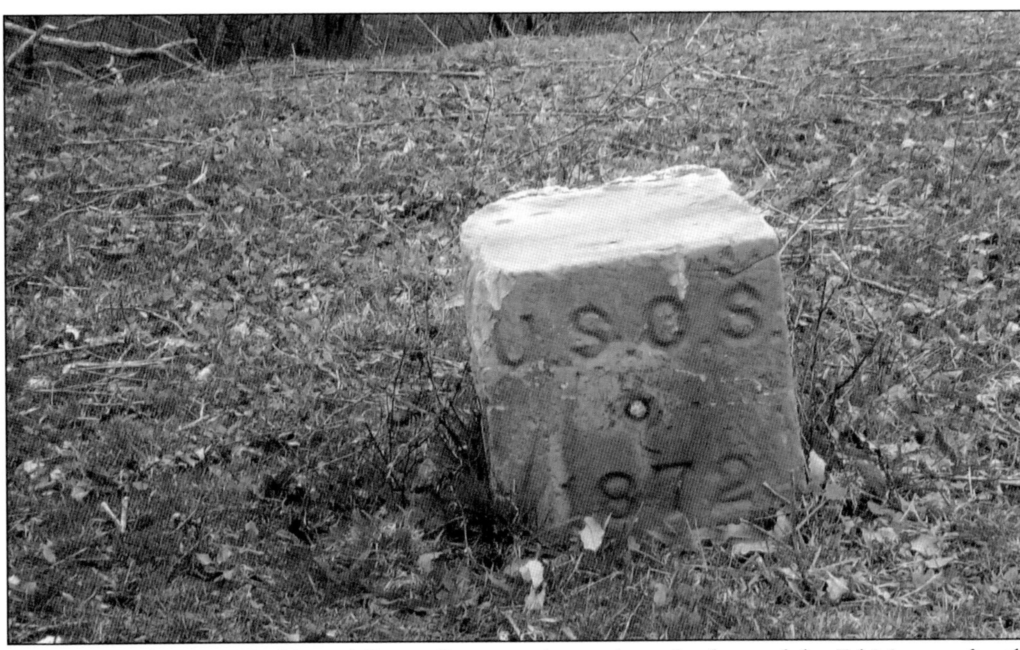

This marker for the 1872 United States Census is located on the farm of the Ed Monroe family just north of Falmouth. The placement of the marker indicates that in 1872 this point was the center of the United States based on population. (Courtesy of Alex Monroe.)

Introduction

Over 200 years have passed since a group of pioneer families traveled from Virginia, Pennsylvania, and other eastern colonies to the wilderness now known as Pendleton County. With lands ranging from rolling hills to rich river bottoms, it seemed a good place to settle. Many of these early explorers were former soldiers of the Revolutionary War who received bounty land grants for their services to the patriot cause. Others found they could obtain cheap land here, while some wished for space and the rich forests for hunting.

Pendleton County was born of lands taken from recently formed Bracken and Campbell Counties through an act of the Kentucky General Assembly on December 13, 1796. The county took its name from judge Edmund Pendleton of Carolina County, Virginia, who was a statesman, surveyor, and member of the House of Burgesses. It comprised approximately 300 square miles of land including a small portion bordering the Ohio River. This area gave access to the large waterway and provided a means by which commerce was available with Cincinnati, Louisville, and towns back east.

The county is dominated by its rivers, the Main Licking and the South Fork Licking, with many tributaries feeding their water supply. These creeks and springs made the area a most habitable place. Rich bottomland, with its dark soil, encouraged crops, but the area remained almost wilderness for more than 50 years until the coming of the railroad and bridges. Falmouth (or "Forks of the Licking" as it was first called) received its charter in 1793, three years before the county was established. Located at the confluence of the two Licking Rivers, Falmouth had been noted by early surveyors. Upon receiving parcels of these lands, three early Virginians—John Cook, William McDowell, and John Waller—divided the land and auctioned it. Thus the town of Falmouth was organized. Most people believe the name was chosen as a reminder of Falmouth, Virginia.

Many smaller communities were founded during later years. Four besides Falmouth were large enough to incorporate. In March of 1860, Catawba and DeMossville incorporated, while Boston Station and Butler did so in February 1868. Today many members of the older families continue to identify themselves as living in places like Flower Creek, Peach Grove, Gardnersville, Four Oaks, McKenneysburg, Mount Auburn, Knoxville, and Carntown. These smaller communities were once centers of much activity supplied by their churches and schools, general stores, mills, blacksmiths, and many other small businesses. Today most are gone, leaving only a church or cemetery to mark what once was.

The roadways connecting these towns were old war roads or wagon roads made by early explorers traversing Native American lands. In 1852, Pendleton County saw the arrival of the Kentucky Central Railroad, later a part of the Louisville and Nashville Railroad. In 1854, the first suspension bridge was built over the Main Licking River at Falmouth; in 1871, there was one at Butler, and another in Morgan about the same time. These two improvements in the means of traveling beyond the borders of the towns and communities brought an increase in the population of Pendleton County and an expansion of trade by allowing a faster and easier connection with the markets in Louisville and Cincinnati. Until this time, Pendleton County had still been seen as a backwoods community.

Schooling was important to the people who settled here, but with the distances between families and the poor means of transportation, providing local children with an education proved to be a great challenge. Only one common school is known to have existed in 1844. By 1876, however, records note 68 schools for whites and 3 for nonwhites. Butler had its first one-room school in 1856. Most of these schools offered very basic courses of study, and the quality of the buildings and instructors varied greatly. Few high schools existed early on, but in 1814, the private Pendleton Academy (or Seminary) was built in Falmouth. In 1909, Falmouth, Butler, and Morgan all had high schools. By the mid-1960s all the smaller schools had been consolidated into one high school and six grade schools. By 1972, the grade schools had consolidated to two: one at the northern end of the county and another in Falmouth.

The early years found the settlers struggling with nature as they spent their time and energy clearing land for crops and building new homes and businesses. Then many found themselves involved again with new wars. In the War of 1812, large numbers of Kentuckians, including several from Pendleton County, fought against the British at the Battle of River Raisin in Michigan. The Civil War brought years of hardship. Pendleton County, as part of a border state, did not officially side with either North or South, but in truth, there was no neutrality. The high level of partisan feeling could be seen in the large numbers of men who signed up to fight for either the Union or the Confederacy. In some cases, these choices even divided families and friends. Pendleton County saw no true battles and only a couple of skirmishes. Northern troops passed through as they moved south to battle in Central Kentucky, Tennessee, and Georgia. World War I and World War II saw a large number of local young men, some only boys, climb aboard the train and head north to Covington or Cincinnati for induction into the service. Eleven local women have also been identified as having served in World War II. Many others gave of themselves by maintaining the businesses and family back home. Today Pendleton County still has young men and women giving of themselves in service to their country.

Over the years, life in the county was not all work. Plenty of events, gatherings, and activities added fun and pleasure to the days. There have been businesses that offered food and liquid refreshment along with music and companionship. In the early years, the second floor over several businesses was the place where people could find a ballroom for more formal dances and parties. Churches and schools offered plays, concerts, and picnics. Falmouth and Butler had movie houses. There was a skating rink and outdoor dances at the local ice cream shops. One of the all-time favorite events of summer was the Falmouth Fair. Held on grounds just outside town, it brought visitors from the surrounding counties by wagon, train, and, later, by cars. At one time, it was said to be one of the biggest and best fairs in the state of Kentucky.

Pendleton County has also seen times of hardship. In 1937, the area dealt with a flood in Falmouth and Butler, trying the faith and will of the citizens. In 1948, the rivers again rose to new heights. In 1964, the rivers rose even higher to flood the whole west end of Falmouth and large areas in Morgan, McKinneysburg, Demossville, and Butler. The high-water mark set during the flood of 1964 stood until 1997, when the Licking Rivers bested the old record by 5 feet. This time the rivers flooded most of Falmouth, a large area of Butler, and the lowlands throughout the county. This flood inundated homes and businesses, and left most people with only fragments of their earlier lives. Between the floods, the county experienced a devastating tornado in 1968, which tore apart numerous homes in the east end of Falmouth.

Even with all the trials, tribulations, and changes felt by this community, it stands tall and proud of its citizens and what has been accomplished over the years. Please enjoy this journey through past times in Pendleton County, Kentucky.

One

Schools and Churches

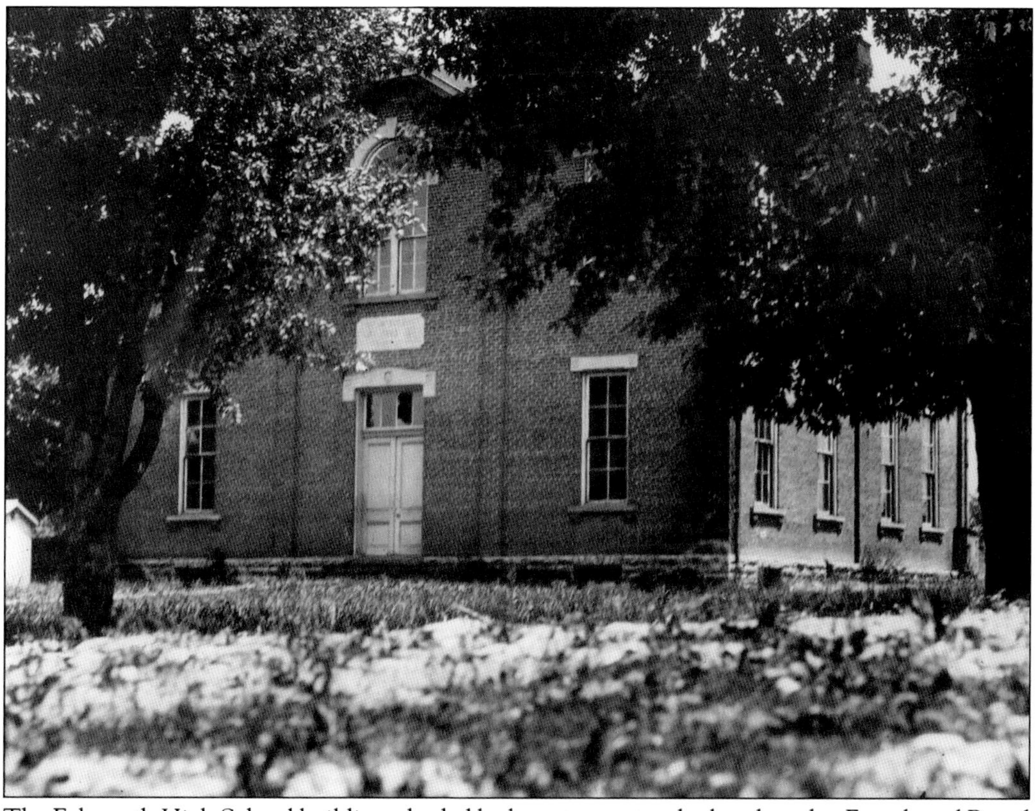

The Falmouth High School building, shaded by large trees, stands abandoned at Fourth and Broad Streets. It was a two-story structure of eight classrooms. For a time the building also served as Pendleton County High School. In the late 1920s, this building was torn down, and a new one was built on Chapel Street. That building served students from first grade through high school until 1968. Today several beams and lentils from the old building can be found as architectural parts of at least one home on Robbins Avenue.

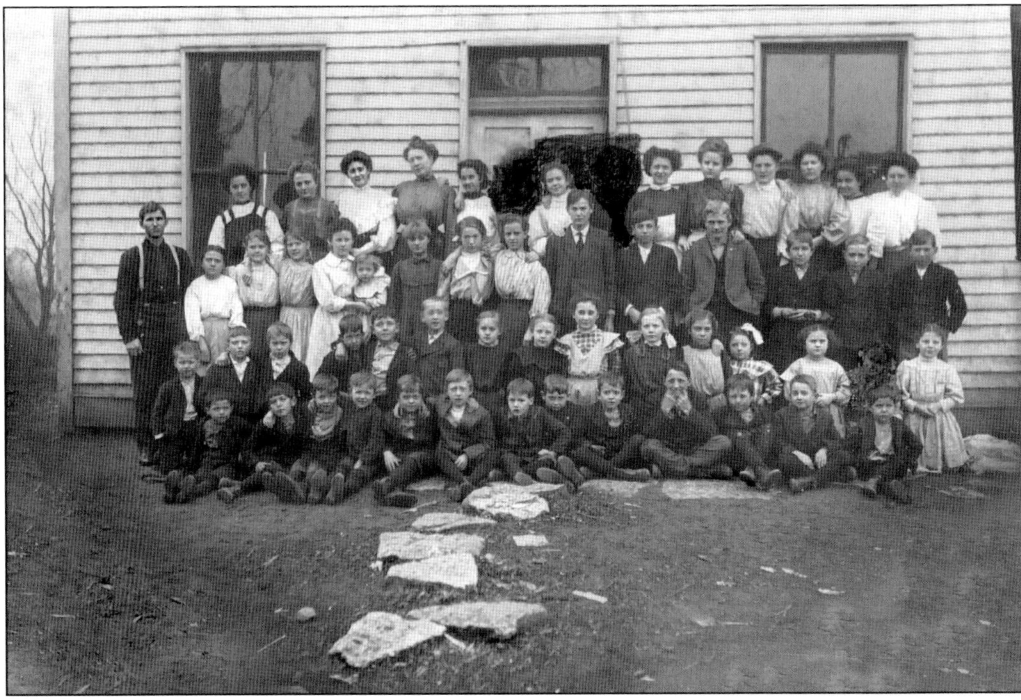

New Hope School could be found on the road that connected Foster with the crossroad, giving a view of the river area and valleys. In 1914 it served 32 pupils for 14 families with Jessie Rush as the teacher. In this photograph, Elizabeth Nordheim is the fourth girl from the right in the back row, and Anna Nordheim, her sister, is the fifth girl from the left in the back row. (Courtesy of Keith Gunkel.)

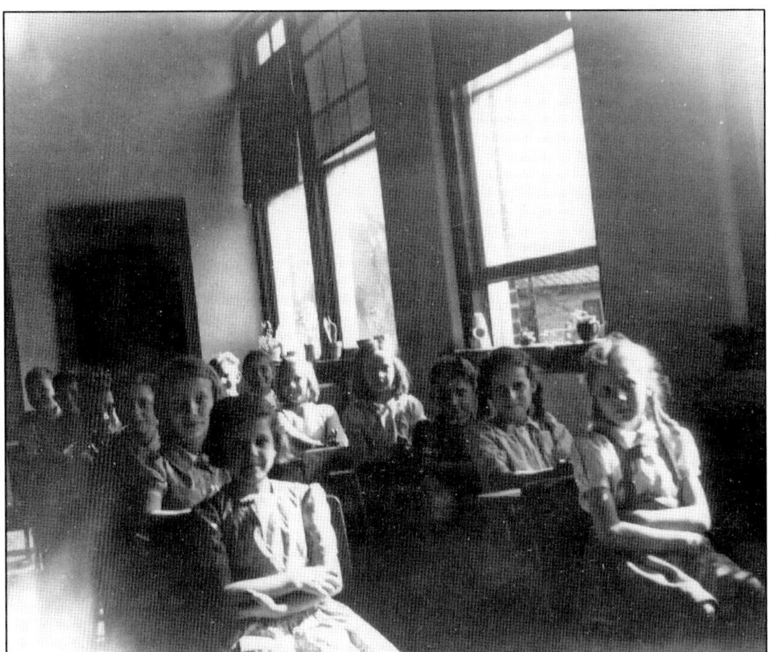

Seen here is the inside of a typical schoolroom around 1950. Note the wooden desks, which would have been bolted to the floor and arranged one behind another, with a drop-down seat at the front. The windows were quite tall, allowing the natural airflow needed before the days of air conditioning. (Courtesy of Billie Newman.)

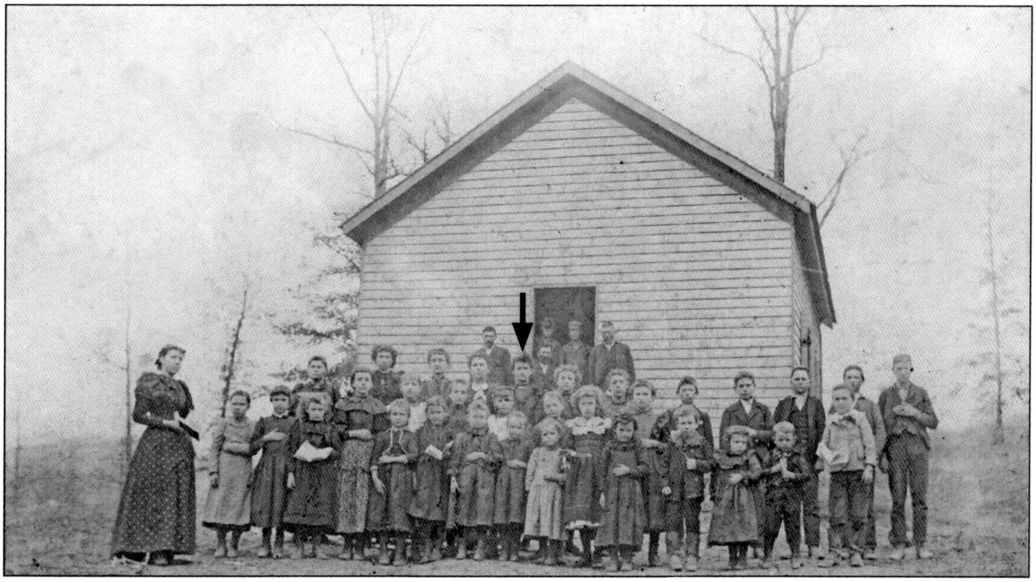

In this picture taken about 1914, a group of students from the Hall School are seen posing for a traveling photographer with their teacher, Nona Wright. Bessie Lee Hall is noted with the arrow. (Courtesy of Joyce Carson.)

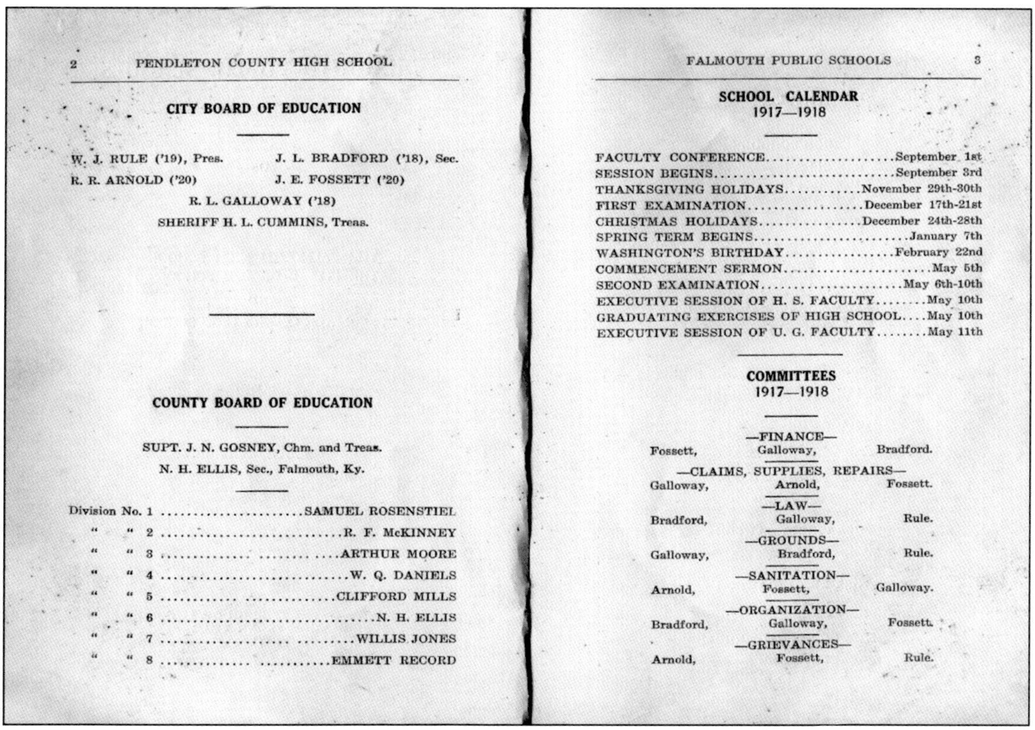

2 PENDLETON COUNTY HIGH SCHOOL

CITY BOARD OF EDUCATION

W. J. RULE ('19), Pres. J. L. BRADFORD ('18), Sec.
R. R. ARNOLD ('20) J. E. FOSSETT ('20)
R. L. GALLOWAY ('18)
SHERIFF H. L. CUMMINS, Treas.

COUNTY BOARD OF EDUCATION

SUPT. J. N. GOSNEY, Chm. and Treas.
N. H. ELLIS, Sec., Falmouth, Ky.

Division No. 1 .... SAMUEL ROSENSTIEL
" " 2 .... R. F. McKINNEY
" " 3 .... ARTHUR MOORE
" " 4 .... W. Q. DANIELS
" " 5 .... CLIFFORD MILLS
" " 6 .... N. H. ELLIS
" " 7 .... WILLIS JONES
" " 8 .... EMMETT RECORD

FALMOUTH PUBLIC SCHOOLS 3

SCHOOL CALENDAR
1917—1918

FACULTY CONFERENCE .... September 1st
SESSION BEGINS .... September 3rd
THANKSGIVING HOLIDAYS .... November 29th-30th
FIRST EXAMINATION .... December 17th-21st
CHRISTMAS HOLIDAYS .... December 24th-28th
SPRING TERM BEGINS .... January 7th
WASHINGTON'S BIRTHDAY .... February 22nd
COMMENCEMENT SERMON .... May 5th
SECOND EXAMINATION .... May 6th-10th
EXECUTIVE SESSION OF H. S. FACULTY .... May 10th
GRADUATING EXERCISES OF HIGH SCHOOL .... May 10th
EXECUTIVE SESSION OF U. G. FACULTY .... May 11th

COMMITTEES
1917—1918

—FINANCE—
Fossett, Galloway, Bradford.
—CLAIMS, SUPPLIES, REPAIRS—
Galloway, Arnold, Fossett.
—LAW—
Bradford, Galloway, Rule.
—GROUNDS—
Galloway, Bradford, Rule.
—SANITATION—
Arnold, Fossett, Galloway.
—ORGANIZATION—
Bradford, Galloway, Fossett.
—GRIEVANCES—
Arnold, Fossett, Rule.

The officials in charge of the Pendleton County city school in 1917–1918 were W. J. Rule, R. R. Arnold, J. L. Bradford, J. E. Fossitt, R. L. Galloway, and Sheriff H. L. Cummins. County Superintendent J. N. Gosney was the chairman and treasurer, with N. H. Ellis as secretary of the eight divisions of the county schools. Each division had a principal. Note that the school year stretched from September to early May. (Courtesy of Cheryl York.)

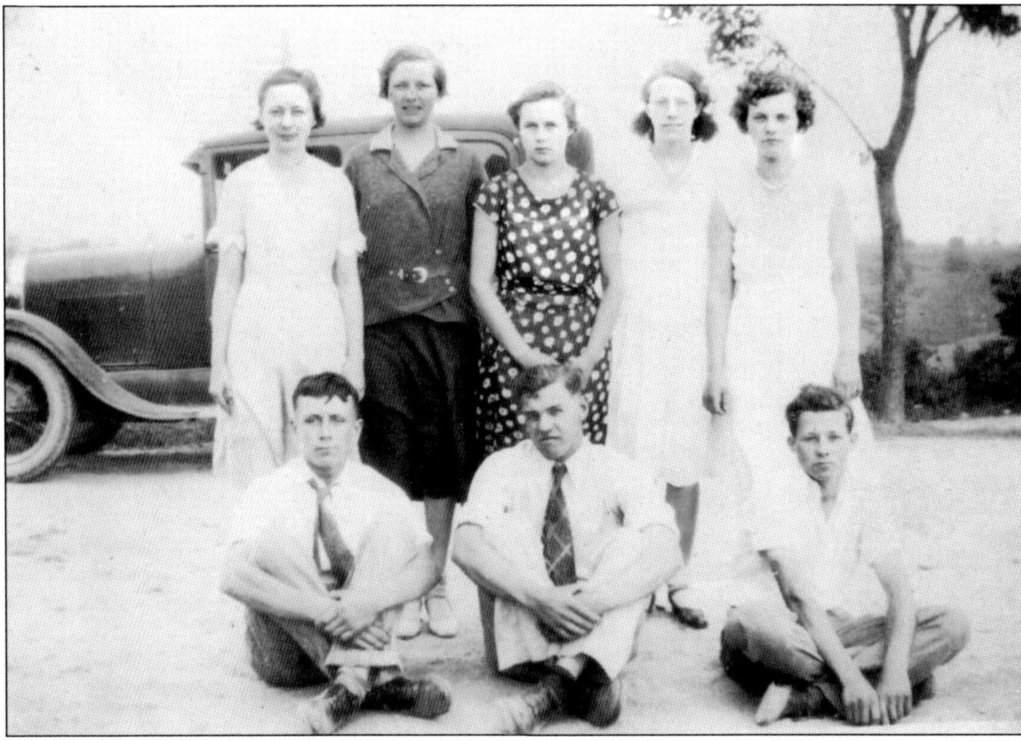

Shown here taking a break from studies is the Goforth School sophomore class of 1932. From left to right, the students are (first row) Orman Conrad, Clyde Buckley, and James Chiles; (second row) Agnes Poor, Emma Lou Dance, Virginia Blackburn, and Roberta Hutchison. At this time, Goforth held classes for grades one through twelve.

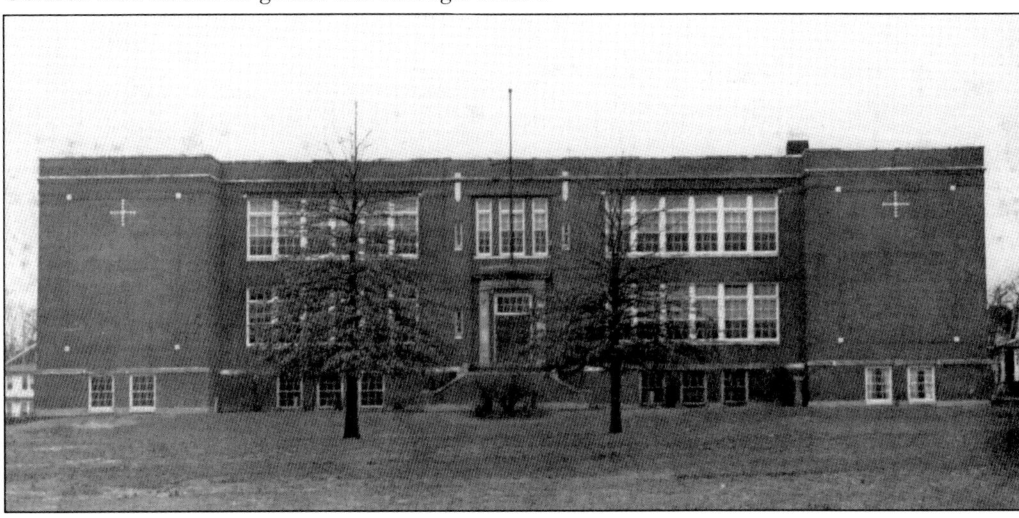

This Falmouth School building served the Falmouth community from about 1928 until 1968, accommodating first through twelfth grades. In 1968, it became an elementary and junior high school for first through eighth grades. The high school students merged with the existing county high school. In 1972, the school's role changed again when it became a middle school housing the county's seventh and eighth grades. When a new middle school was built in 1998, it became the Falmouth School Center and serves as such today. (Courtesy of Hallie Hart.)

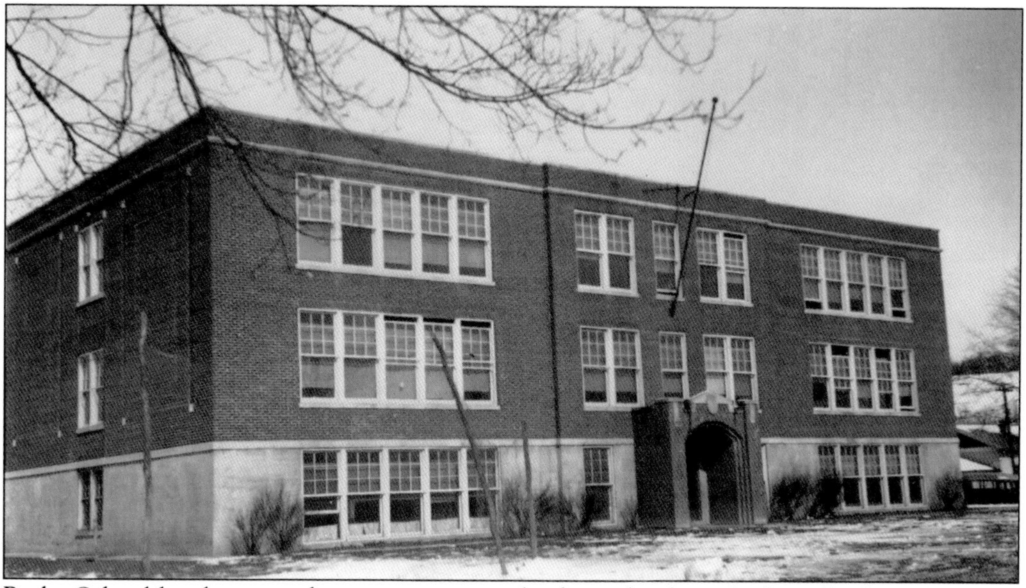

Butler School has been on the same site since the first school was built in the late 1860s as a one-room school. In 1931, Butler School consolidated and became a part of a county system. It held a high school until a new county school, Pendleton Memorial High School, opened in 1959. Today the school is an apartment complex.

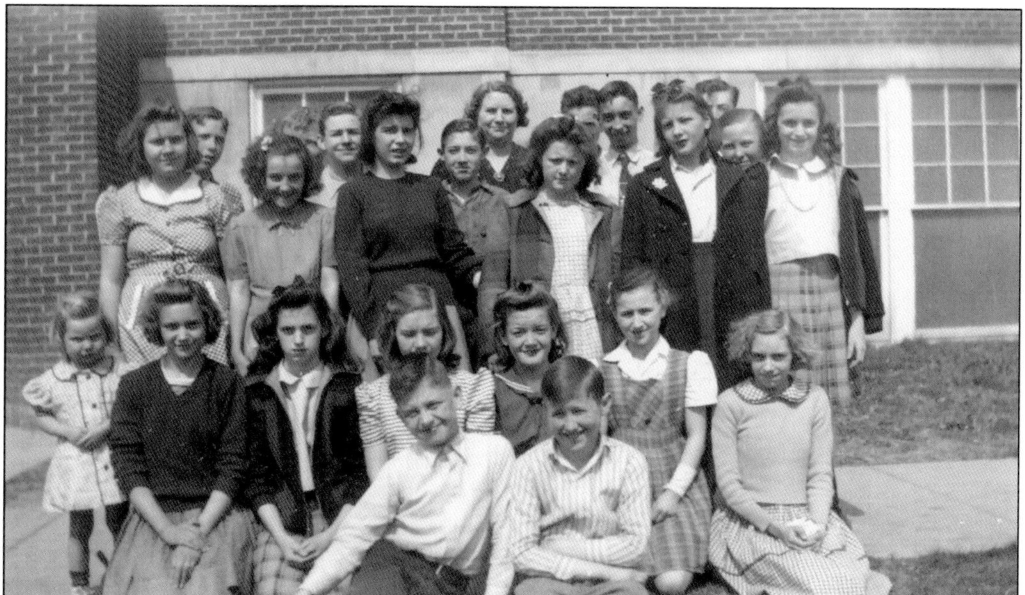

Butler seventh graders pose for a class photograph in 1943–1944. From left to right, they are (first row) Carl Eckert and J. B. Whitaker; (second row) two unidentified, Alta Mae Fryer, Mary Helen Pribble, Betty Brownfield, Carletta Jenkins, and Bonnie Clifford; (third row) ? Lunsford, Joyce McLaughlin, Roma Burlew, John Goins, Ann Buchanan, unidentified, and Alma Faye Fryer; (fourth row) "Corky" Burlew, unidentified, Virgil Hale, teacher Edna Nagel, Ray Wolfe, Melvin Jenkins, unidentified, and Earl Hart.

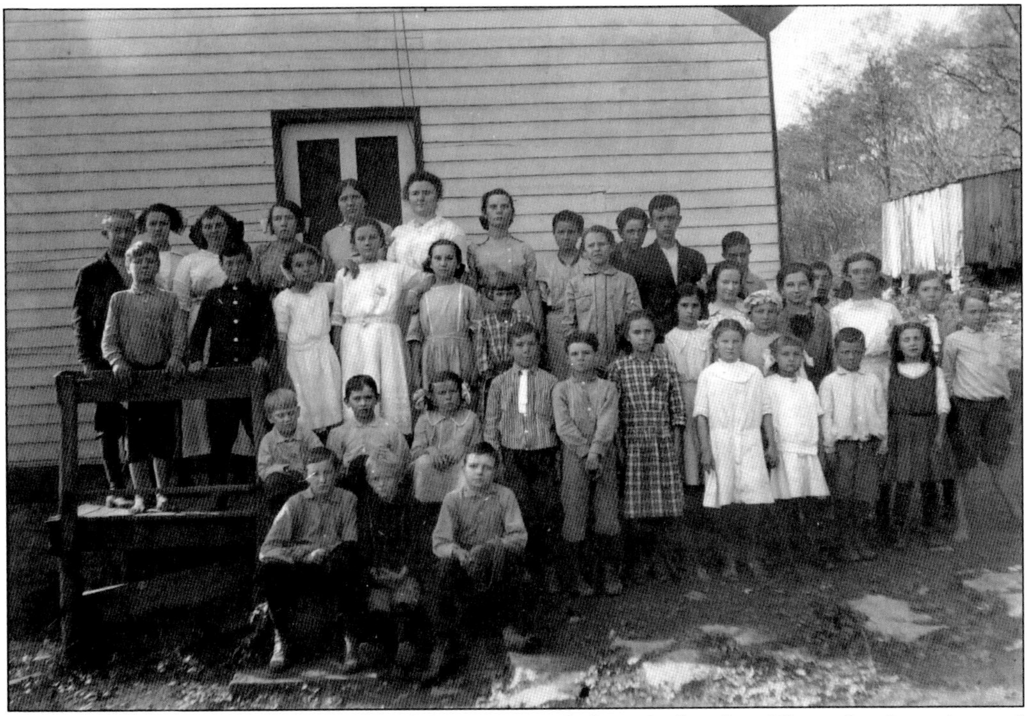

Concord School had an enrollment of about 43 pupils from 21 families. This school was located northeast of Falmouth on the Concord-Lenoxburg Road. Emma Stevens served as the teacher during this time. (Courtesy of Velma Steele.)

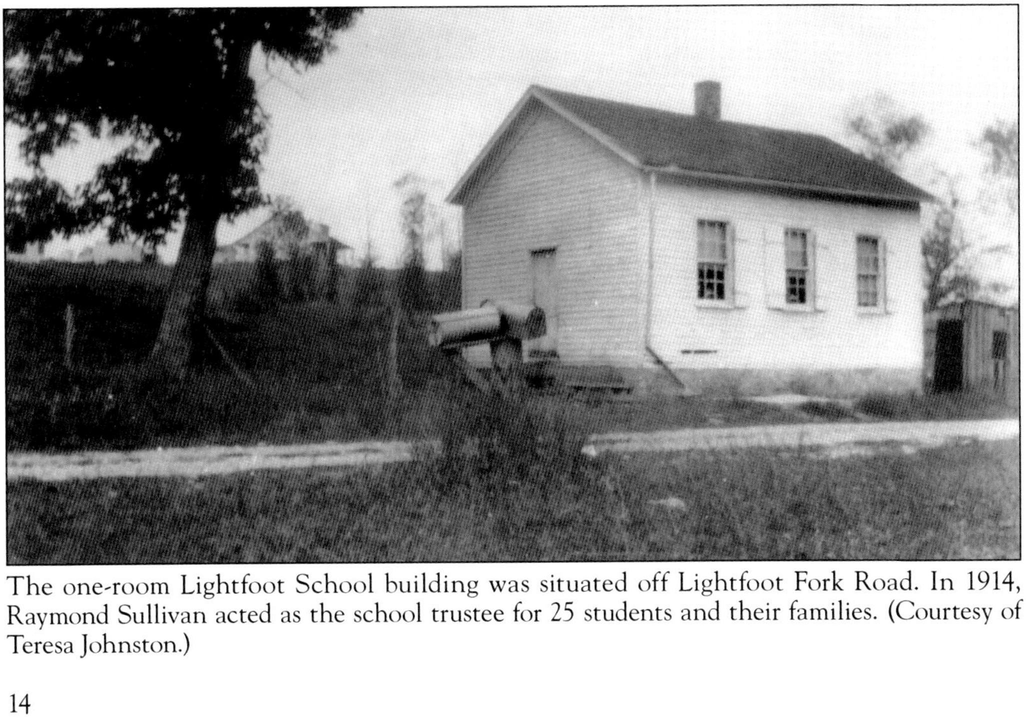

The one-room Lightfoot School building was situated off Lightfoot Fork Road. In 1914, Raymond Sullivan acted as the school trustee for 25 students and their families. (Courtesy of Teresa Johnston.)

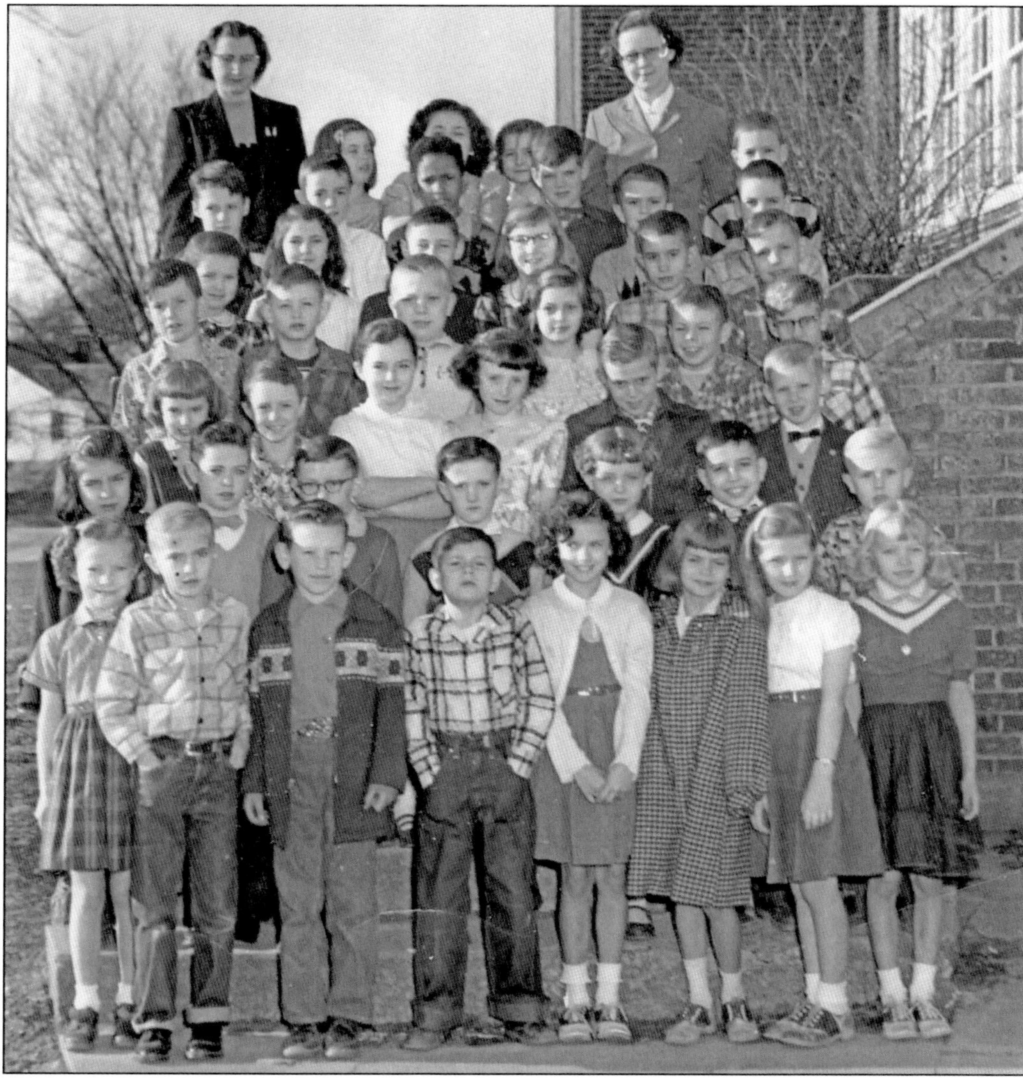

Standing on the entrance steps to Falmouth School in 1957 are the two third-grade classrooms taught by Ella Bishop and Ruby Wright. From left to right, the students are (first row) Lois McNees, C. W. Snodgrass, Ronnie Lawrence, Roger Justice, Linda House, Brenda Smith, Cheryl Hughes, and Janice Thompson; (second row) Ruth Allender, Donald Leadingham, Wendel Miles, Clay Ramsey, Carolyn Hesler, Franklin Thompson, and unidentified; (third row) Jonna Lynn Bass, Roger Wolfe, Barbara Slocum, Diane Arnold, unidentified, and Russ Conrad; (fourth row) unidentified, Lamen Goins, Jim Thomlin, Joyce King, Terry Florence, and Ray Bishop; (fifth row) Patsy Harrison, Beverly Piercefield, Billy Daugherty, two unidentified, and David Klee; (sixth row) Curtis Reeves, Gary McMillin, Alonzo Allen, Roger Winkle, unidentified, and Mark Browning; (seventh row) teacher Ruby Wright, Wanda Allender, Connie Clemons, Connie Finley, teacher Ella Bishop, and Steve Craig.

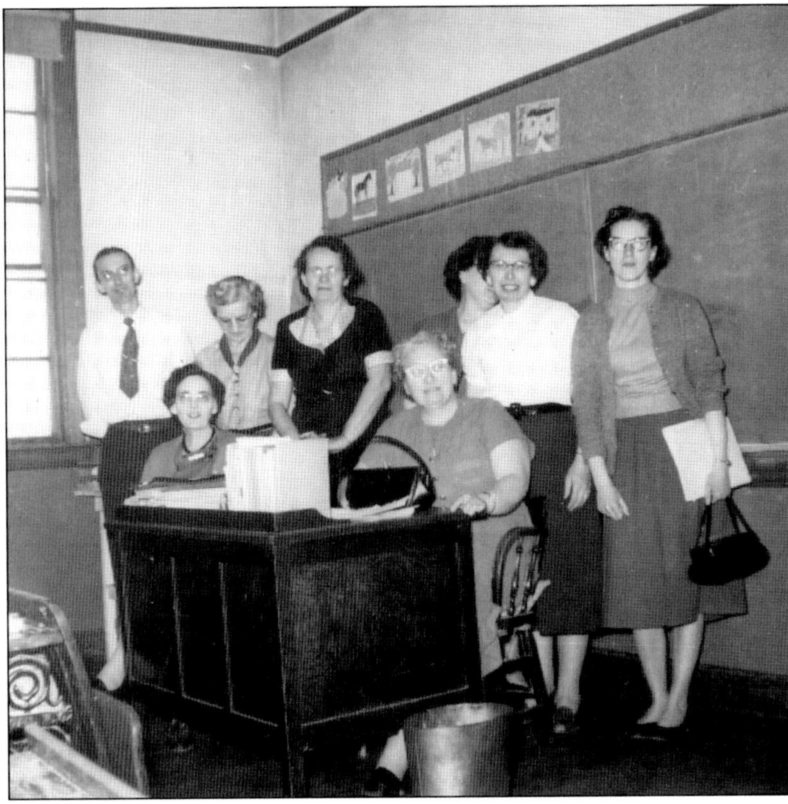

Several teachers from Mount Auburn School met after school to discuss the day's events. From left to right are (seated) Ethel Norris and Margaret Morford; (standing) J. W. McKinney, Anna McClanahan, Ardina Sharp, Gertrude Morris, Lena Cooper, and Lona Kemplin. (Courtesy of J. W. McKinney.)

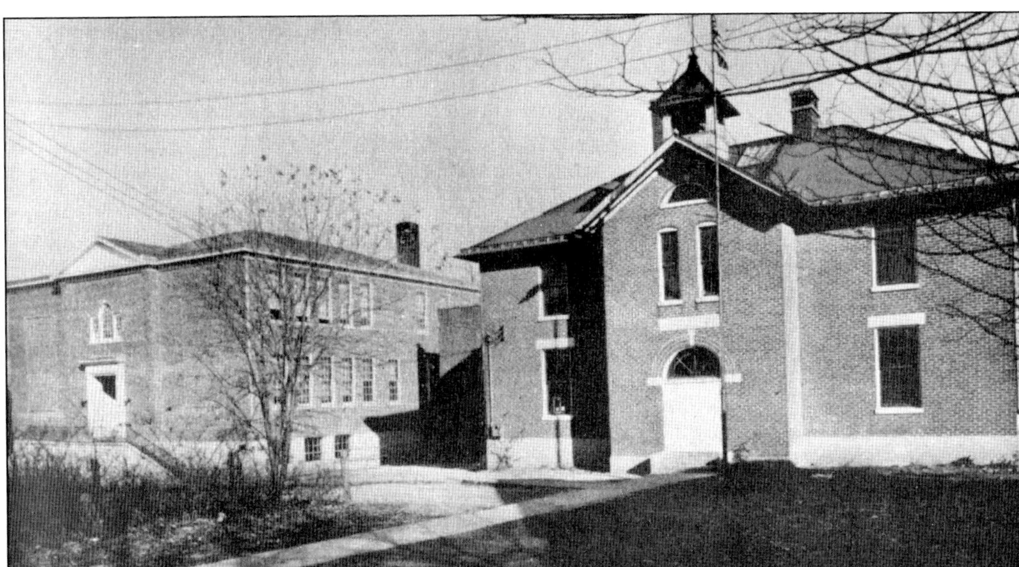

In 1909 Morgan High School was one of three high schools in Pendleton County. It was a brick building located near the banks of the South Fork Licking River in Morgan. The first graduating class in 1920 was comprised of only two students. One of Morgan's most distinguished graduates was Kenny Price, who later became a popular star of the television programs *Midwestern Hayride* and *Hee Haw*. (Courtesy of Nancy Gulick Harville.)

In 1902 School District #71 had six grades with W. Q. Daniel as their teacher. Thirty-seven students from 15 families were under his leadership. Hattie S. Orr was the superintendent, and Owen Dunaway was the chairman of the board. The two trustees were Calvin Fryer and S. A. Yelton, who also served as treasurer. (Courtesy of the Opal Jackson family.)

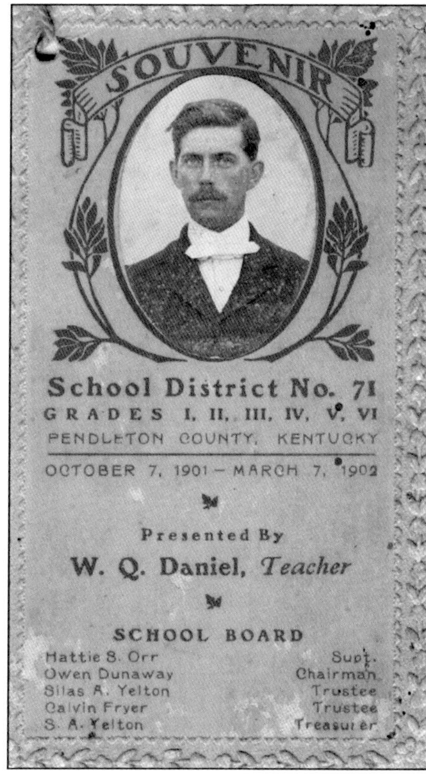

SOUVENIR

School District No. 71
GRADES I, II, III, IV, V, VI
PENDLETON COUNTY, KENTUCKY
OCTOBER 7, 1901 – MARCH 7, 1902

Presented By
W. Q. Daniel, *Teacher*

SCHOOL BOARD

Hattie S. Orr	Supt.
Owen Dunaway	Chairman
Silas A. Yelton	Trustee
Calvin Fryer	Trustee
S. A. Yelton	Treasurer

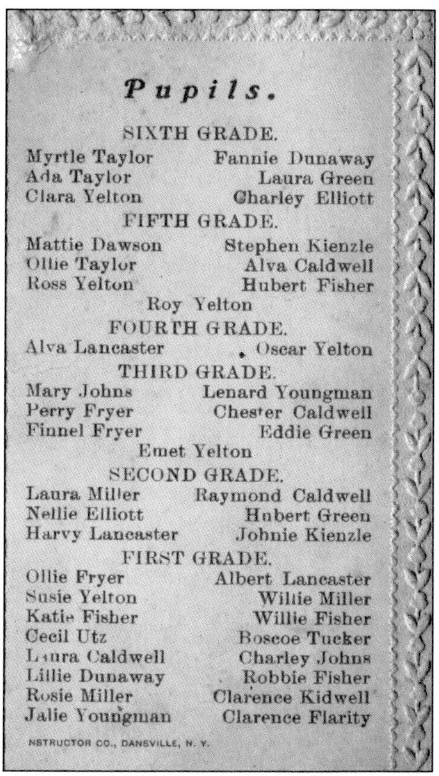

Pupils.

SIXTH GRADE.

Myrtle Taylor	Fannie Dunaway
Ada Taylor	Laura Green
Clara Yelton	Charley Elliott

FIFTH GRADE.

Mattie Dawson	Stephen Kienzle
Ollie Taylor	Alva Caldwell
Ross Yelton	Hubert Fisher

Roy Yelton

FOURTH GRADE.

Alva Lancaster	Oscar Yelton

THIRD GRADE.

Mary Johns	Lenard Youngman
Perry Fryer	Chester Caldwell
Finnel Fryer	Eddie Green

Emet Yelton

SECOND GRADE.

Laura Miller	Raymond Caldwell
Nellie Elliott	Hubert Green
Harvy Lancaster	Johnie Kienzle

FIRST GRADE.

Ollie Fryer	Albert Lancaster
Susie Yelton	Willie Miller
Katie Fisher	Willie Fisher
Cecil Utz	Boscoe Tucker
Laura Caldwell	Charley Johns
Lillie Dunaway	Robbie Fisher
Rosie Miller	Clarence Kidwell
Jalie Youngman	Clarence Flarity

NSTRUCTOR CO., DANSVILLE, N. Y.

For this five-month school year, stretching from October 7, 1901, to March 7, 1902, six students were enrolled in the sixth grade, six in the fifth grade, two in the fourth grade, seven in the third grade, six in the second grade, and ten in the first grade. At the end of the year, a card like this was presented to each student as a gift from their teacher. (Courtesy of the Opal Jackson family.)

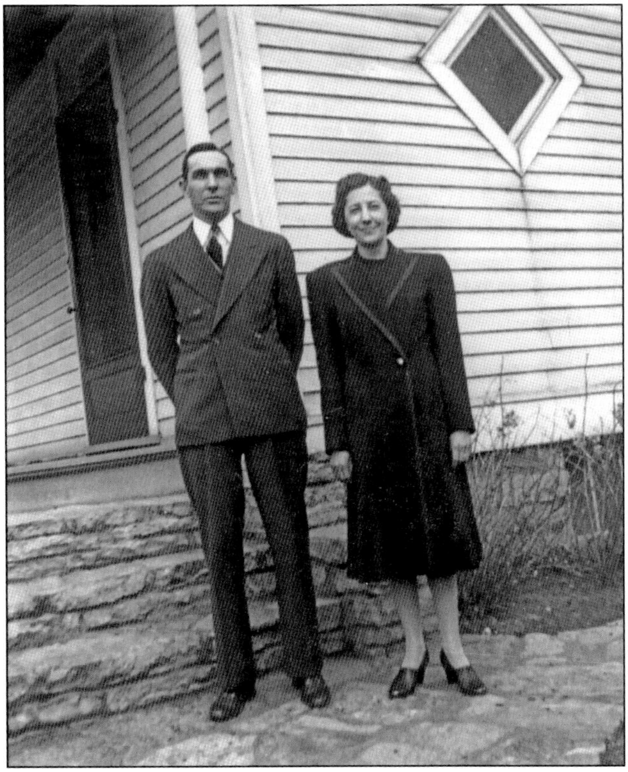

Standing outside their home are Ansel Beckett "A. B." Arnold and his wife, Garnett. Ansel was born in 1902 and died in 1966. During this time he served the community of Butler as a teacher and as the school principal. Later he became the superintendent of Pendleton County Schools. They had one son, Garret, who was a partner in the Fisher and Arnold Trucking Company in Falmouth.

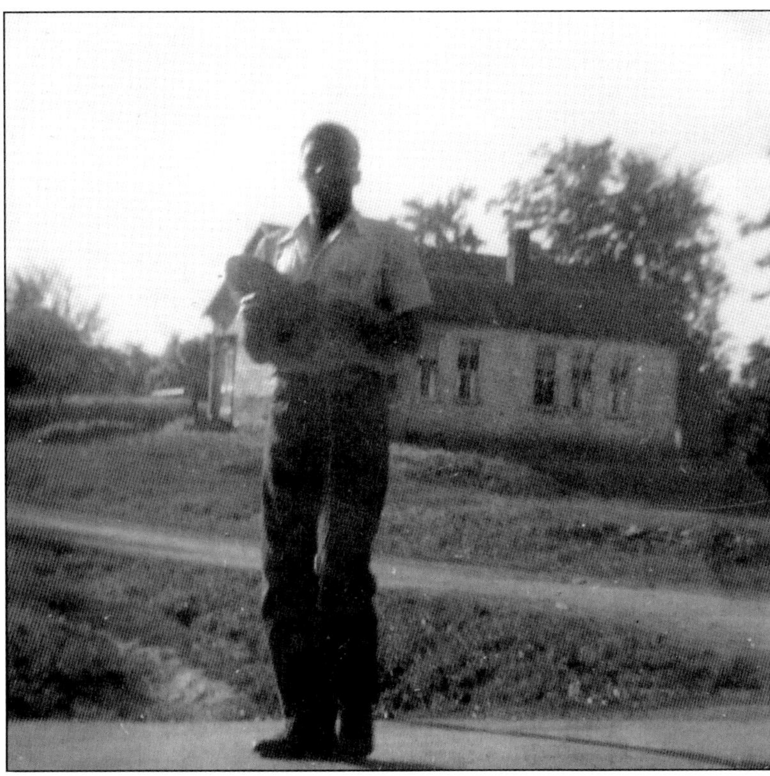

Taken in the early 1940s, this photograph shows Emmett Taylor standing outside of his school house. He was about 17 years old at the time. At this point, this one-room school house was the only school in the county serving the "Negro" students. When this building was no longer available, the students were bused to Cynthiana for classes. The school sat on the corner of Fourth and Licking Streets in Falmouth. (Courtesy of Anne Higgins.)

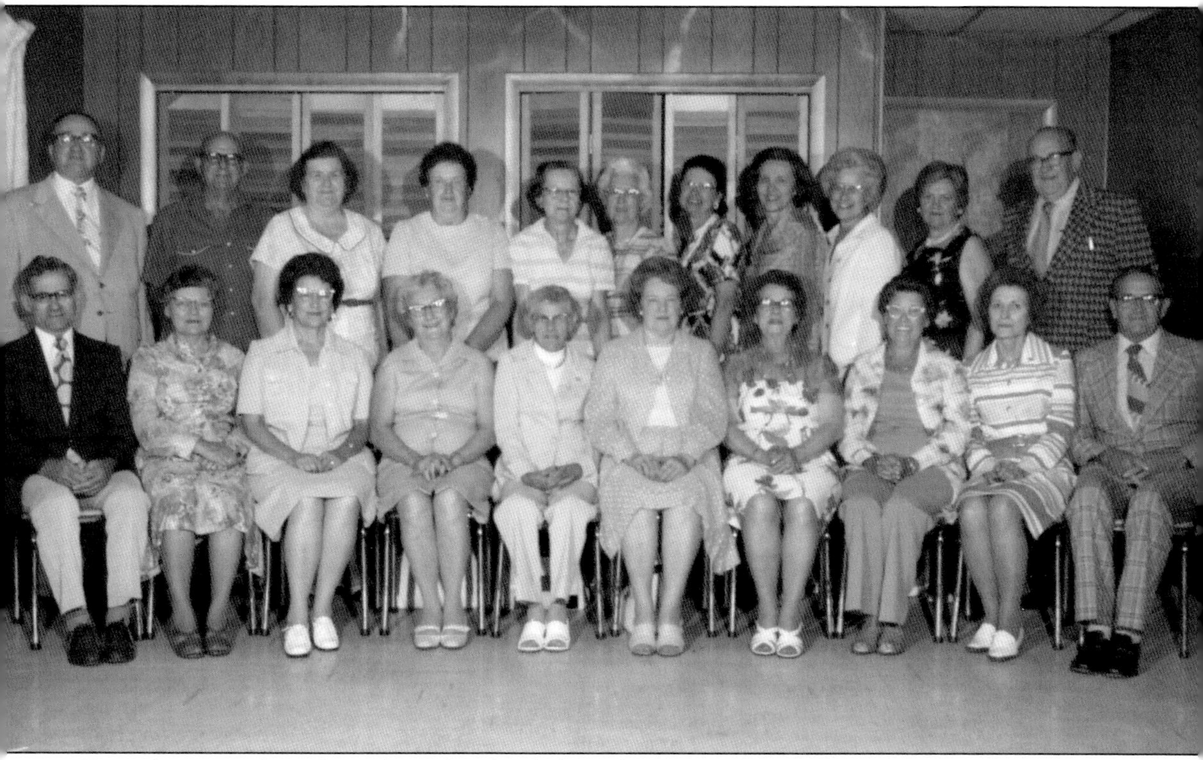

Every five years the Falmouth High School class of 1936 met for a reunion. It was the largest class to graduate from Falmouth High School to that date. The classmates who were in attendance in August 1976 were from left to right: (first row) Chester Conrad, Odella Ashcraft Lane, Helen Hancock Booher, Verna England Dahms, Ruth Epperson Braun, Alice Lees Simpson Accordine, Merta Fowee, Odella Wiggins Hermann, Edith Cummins Franks, and Pickett Wiggins; (second row) James Crawford, Frank Gulick, Elizabeth Elliott, Ruby Baumgartner Simpson, Ella Bishop, Esther Fryer Stout, Bertha Brandt Bush, Carolyn Monroe Brown, Anna Mae Bentle Conrad, Elizabeth Holton King, and Melvin Hart. Carl M. Frazier and Jason Ammerman were remembered during a memorial reading. (Courtesy of Hallie Hart.)

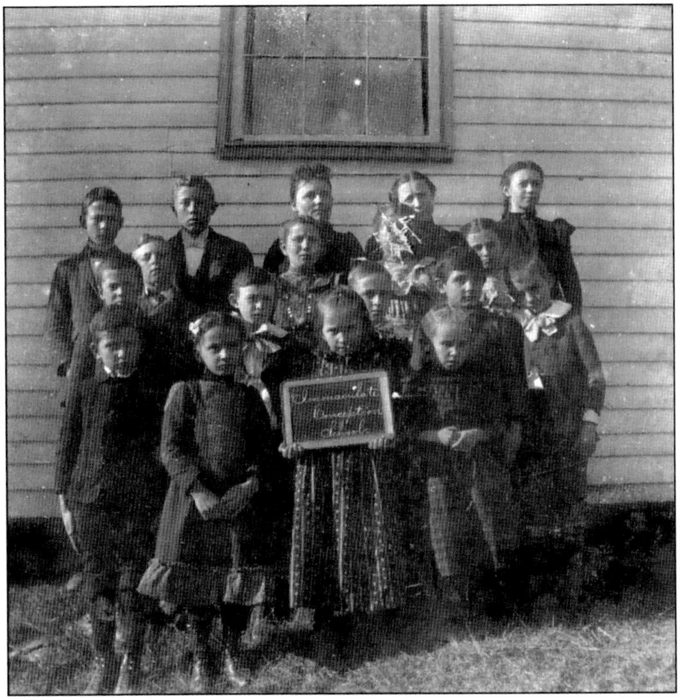

The Immaculate Conception School was situated between the hills near Carntown. In the beginning, it served as a German-language school. In attendance on this day were from left to right: (first row) Frankie Dittleberger, Matilda Faulhaber, Katherine Dittleberger, and Josephine Dittleberger; (second row) John Eshman, Elizabeth Nordheim, Lena (Magdelena) Dittleberger, and Margaret (Maggie) Dittleberger; (third row) John Steiger, George A. Nordheim, teacher Mary Emminger (mother to Albert, Les, and Hilda Emminger and Anna Dougherty), Anne Nordheim, and Anna Mary E. Rust. (Courtesy of Marvin Record.)

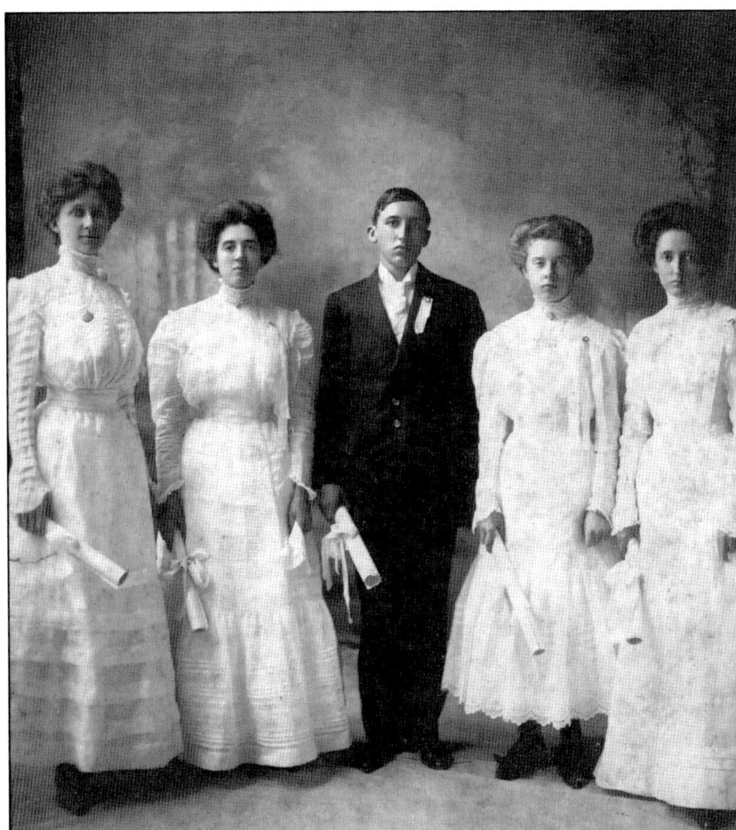

Ollie Beryl Taylor of Butler is pictured here with the 1909 graduating class of Morehead Normal School. At this time Morehead was a school for training future teachers. She married Llano Britton in January 1917. (Courtesy of the Opal Jackson Family.)

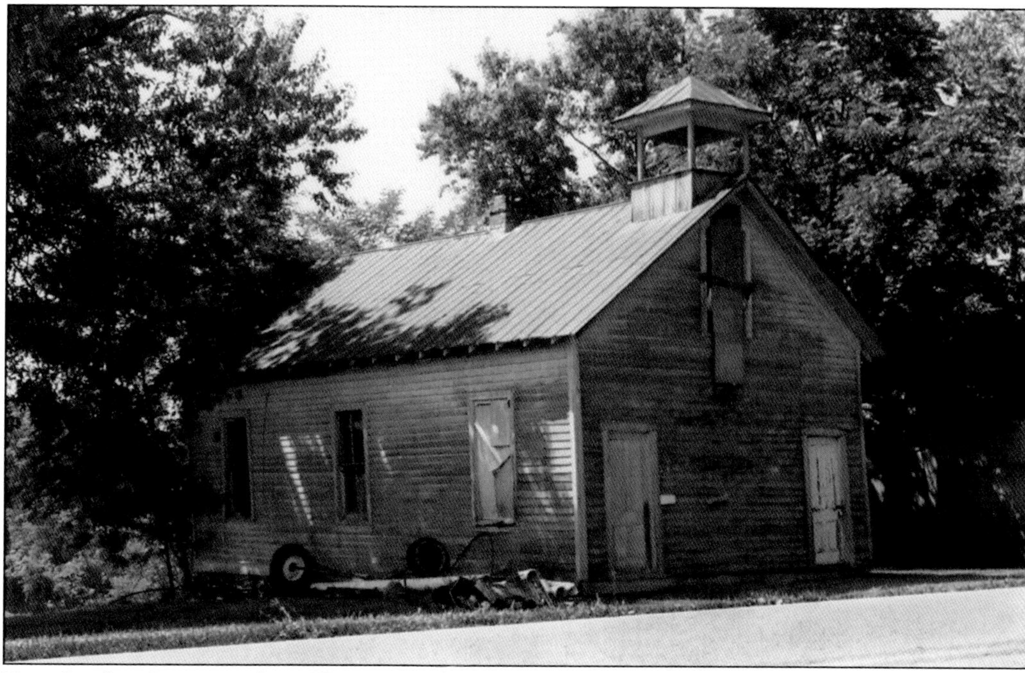

Travelers heading east along KY10 toward Foster pass this building, one of three church buildings used from Baptist to Pentecostal denominations. A larger building known as "The Fishers Tabernacle" had sides which opened to allow better air flow when used in warmer months, while this smaller one was used in winter. It is reported that when services were held and the windows were open, ministers could be easily heard by those seated outside on the grounds. The last services were held about 1945.

The First Baptist Church met most every Sunday at Beech Street in Falmouth with Hope Kimble leading the group. Taken in the 1950s, this photograph shows several regulars and a few visitors. From left to right, they are (first row) Ruth Ann Hinton, Bernice Smith, Rosemary Allen, Barbara Jean English, and Alvina Smith; (second row) "Brother" (a visitor), William Graves, James English, Edwin Thomas, Beverly ?, and an unidentified visitor; (third row) Juanita ?, Adrene Higgins, Nedra English, Jerome Custard, and Joseph Merritt; (fourth row) Mary Graves, Sylvia Graves, Jesse Thompson, Grace Graves, and Thomas Graves; (fifth row) Hattie White, Mae Taylor, and Hope Kimble. (Courtesy of Anne Higgins.)

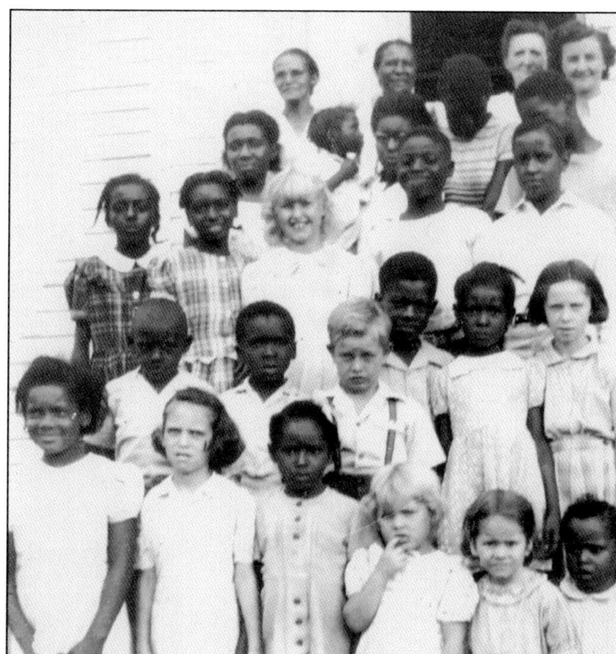

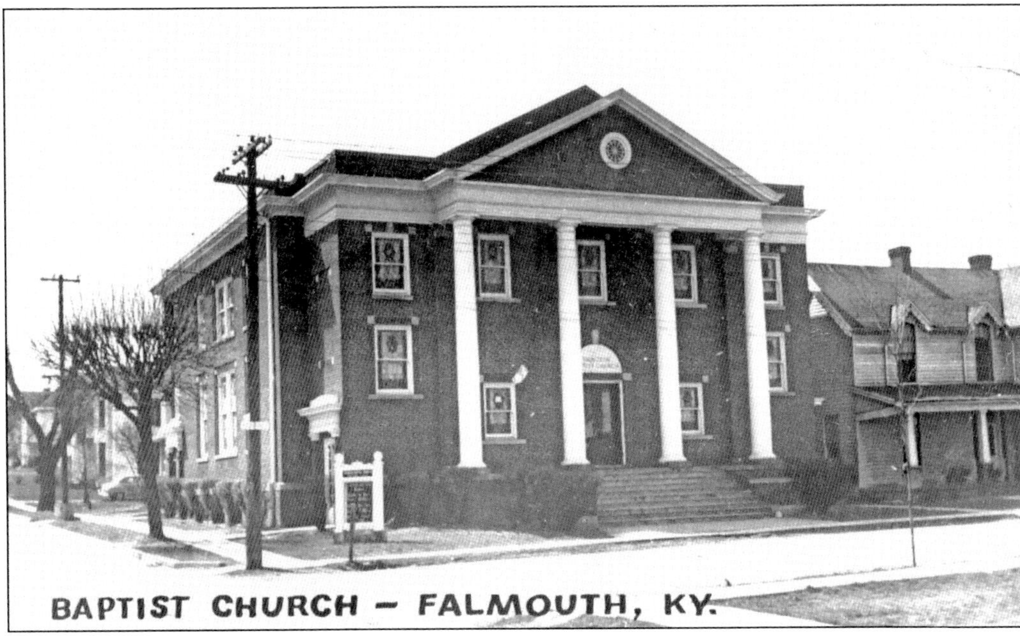

The Baptist denomination was most likely the first to form a church in Pendleton County. A small group gathered in 1795 under Rev. Alexander Monroe. They formed the "Forks of the Licking River Church." A second building constructed on the corner of Main and Fourth Streets was demolished in 1854. The third was constructed in 1861 on the corner of Fourth and Chapel Streets. By 1930 a larger building was constructed on Maple Avenue and Fourth Street, where it still serves today. The church took the name "Falmouth Baptist Church" in 1872.

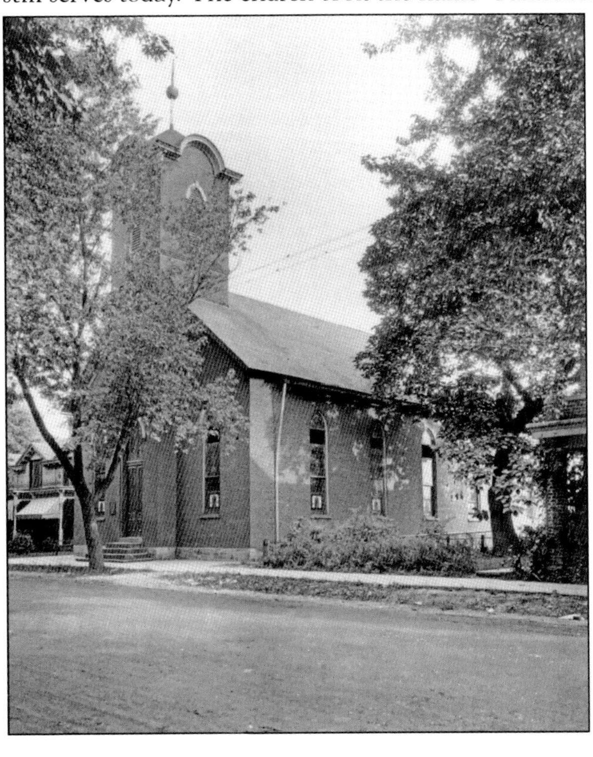

The earliest records of the Falmouth Christian Church were destroyed by fire, leaving little data about the organization of the church. The pioneer preachers John T. Johnson, William Patterson, and John A. Gano have been credited with the first missionary work of New Testament Christianity done with this church. The present meeting house on Shelby Street was begun in 1872 on land sold to the church from the estate of Reuben McCarty and was competed in 1876 when a dedication officiated by Esaac Errett was held.

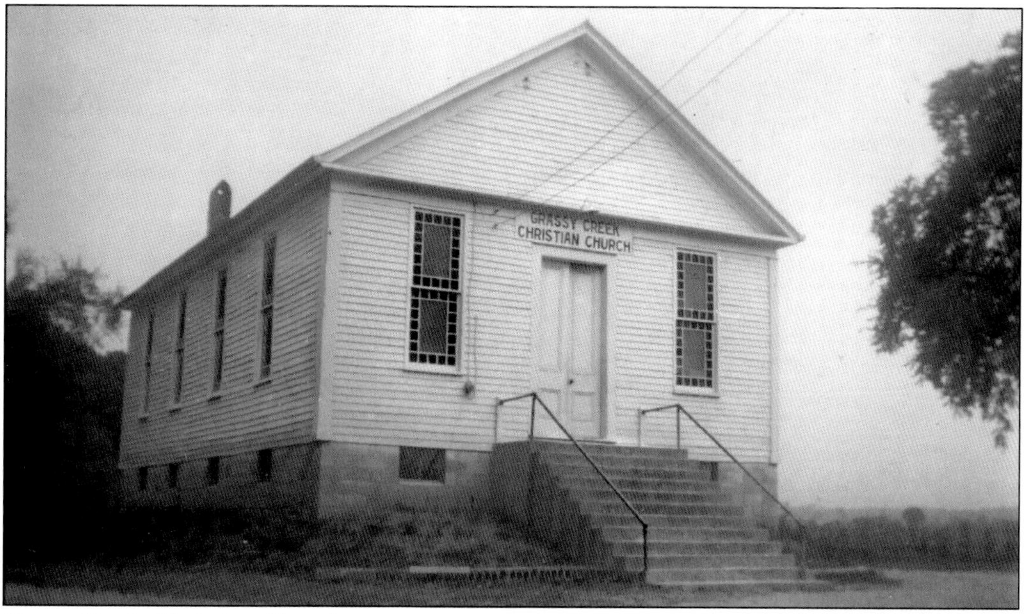

Grassy Creek Christian Church organized in 1838 in a log building on the South Fork of Grassy Creek. The congregation later moved to a frame building on land given by Richard Mullins. After the flood of 1937, several changes were made in hopes that the church would not be damaged again, but the 1964 flood put 4 feet of water inside. In January 1965, a fire burned the church to the ground. Dedication services for a new building placed on higher ground off Grassy Creek Road were held in October 1965. (Courtesy of Margaret Longworth.)

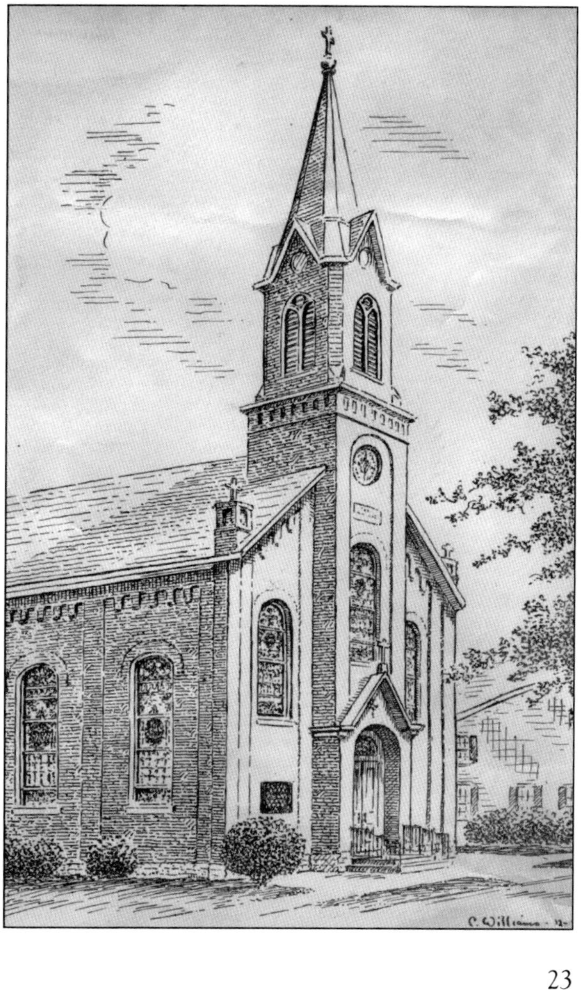

As early as 1851 missionary priests from Frankfort and Lexington provided services for local Catholic families. In 1860 the first Catholic church was built on Main Street close to the Licking River. By 1876 the population had greatly increased, and a new church structure on Second Street was begun under the leadership of Father Gadker, with the old building being used as a parishioners' school. This sketch was done for a centennial celebration. (Courtesy of Veronica Hargett.)

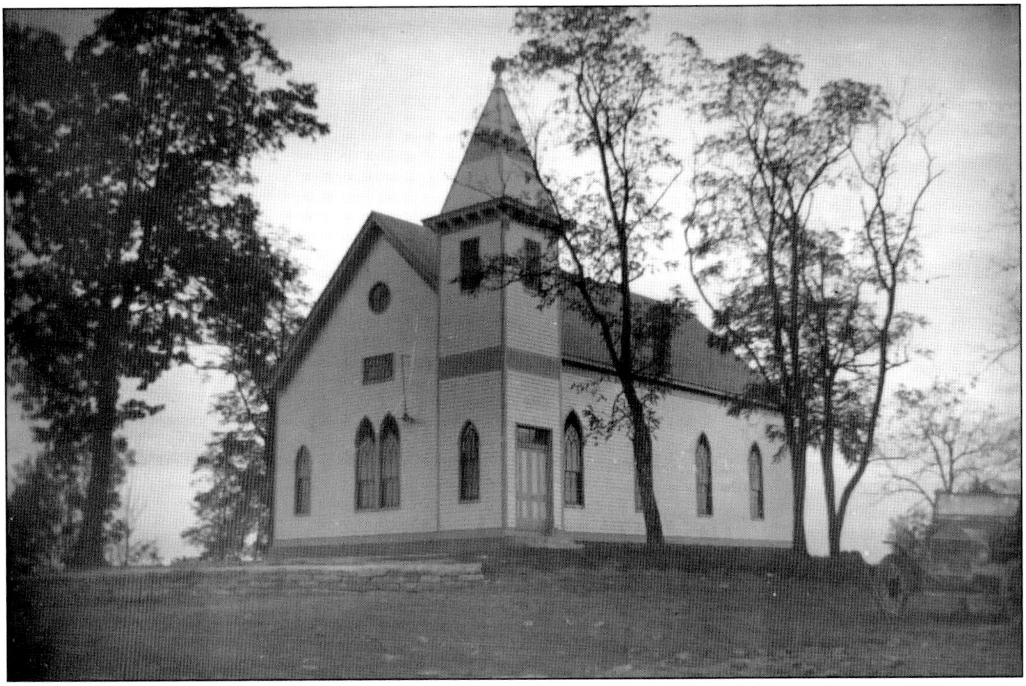

In the mid-1860s, daily discussions held at the general store about life and the teachings of Alexander Campbell led a small group of men to form a Bible study group. This was the beginning of the Browningsville Christian Church. The group met during their first year in the log school house. The congregation continued to grow and in 1869, with a new name, Oakland Christian Church was built. A new church building, seen above, was erected on the old foundation in 1916, where it stands today. (Courtesy of Clara Holmes.)

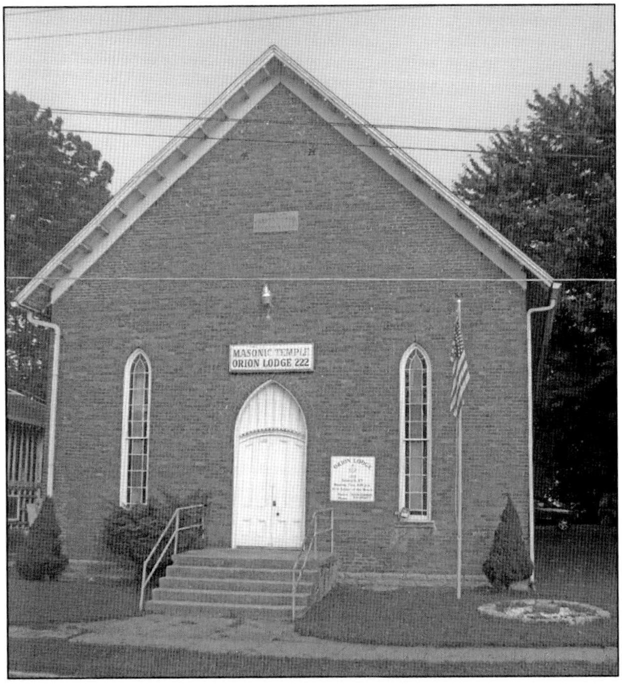

The Falmouth Presbyterian Church, at left, was built in 1873 by D. E. Redmon. It was completed and a dedication held in January 1874. Twelve years later, a new Presbyterian church was organized at Concord, and most members of the Falmouth church requested that their memberships be transferred to this new church. In 1932 it was decided to sell the building to the Orion Lodge, the present owners.

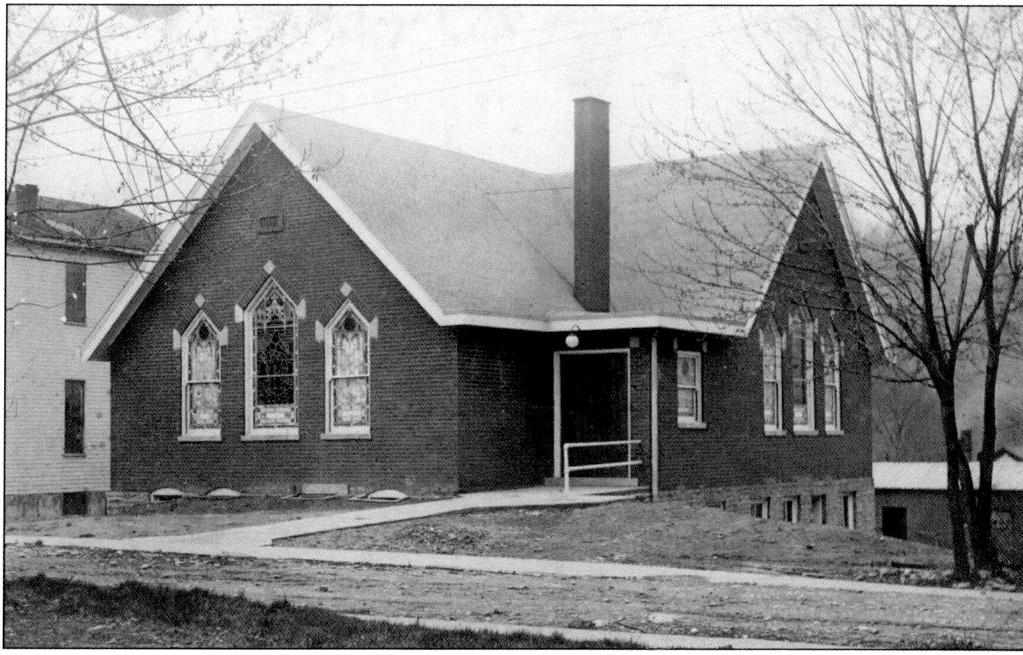

For many years Butler had no Methodist Church even though records indicate that a church group had been organized in 1868 by P. H. Hoffman. In the early 1900s a group of Methodists organized and held church meetings in the building owned by the Masonic Lodge. Although work toward the erection of a building for their needs progressed over the years, it wasn't until 1918 that the First Methodist Church was dedicated. (Courtesy of Lois Wilson.)

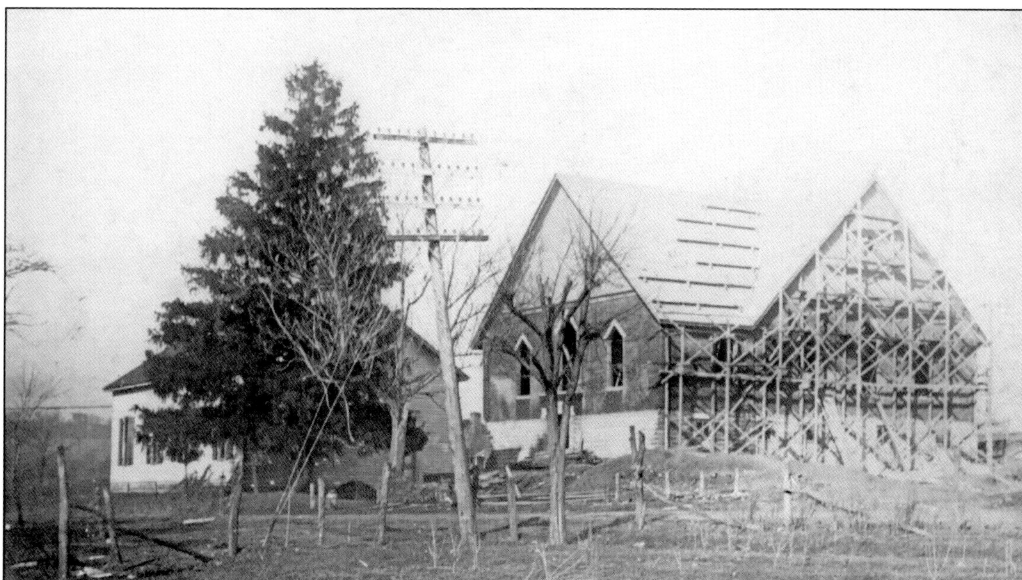

Seen in this photograph is the Flour Creek Christian Church as it was being constructed beside the older frame church building. The church was organized in 1826 with five charter members. Over the next 50 years the membership increased so much that two "daughter" churches were formed. By the time the new church was dedicated in 1920, more than 979 people were noted as having been a member of Flour Creek Christian Church. (Courtesy of Teresa Johnston.)

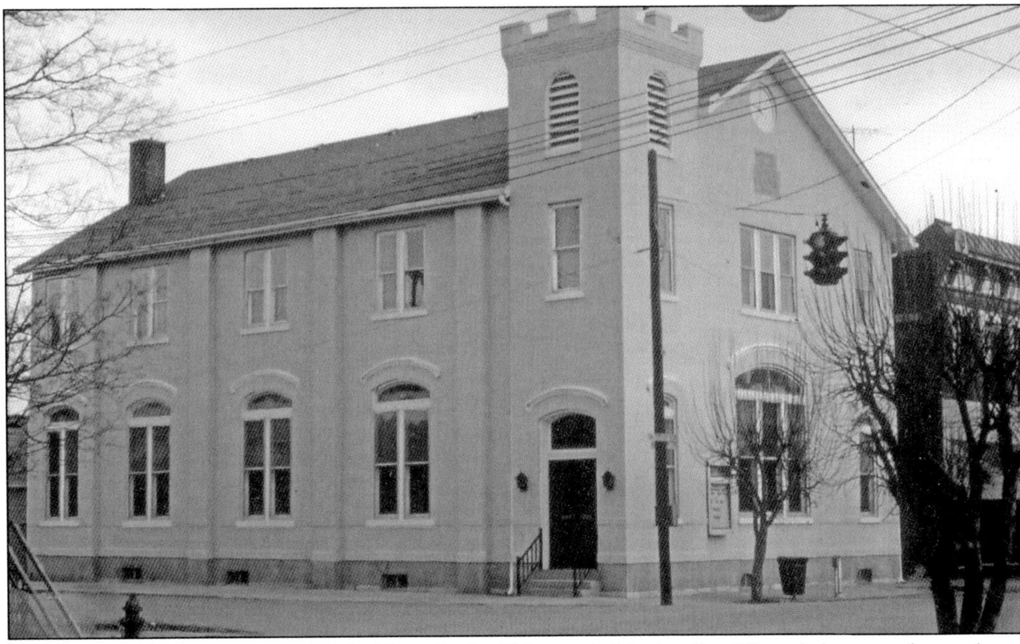

Known at its beginning as Mary's Chapel, the Falmouth Methodist Church began when a lot in Falmouth was donated to the Falmouth Methodist Society. The church building was completed through generous donations from Augusta Robbins, and dedicated in 1855. The three art glass windows seen in this photograph replaced the vestibule opening at the front of the church before 1890. The church was enlarged and a belfry added in 1926; the disbanded Presbyterian church donated their bell. (Courtesy of George Lach.)

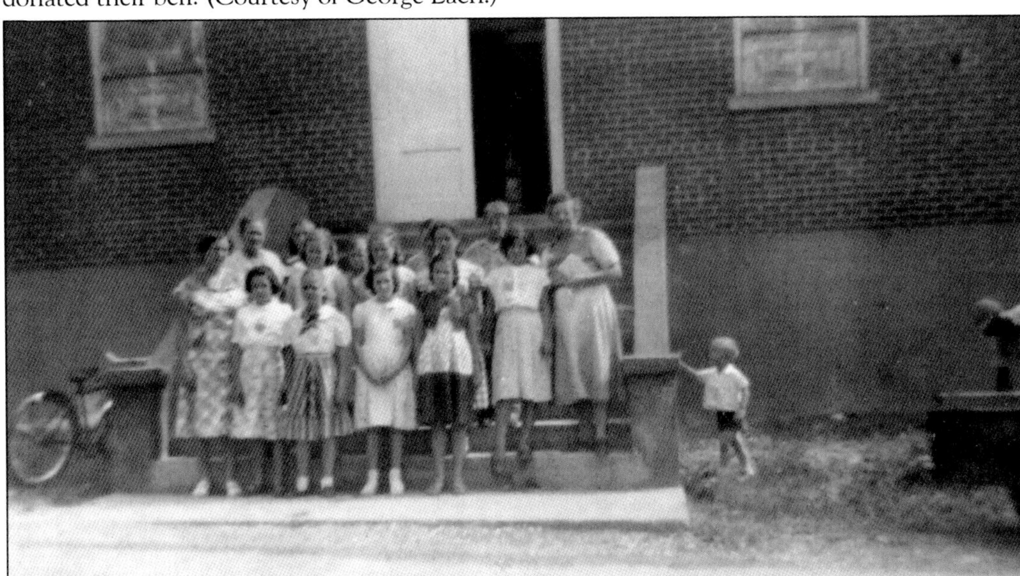

Standing on the steps of Morgan Christian Church are a group of young women and their leaders. The church was built on land adjacent to the South Licking River, deeded from Richard Lowers to the church trustees in 1862. William Kirkwood was their first minister. In 1863 the frame building was destroyed by fire. A second building was completed that same year and served church needs until 1914, when it was torn down and the present brick building constructed. (Courtesy of Nancy Harville.)

Originally known as the Regular Baptist Church of Christ, Short Creek Baptist Church began in 1833 with only six people who met in a log school house for seven years before building a church. In 1851 a growth surge resulted in the construction of new quarters at the intersection of Fishing Creek Road and KY22. This building burned in 1908 after being struck by lightning. The church building seen in the photograph was built soon after on the same site.

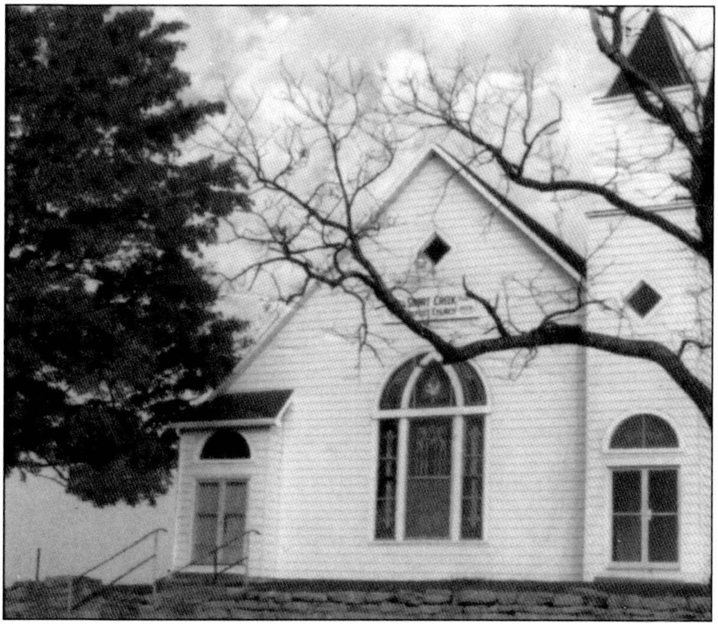

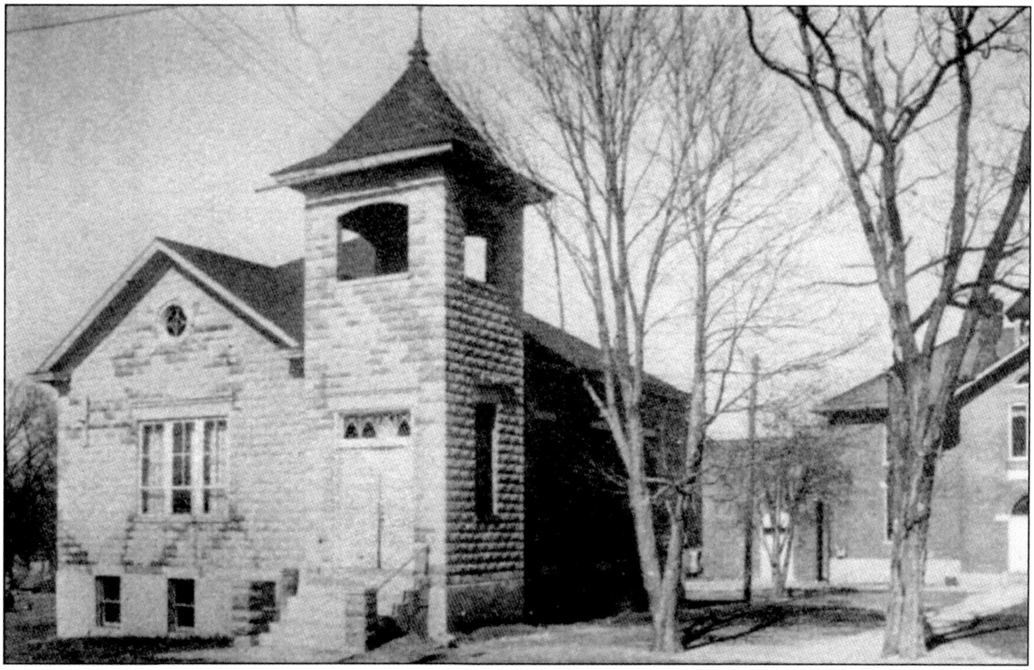

The Morgan Baptist Church sat on KY1054, just across the bridge into Morgan. It was also directly in front of the Morgan School. After the church congregation disbanded about 1940, the Morgan School purchased the building to use for a home economics classroom. (Courtesy of Nancy Bray.)

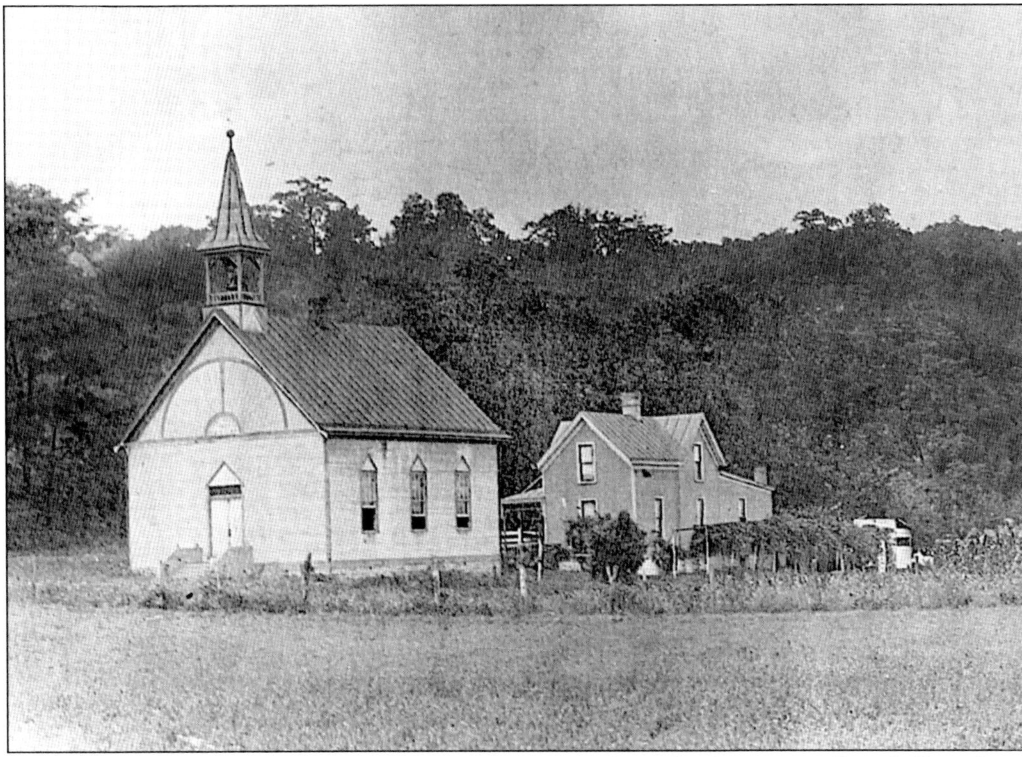

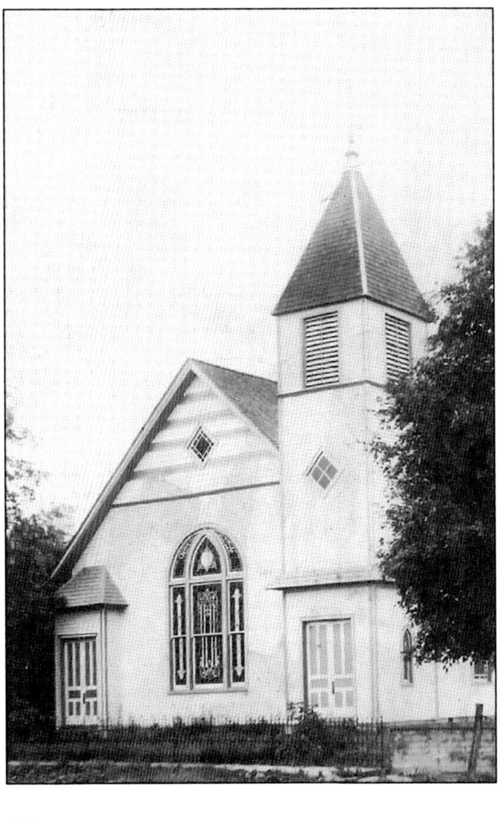

Set in the valley between rolling hills and the Ohio River, the Carntown Methodist Church provided a place of worship for years. Years after services ended there, it became an office building for the Black River Mining Company. Today, it, like all of Carntown, is gone to the changing needs of our society. (Courtesy of Chris Fossitt.)

In May 1841, some 30 people from the Baptist Church of Christ in Campbell County met to organize a new church. The congregation gathered in a local school or in members' homes until a brick building was completed in 1843. The first name given this church was "Fellowship Baptist Church." The name change to Second 12 Mile Baptist Church was most likely due to its location at the beginning of 12 Mile Creek—another church was located at the mouth of this same creek. (Courtesy of Chris Fossitt.)

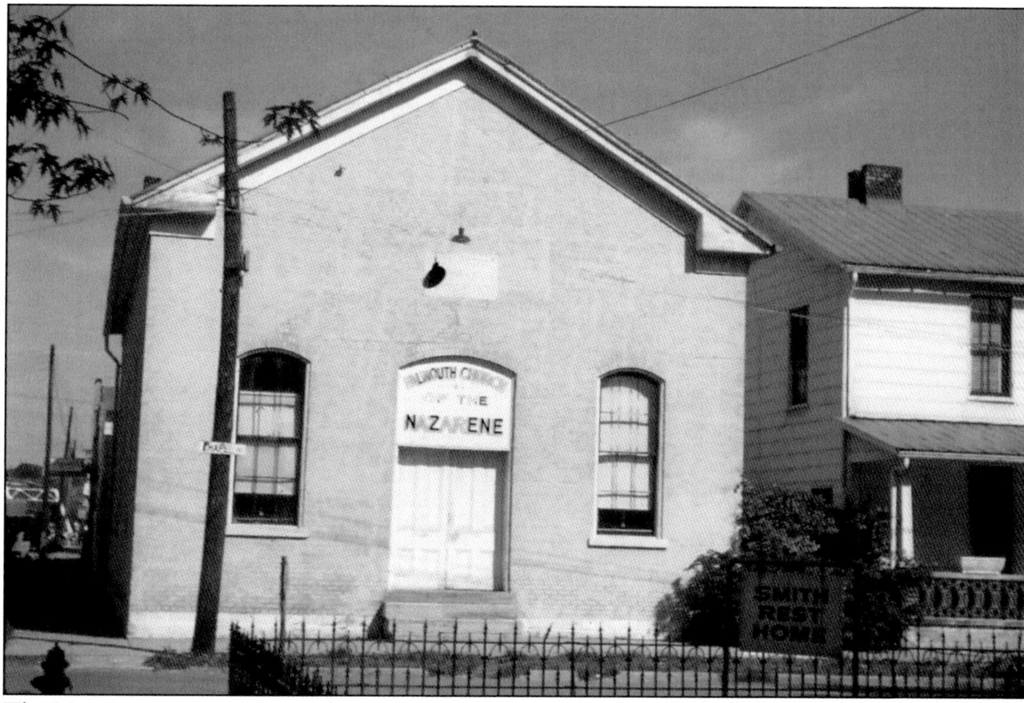

The Nazarene Congregation that met in the building shown was organized in the 1950s and served this community until the mid-1990s. The building was used in services conducted as far back as 1870 for members of the Lutheran Protestant St. Paul Church. In 1917 it was deeded for possible use as a town hall. In the late 1940s the building was used for the city offices. Today the building serves as the county sheriff's office. (Courtesy of George Lach.)

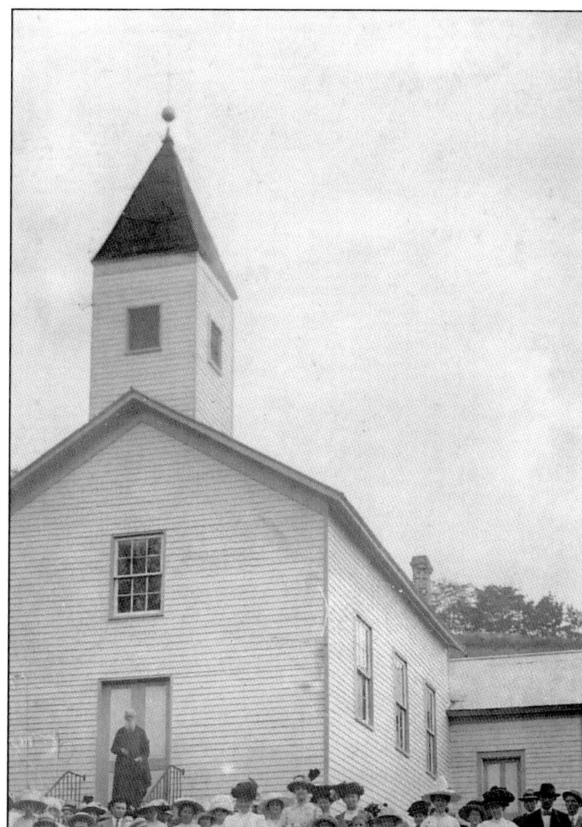

The Immaculate Conception Church has a long history in Pendleton County. There was no organized Catholic group in Carntown from 1840 to about 1861, but families met in homes and later built a log structure. In 1861 the present building was completed, and the log building became a German school. This church, along with the cemetery, is now listed on the Kentucky Historical Register as the oldest frame church in the Diocese of Covington. (Courtesy of Marvin Record.)

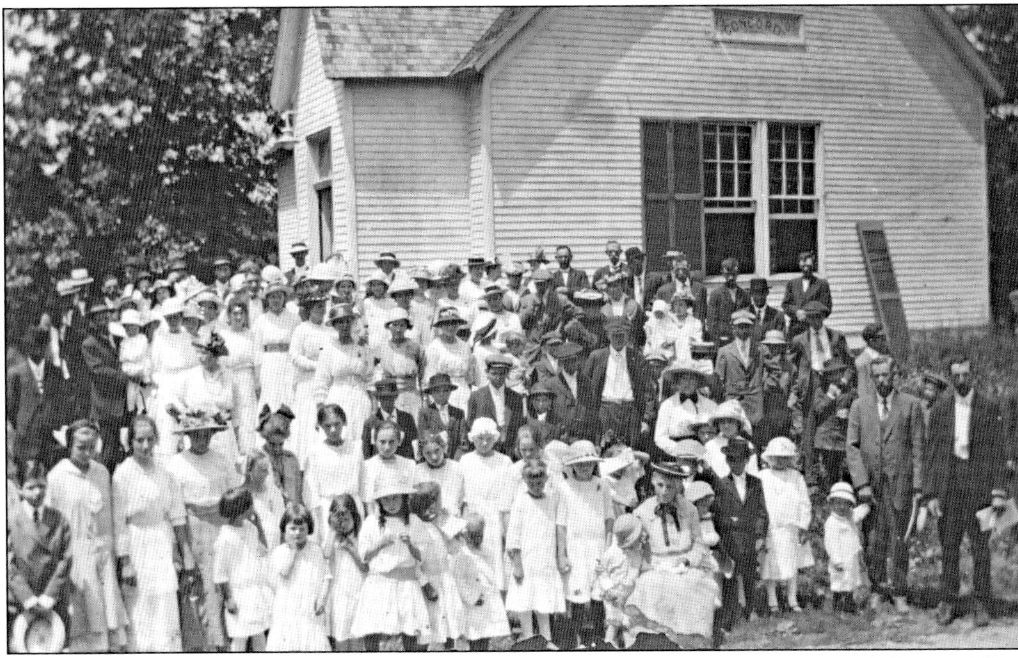

Concord Methodist Church began in 1800 when a Methodist Society organized. By 1844 land was set aside for a church and cemetery on KY159. A building was constructed, but it burned in 1904. During this time, a local Presbyterian church was also using the building, so they joined together and built The Concord Methodist and Presbyterian Union Church across the road. In 1928, the Presbyterians disbanded, and the church was renamed the Concord Methodist Church. (Courtesy of Velma Steele.)

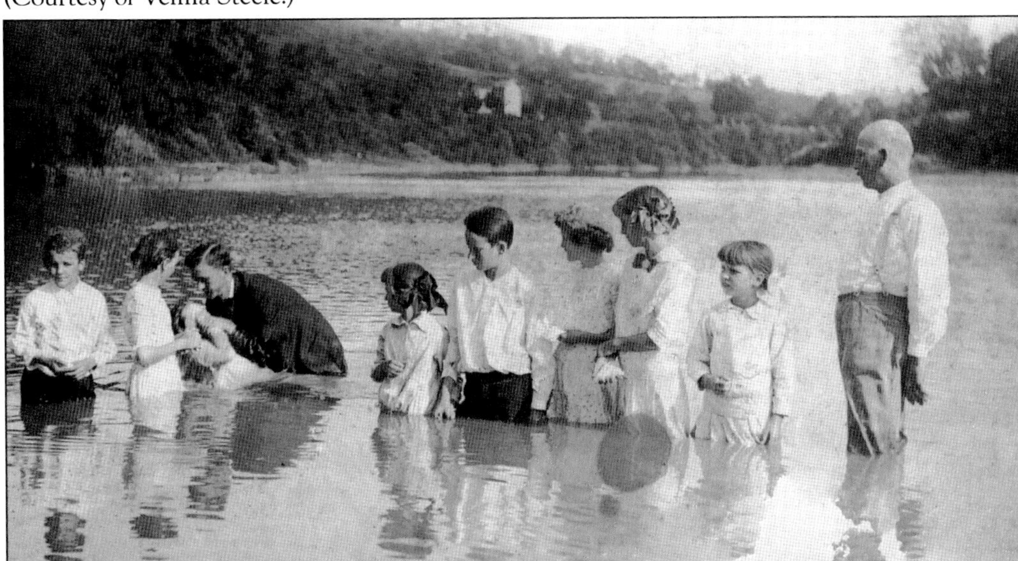

River baptisms were a regular occurrence with many early churches, especially with the number of creeks and the shallow waters of the Licking River. A group of young people await their turn at this baptism service. The house in the background is off KY177 near Flour Creek. (Courtesy of the Opal Jackson family.)

Two
BRIDGES AND MODES OF TRANSPORTATION

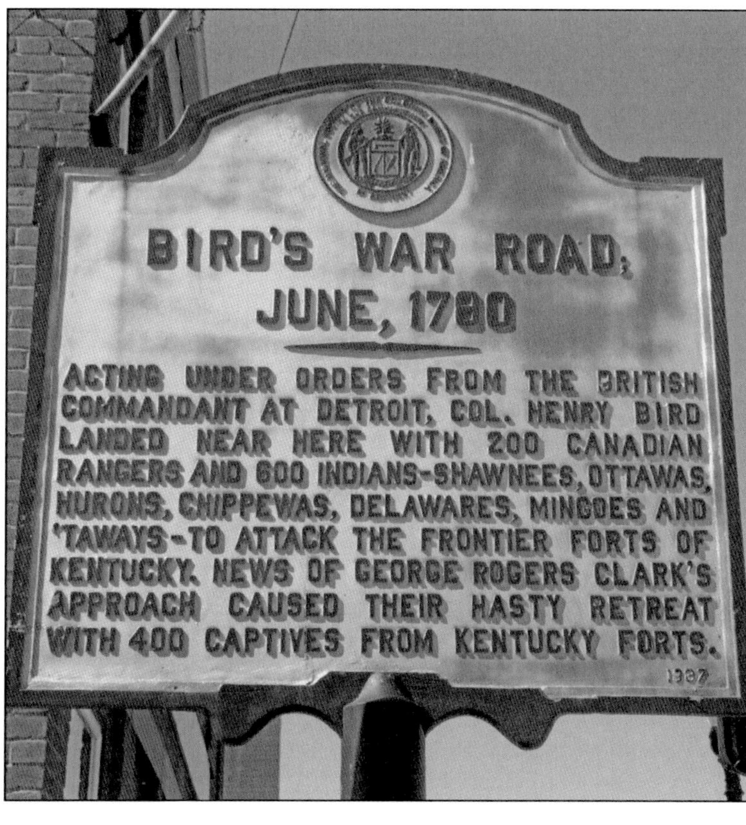

Byrd's Road was carved when Col. Henry Byrd, acting on orders from the British commandant in Detroit, followed the buffalo trails through southern Ohio and into Kentucky. He led a large contingent of Canadian Rangers and bands of Native Americans to the frontier forts of Kentucky, raiding them and taking over 400 prisoners before quickly heading north. It has been told that they camped in the area of Riverside Cemetery, leaving the area with no harm done to persons here.

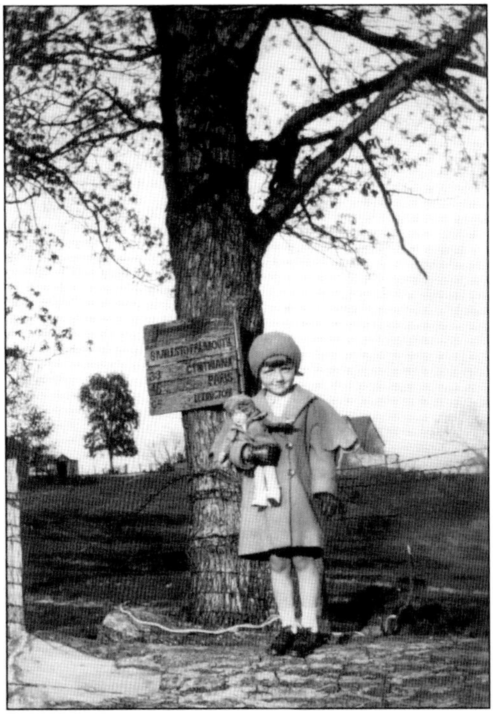

In this 1930s photograph, little Virginia Young stands beside a road sign directing a traveler from the Morgan area south to Falmouth, Cynthiana, Paris, and then on to Lexington. Virginia later married Leonard "Red" Shotwell and became a well-known teacher in the county.

Almost hidden behind the tree foliage is the home of the Bradford family. This house sits on one of many curves found on KY17. The stone walls are from the many rocks found on the hills as the farmers tilled the land. For many years, persons heading north would use this route to reach Butler and then Covington, Kentucky. (Courtesy of Russ Conrad.)

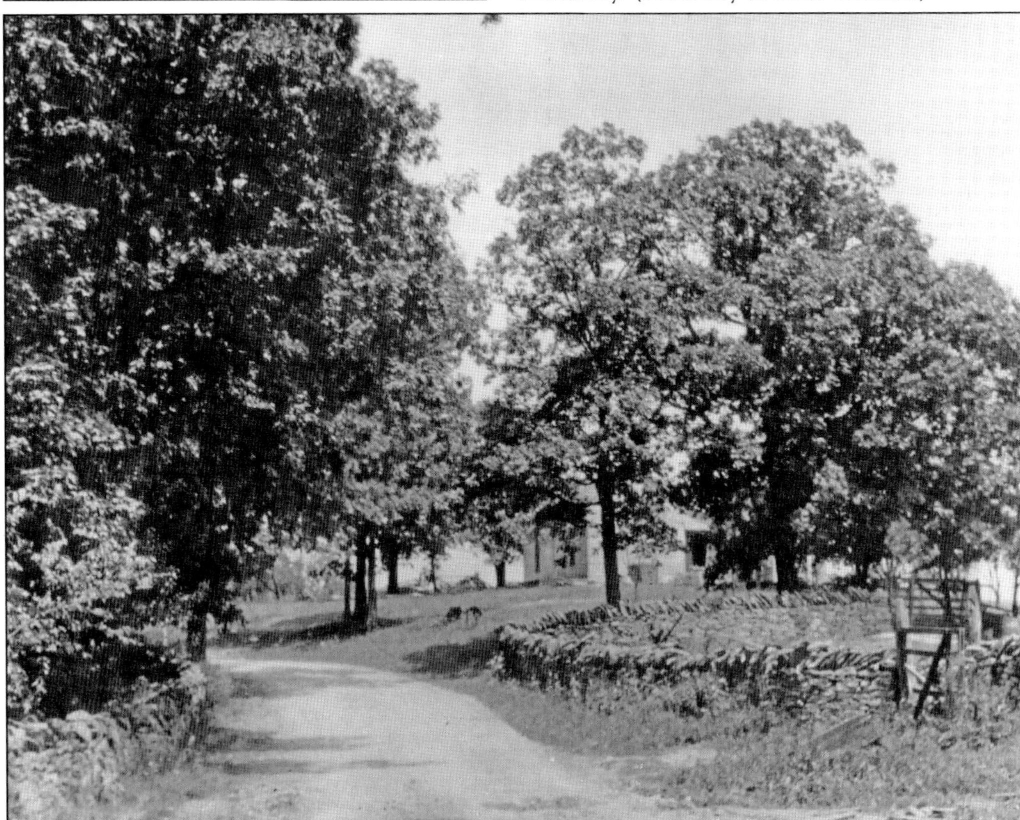

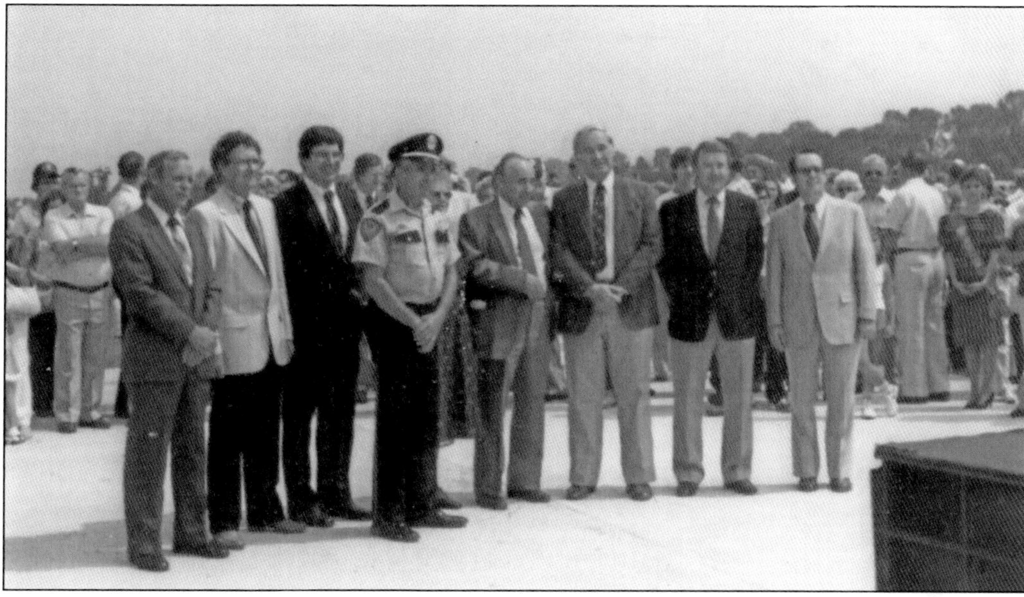

From as early as 1930, there have been small runways near Falmouth. Most were no more than dirt strips on the top of hills, along river valleys, or on the edge of crops. Then in 1985, a dream of local pilots was realized. A regional airport was completed off KY22 and named Gene Snyder Airport, after the Kentucky state representative. Shown at the dedication from left to right are county judge David Pribble, local businessman and pilot Paul Tuemler, attorney Robert Bathalter, Pendleton County sheriff Loyd Spaulding, Falmouth mayor and pilot Max Goldberg, Gene Snyder, and local doctor and pilot Robert McKinney. (Courtesy of Shirley Tuemler.)

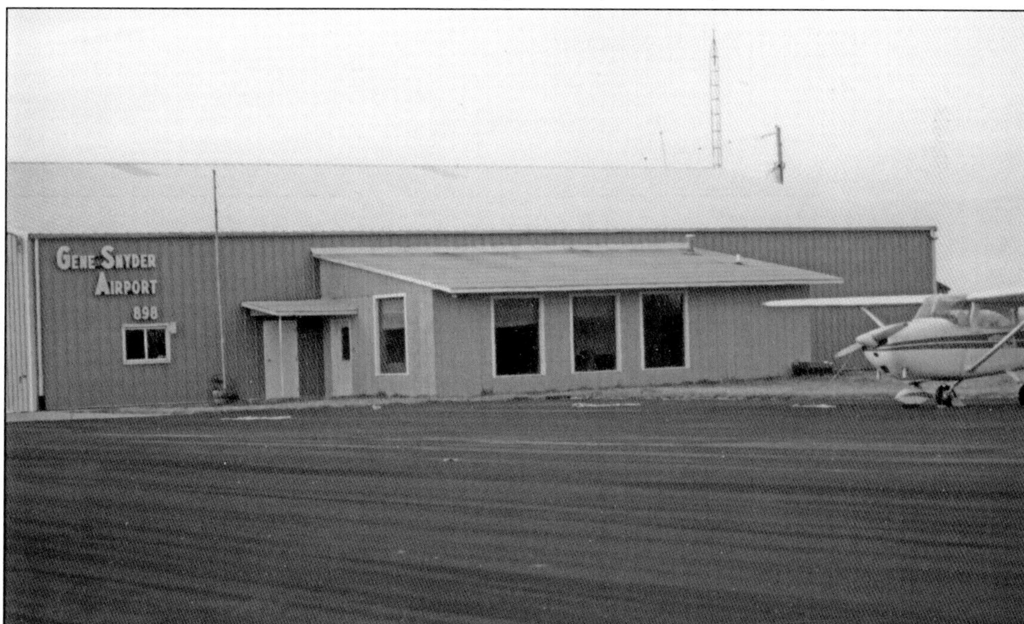

Shown is the newly completed hangar and office of the Gene Snyder Airport built by Paul Tuemler. The airport has expanded the number of hangars since then and continues to serve the region. (Courtesy of Shirley Tuemler.)

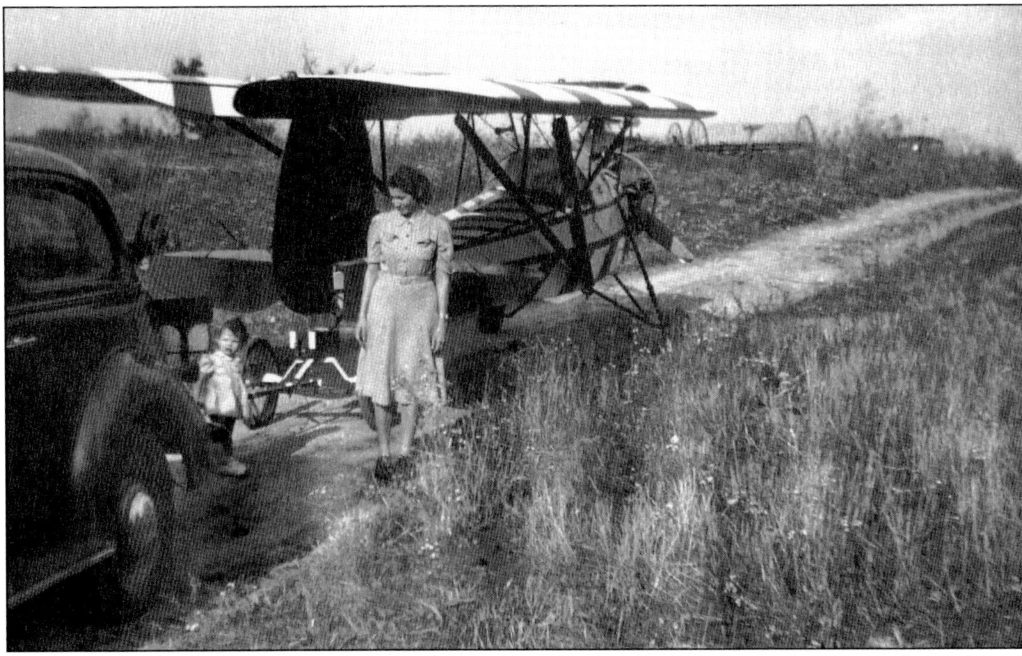

Local flying enthusiasts involved their families, as seen in this photograph of Dorothy Caldwell and her daughter Dora Helen. Farm fields turned runways were common at this time. The plane shown above and in the photograph below was owned by Alex Caldwell, who served in the civil service of the Army Air Force. (Courtesy of Dora Helen Fields.)

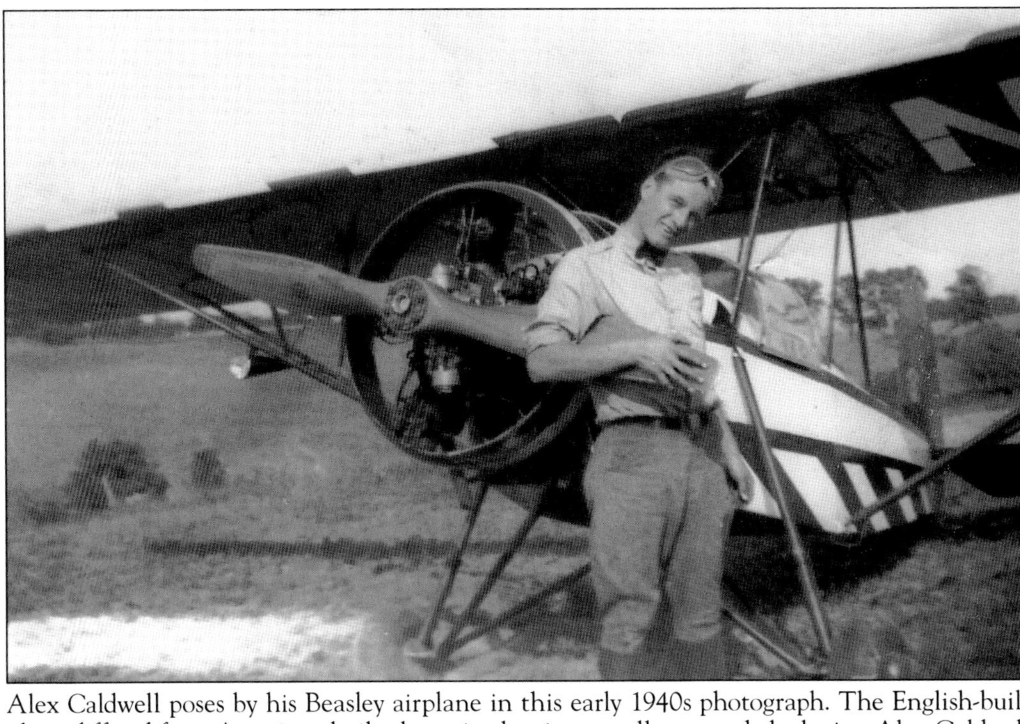

Alex Caldwell poses by his Beasley airplane in this early 1940s photograph. The English-built plane differed from American-built planes in that its propeller turned clockwise. Alex Caldwell was one of the county's first licensed pilots. (Courtesy of Dora Helen Fields.)

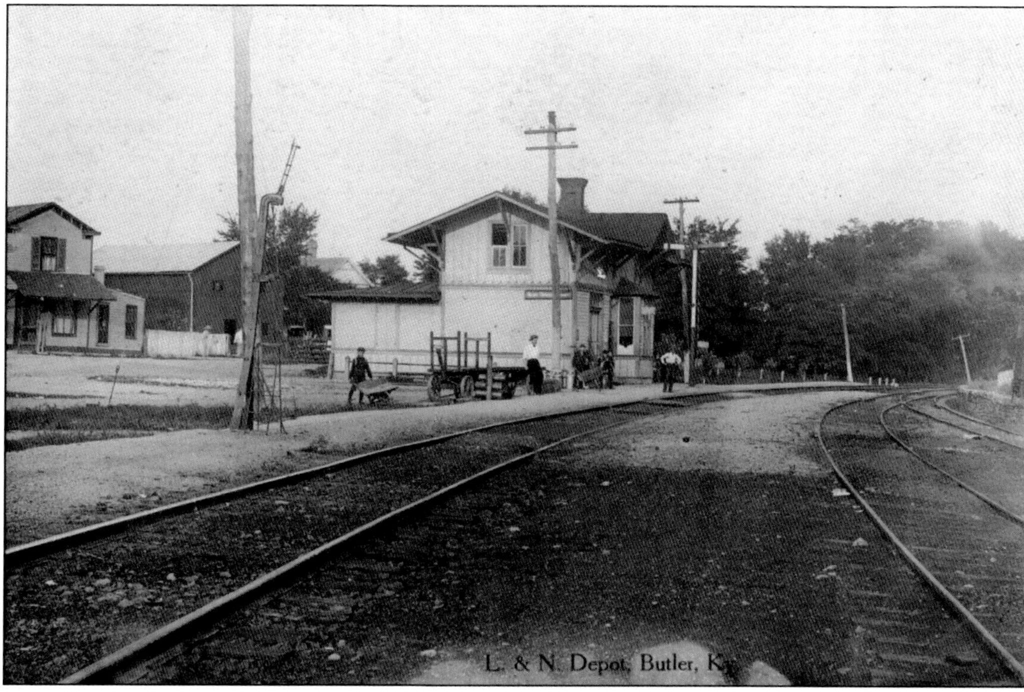

These pictures show the Butler Depot, built in 1882. The first railroad to come through Butler was the Kentucky Central Railroad, which traveled from Covington to Lexington. Its successor, the Louisville and Nashville Railroad, traveled this line and on to Nashville, Tennessee. The photograph above comes from a postcard of the depot taken in the early 1900s. From the posture of the men, it appears that a train is due. Located on Front Street, the Butler Depot served the area's businesses, allowing for quicker and more reliable transport of goods. The railroad also served as an easier transportation mode to jobs for Butler citizens who worked in Covington and Cincinnati, as many still did not have automobiles, and traveling by road was long and difficult. In the photograph at right, the depot is seen as it was after the 1940s. A cart still sits waiting for packages, but the roofline has been lowered, electricity has been brought to town, and automobiles are not unusual. The depot was dismantled in 1966, leaving it just a memory. (Above courtesy of Lois Wilson.)

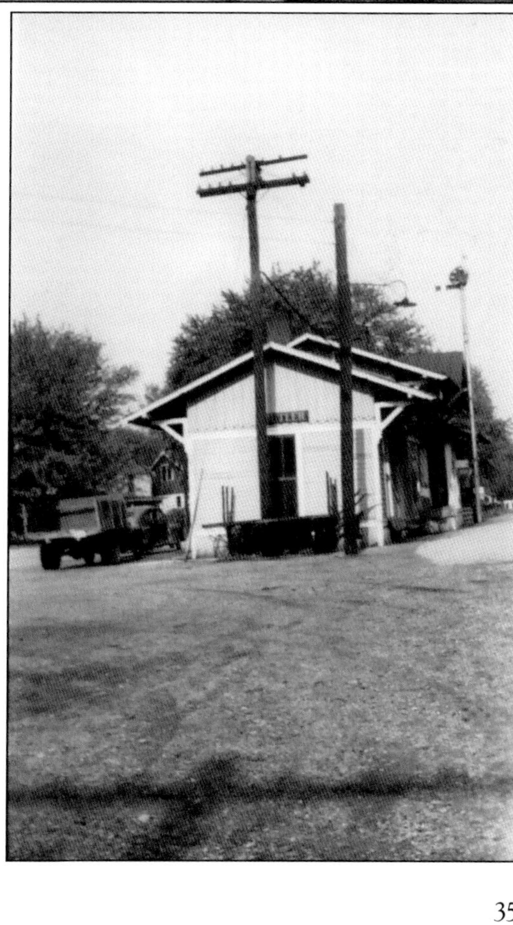

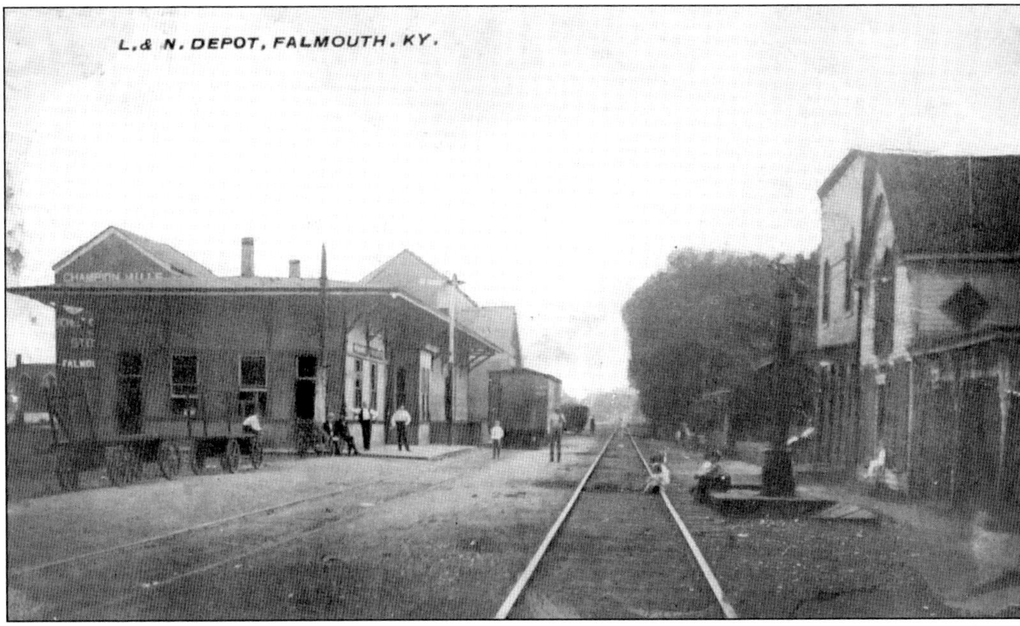

The Falmouth Depot, built in 1912, sat between Railroad Avenue and Park Street. Falmouth was also served in the early years by the Kentucky Central Railroad and the Louisville and Nashville Railroad. The photograph above is looking to the west from Shelby Street. Note the children sitting on the rails. The building to the left, behind the depot, is the Champion Mill. In the 1950s photograph below, the depot has been enlarged and lengthened, and the Champion Mill is no longer there. In 1956 the last steam locomotive passed through Pendleton County, and in 1968 the last passenger train was discontinued. The depot was certified as a Kentucky Landmark in 1973 and was destroyed by fire in 1980. (Above courtesy of Cheryl York, below courtesy of George Lach.)

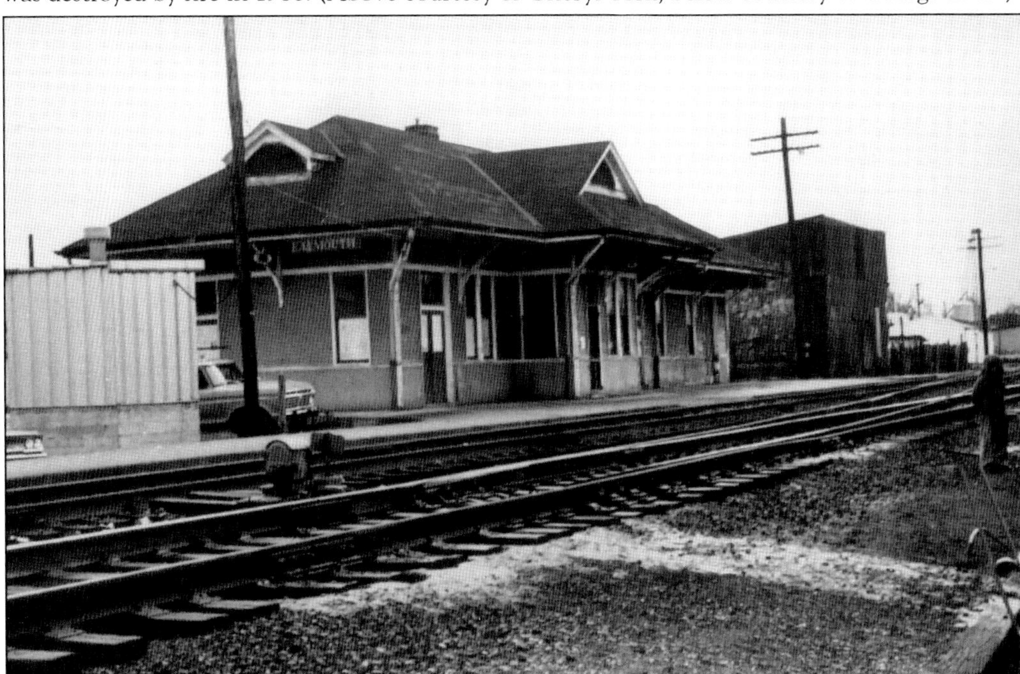

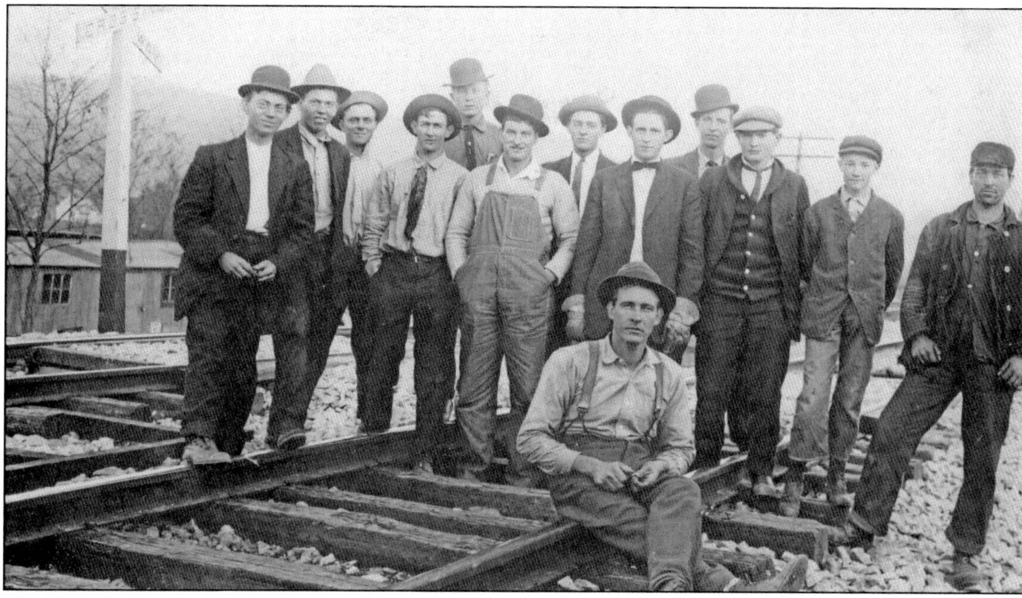

The Works Projects Administration (WPA) railroad crew seen here pauses from its labors for a photograph. Many construction projects and repairs on public buildings were done throughout the county by these WPA crews. The worker fourth from the left with no coat is identified as George Nordheim of New Hope Road. (Courtesy of Keith Gunkel.)

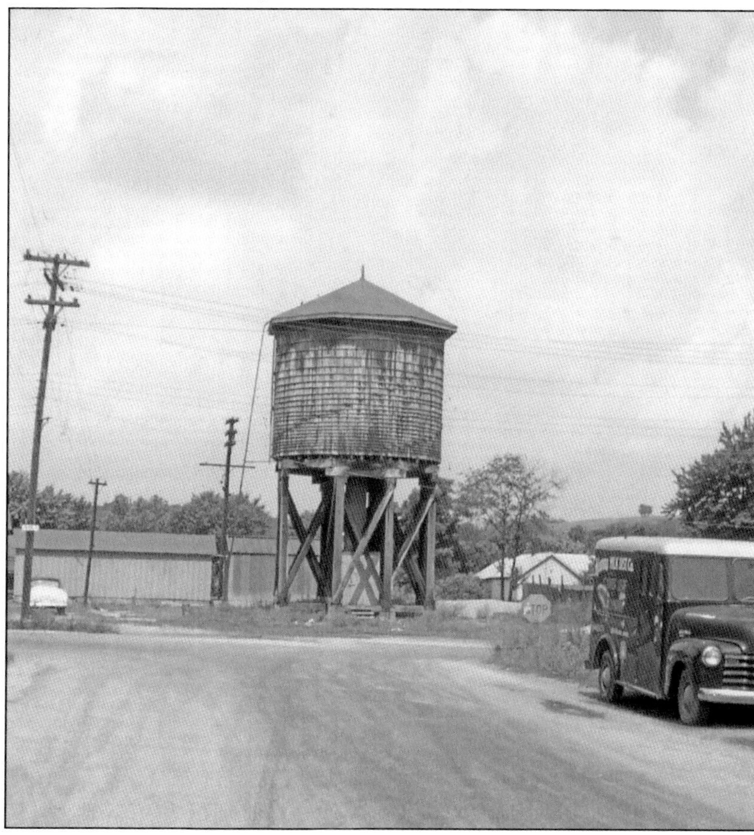

The water tower that sat at the corner of Park and Fourth Streets in Falmouth was a local landmark for years. It was built to serve as the water supply for the steam engine locomotives that traveled through town. The water tower stood for many years after its original purpose had ended; it was finally torn down in April 1957. (Courtesy of George Lach.)

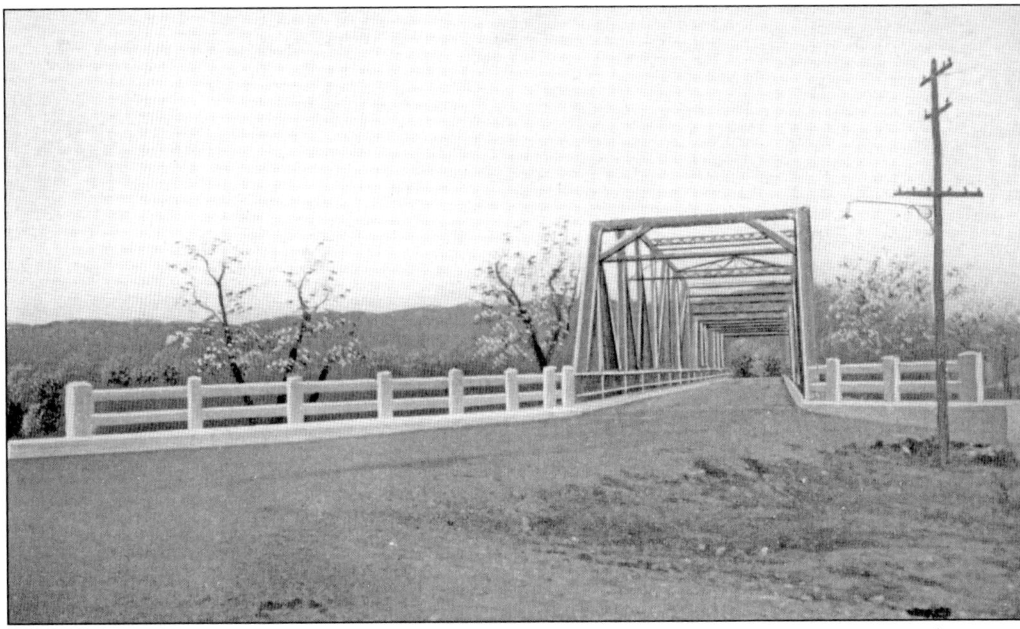

The iron and concrete bridge shown in this c. 1935 picture was built in 1928. This modern two-lane bridge replaced the old covered bridge, which burned in the summer of 1926 when a spark ignited a nearby trash pile. A great celebration took place to mark the new bridge. There was a parade with a marching band, a beauty pageant, a special couple selected to be married at the event, and hundreds who thronged to watch the first vehicle cross. The same bridge, now painted blue, still carries traffic across the river. (Courtesy of George Lach.)

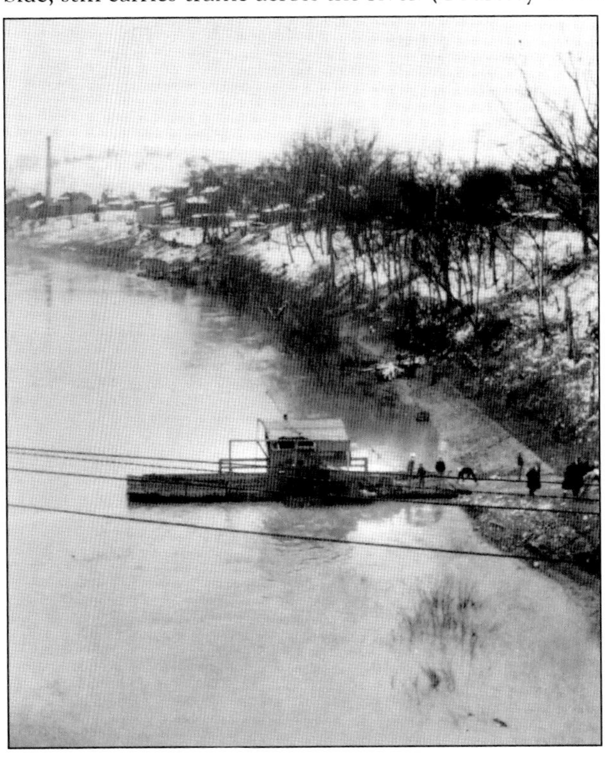

After the old covered bridge burned, the ferry was used for transportation across the river when it was too high to ford. The ferry had a canopy for protection from the elements when needed. There was an access road and small parking area used for the ferry that followed Burnes Branch Creek to the river along Barnes Street. This road was behind the buildings now housing the Outlook Office and Pendleton County Library. (Courtesy of George Lach.)

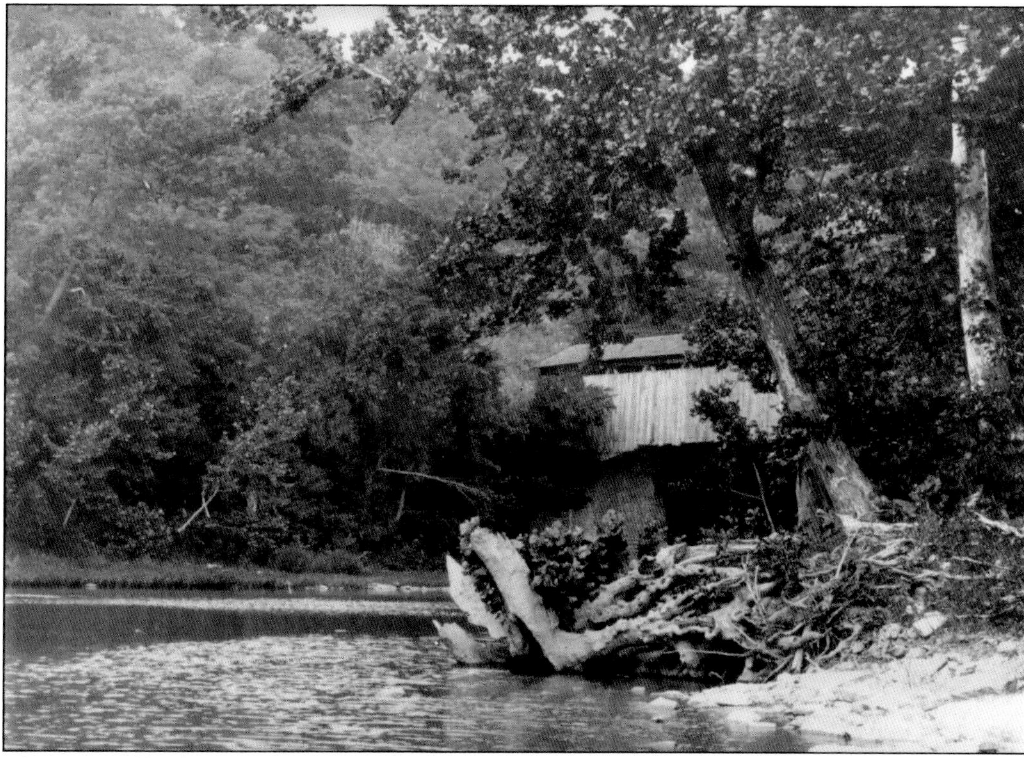

The covered bridge over the South Fork of the Licking River, seen in this photograph, spanned the river from about 1870 until it was torn down in 1929. It was taken down in stages, starting with the sides, until there was nothing remaining except the piers. They still stand at the end of Pike Street today. (Courtesy of Jim Kimble.)

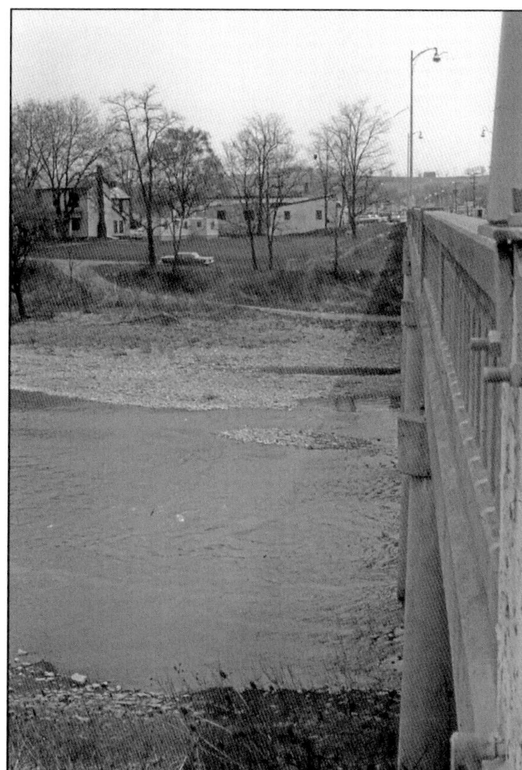

In 1960, as motorists traveled south across the US 27 concrete bridge, they saw immediately to the left Fisher's Garage and Chevrolet Dealership. Behind Fisher's sat the two-story frame home of Grace Lee Browning, wife of Orval Browning and their children, Gladys, John, Ruby, and Ada. The road in front of their home led to the Southfork Licking River dam, which was a popular fishing and swimming spot. (Courtesy of Jerry Conrad.)

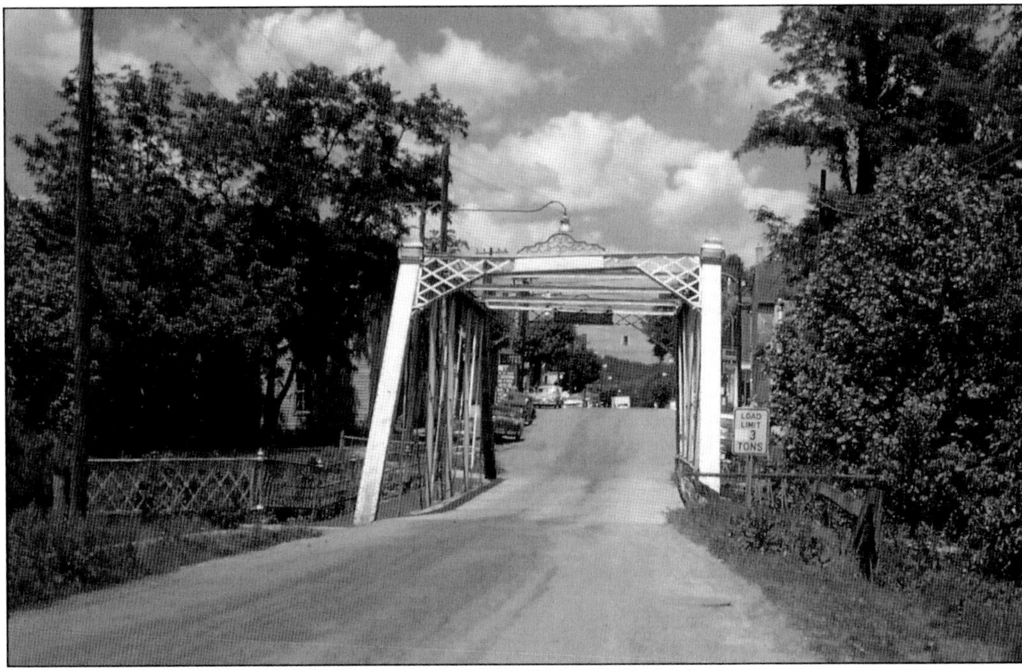

On this page are two views of the "Little Iron Bridge" on East Shelby Street, or High Street as it was originally called. This bridge stood at this site for close to 100 years, serving the foot and road traffic crossing over Burn's Branch, which runs into the Main Licking River near Shoemakertown. In the 1960s photograph above, Falmouth is seen from the east, looking west toward the downtown area. The walking path can be seen on the left side of the bridge. The picture below shows the side of the Little Iron Bridge and the rocks laid up to form the pier. After years of use, the sagging bridge was replaced by a culvert and new roadway. (Both courtesy of George Lach.)

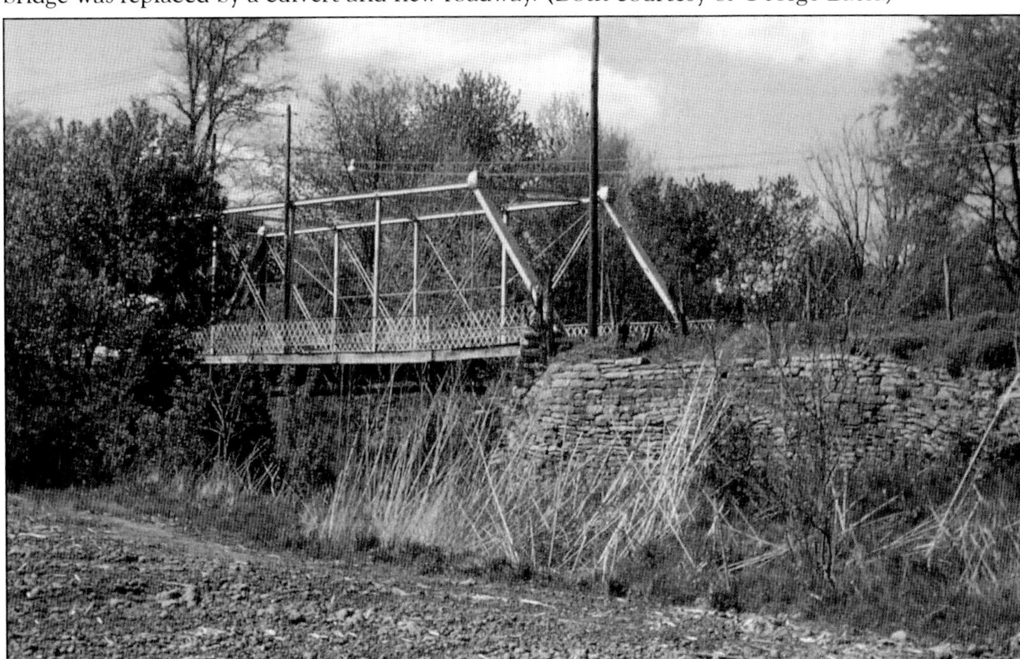

Shortly after 1869, a covered bridge was built across the South Licking River at Morgan. Like the other bridges built in Pendleton County about the same time, this bridge made travel much easier and safer for residents wishing to access the many parts of Pendleton County. (Courtesy of Billie Newman.)

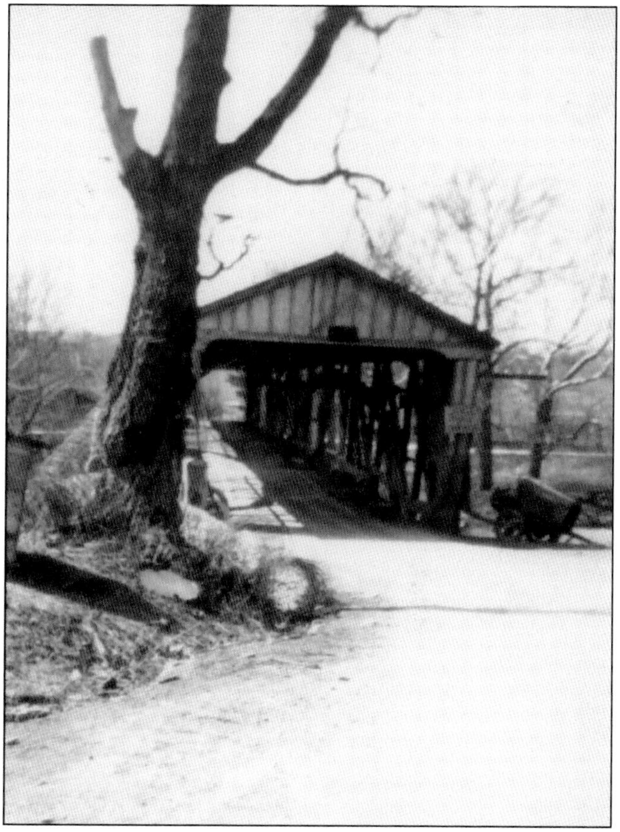

Pendleton County not only had the two Licking Rivers to cross as people traveled around the county, but there were numerous creeks, small and large, that also needed an easier year-round method of crossing. This iron bridge once spanned the Middle Fork of Grassy Creek on Center Ridge Road between Pleasant Ridge and Gardnersville. It was demolished and replaced with one of concrete around 1982. (Courtesy of Millie Belew.)

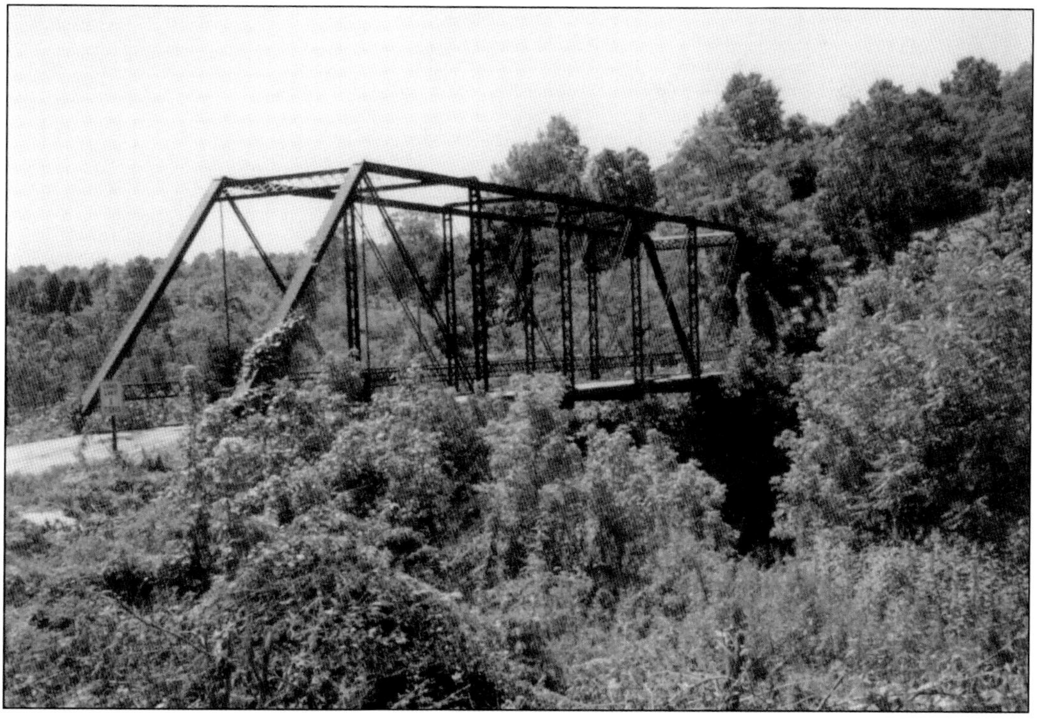

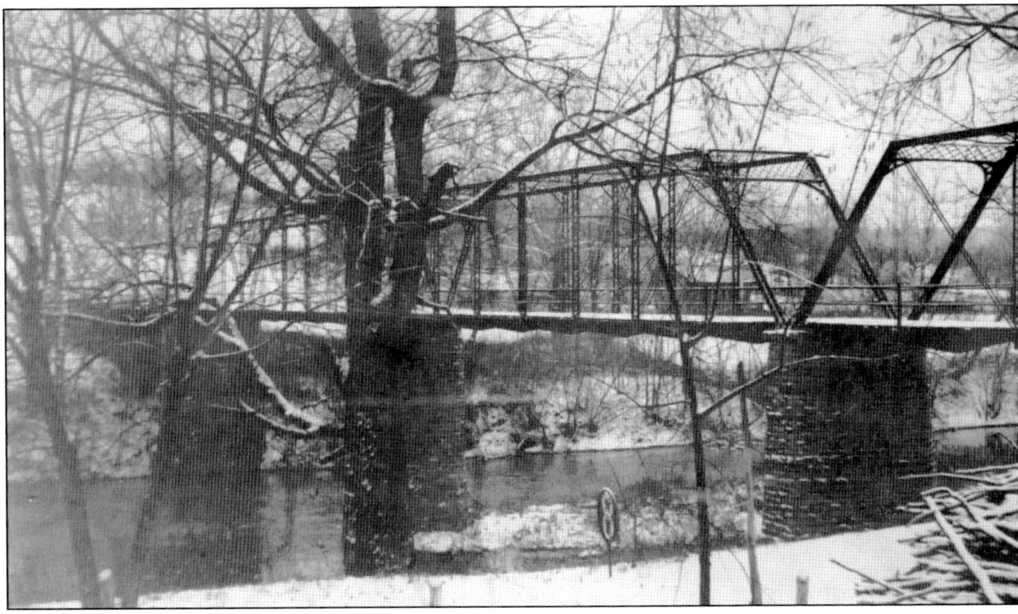

This winter photograph gives a peaceful look to the McKennysburg Bridge, which crossed the Main Licking River at McKennysburg. While the bridge withstood many years of use, the flood of 1997 finally washed it off its rock piers. The piers and the memories are all that remain. A wider and higher concrete bridge was built to take its place around 1999. (Courtesy of Pearlie Wright.)

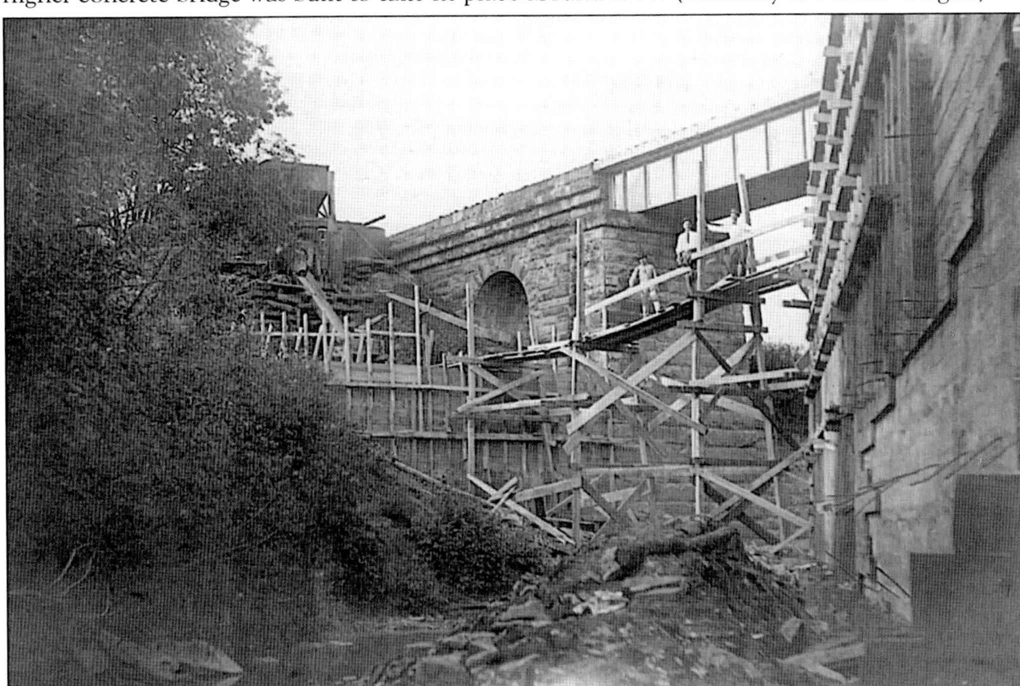

The railroad was a very important part of the development of communities over the years. Here a photographer captured the time when three unidentified workmen were inspecting the concrete construction work being done on the Chesapeake and Ohio Railroad Bridge in the area of Carntown. (Courtesy of Chris Fossitt.)

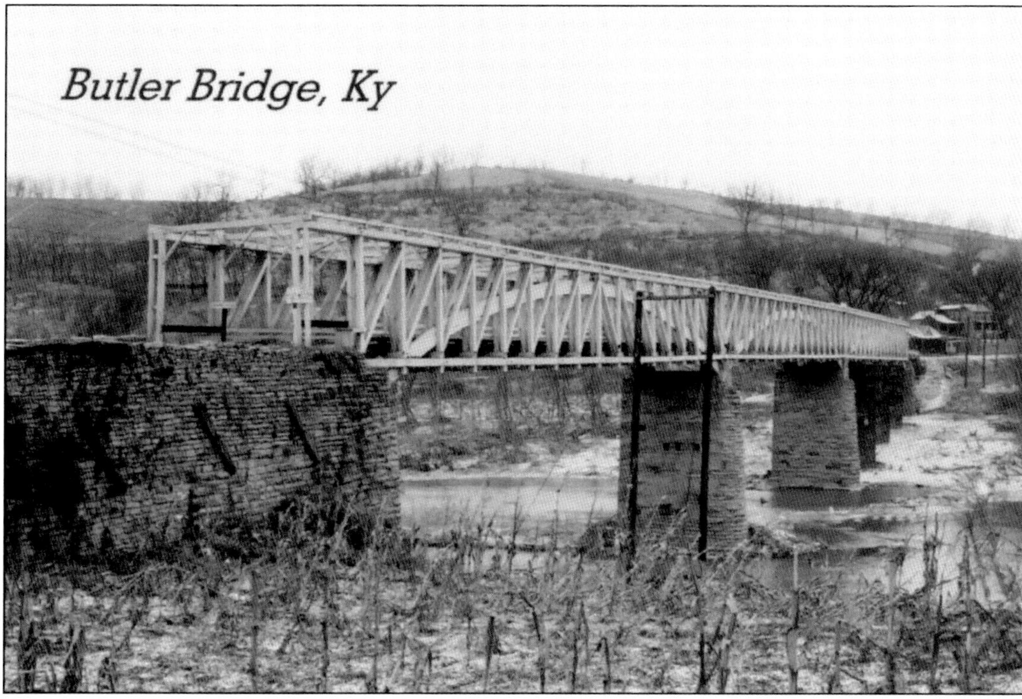

The old wooden covered bridge seen here leading into Butler was built in 1871. It was considered the longest covered bridge in the world at the time of its construction, a wonder for its time. The bridge was damaged beyond repair when the waters of the 1937 flood piled ice against the supports, almost reaching the floor of the bridge. While a modern three-arch bridge was being built, the damaged bridge was used for pedestrian travel only. Gov. A. B. Chandler dedicated the Pendleton County American Legion Memorial Bridge in Butler on October 20, 1937. (Above courtesy of Cheryl York.)

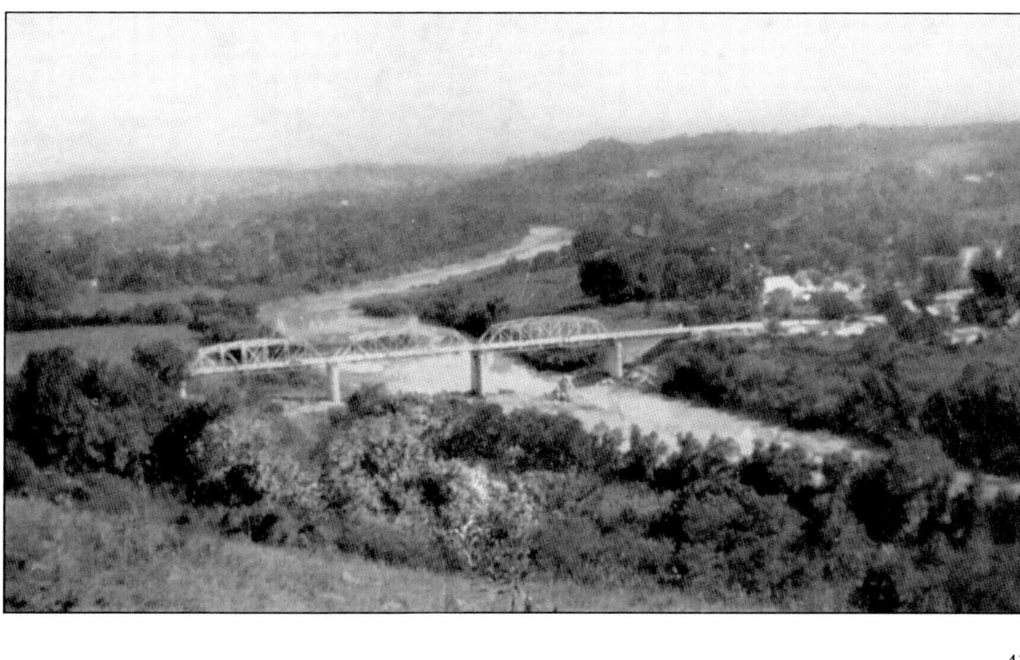

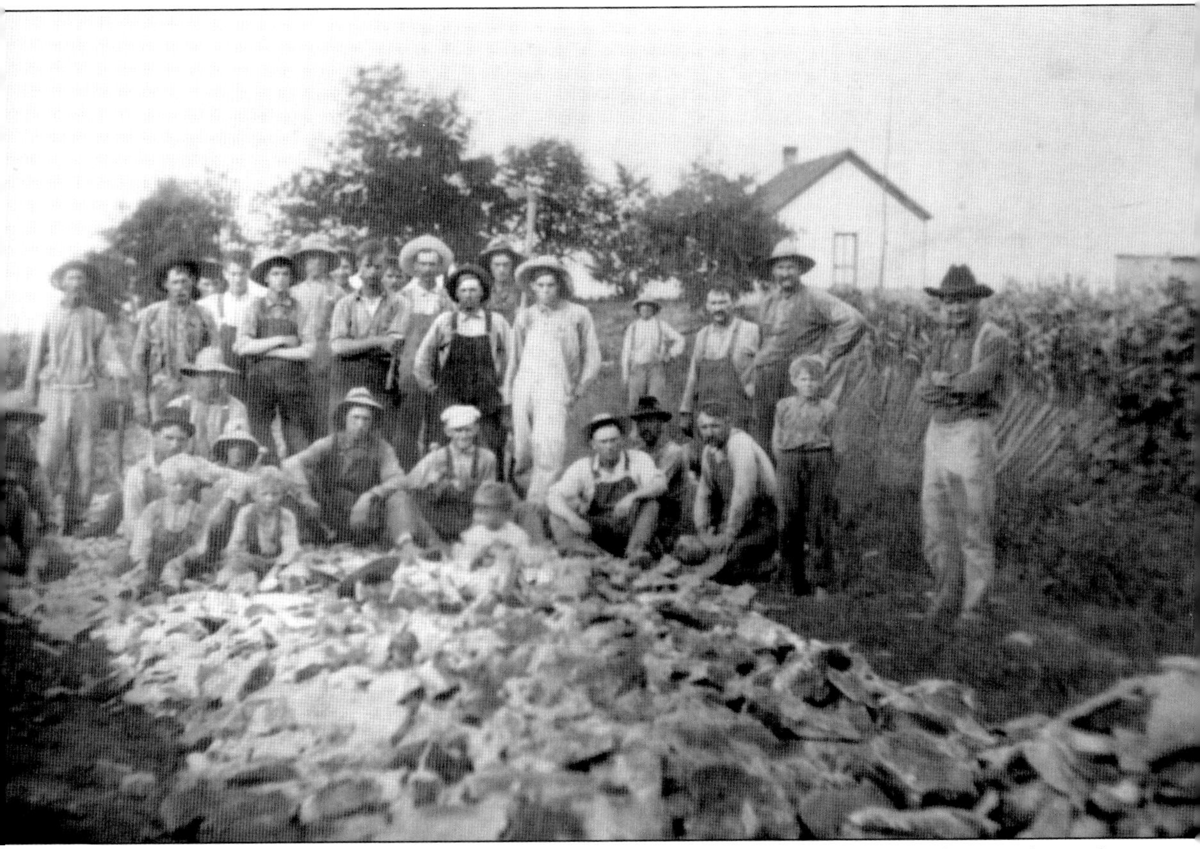

Landowners who had property bordering a road were expected to do their share to keep the roadways passable. This frequently involved cracking rocks into smaller stones and spreading them on the roadway nearest them. Here a group of neighbors in front of Unity School are performing this job. From left to right, they are (first row) Frank Bailey, Emmitt Bush, George Baker, Eddie Carr, Less Tomlin, Charles McMillian, Willie McMillian, Wesley Straub, Hick McMillian, Nelson Huffel, Bart Taylor, Simeon Straub, Ezery Straub, and Russ McMillian; (second row), Jim Hyland, Buck McMillian, Tom Tomlin, Dan Boone, Roy Courtney, Ira Boone, Laff Hutsell, Eddie Straub, Mose Belew, Louis Bailey, Emery ?, Bit McLafferty, Johnnie Straub, and Tom McMillian. The four men in back are unidentified. (Courtesy of Alice Conrad.)

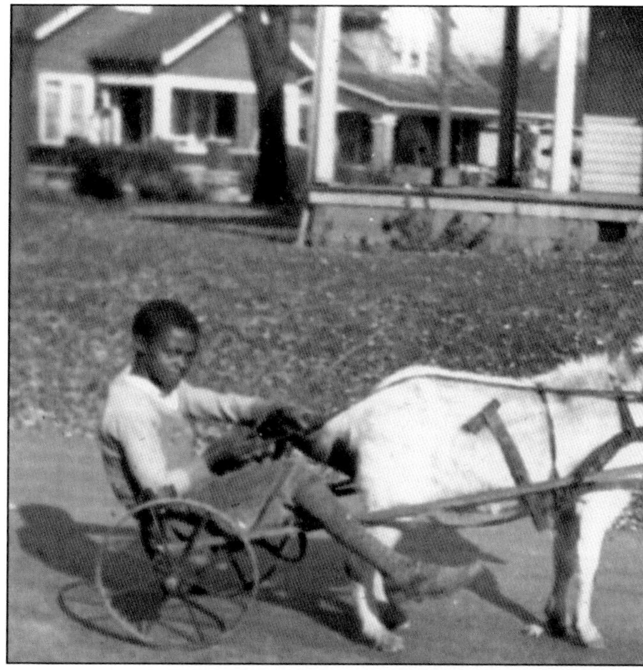

A not-uncommon mode of transportation was the use of carts drawn by farm animals. In this photograph, Calvin Hood uses the family goat to pull his cart as he travels about town. Calvin was the son of Mr. and Mrs. Warren Hood. He and his brother, Walter, served in World War II. While serving with the U.S. Army in the South Pacific, Corporal Hood was wounded. After his return to Falmouth, he lived and raised his family at the corner of Beech and Fourth Streets while working for the city. They later moved to the Cincinnati area. (Courtesy of David Belew.)

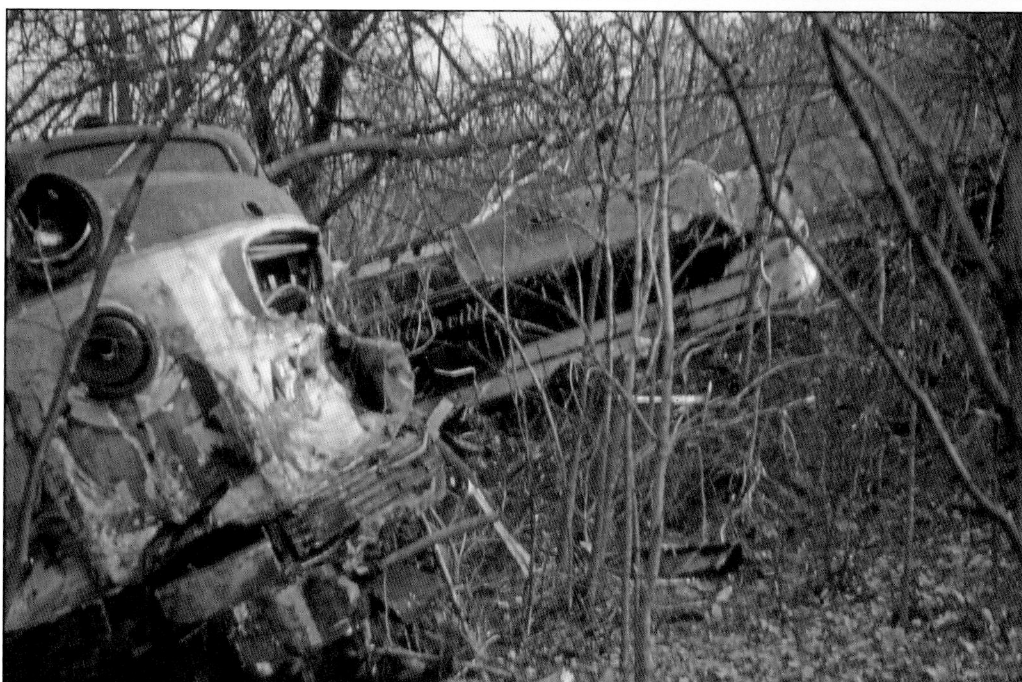

It is 1957, and the southbound Flamingo has just passed through Falmouth. The Flamingo, a Louisville and Nashville Railroad passenger train, wrecked when it was struck by an empty oil tanker that had come loose from a passing freight train heading north. The twin diesel engine was stopped on the edge of the steep banks of the South Fork Licking River by the large sycamore trees. The injured were treated by a local physician and then taken to St. Elizabeth Hospital for further examination. Both engineers were native to the Morgan area. (Courtesy of George Lach.)

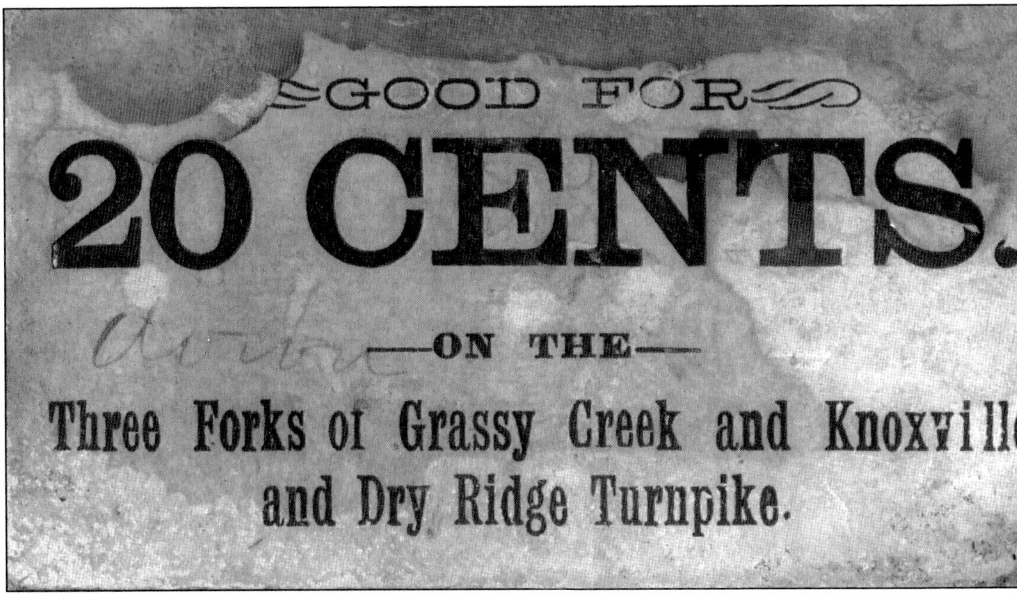
GOOD FOR
20 CENTS.
—ON THE—
Three Forks of Grassy Creek and Knoxville and Dry Ridge Turnpike.

Tollhouses could be found along several roads throughout the county. The ticket shown here is for the Three Forks of Grassy Creek and Knoxville and Dry Ridge Turnpike. Different prices were charged for the various types of vehicles driven over the roadway. This one was for 20¢ and indicates that the travelers were heading down the turnpike. (Courtesy of Sherry DeWald.)

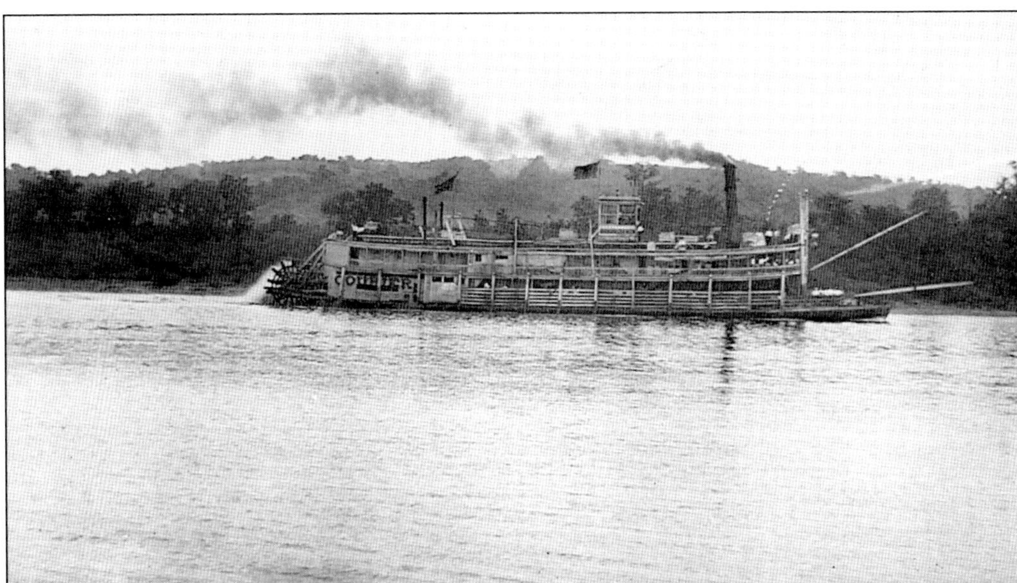

A small strip of Pendleton County borders the Ohio River. Very early in the county's history, the road from this area to Falmouth was well-traveled, even though it was a rough and rocky stagecoach route. The steamboat landing at the mouth of the Stepstone Creek near Carntown and the steamboat landing at Foster provided a means for goods to be shipped to and from Cincinnati and then packed into wagons traveling to Falmouth and other stops along the way. (Courtesy of Chris Fossitt.)

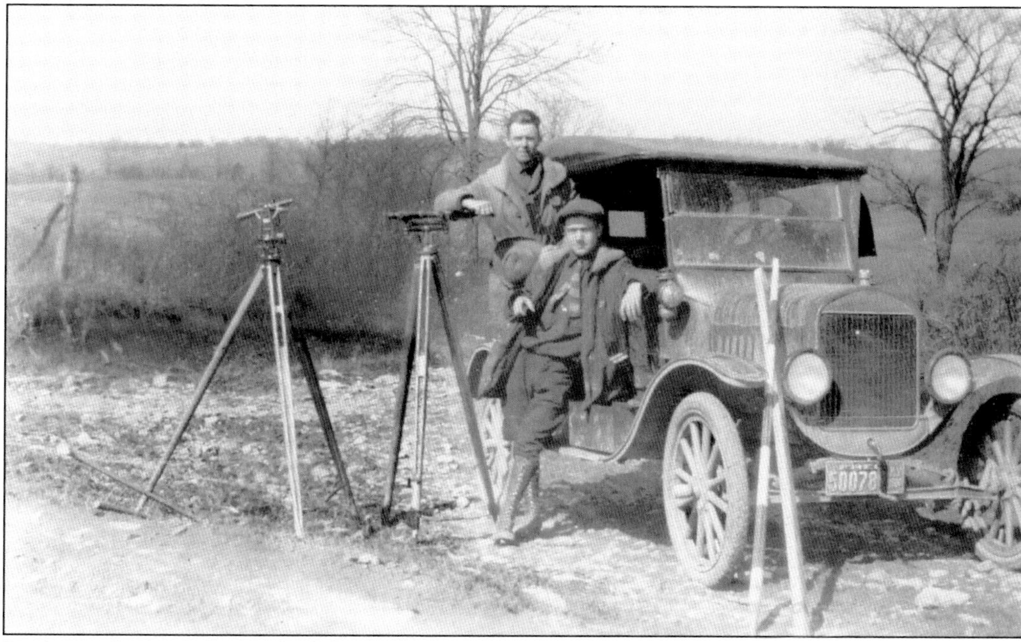

In the early 1920s, several of the main roads were surveyed and straightened from the original paths that followed the ridge tops. Some were little more than the buffalo paths traveled from the very early years in the county's history. Here two young men with their surveying gear stop work for a moment to be photographed. (Courtesy of Bill Pettit.)

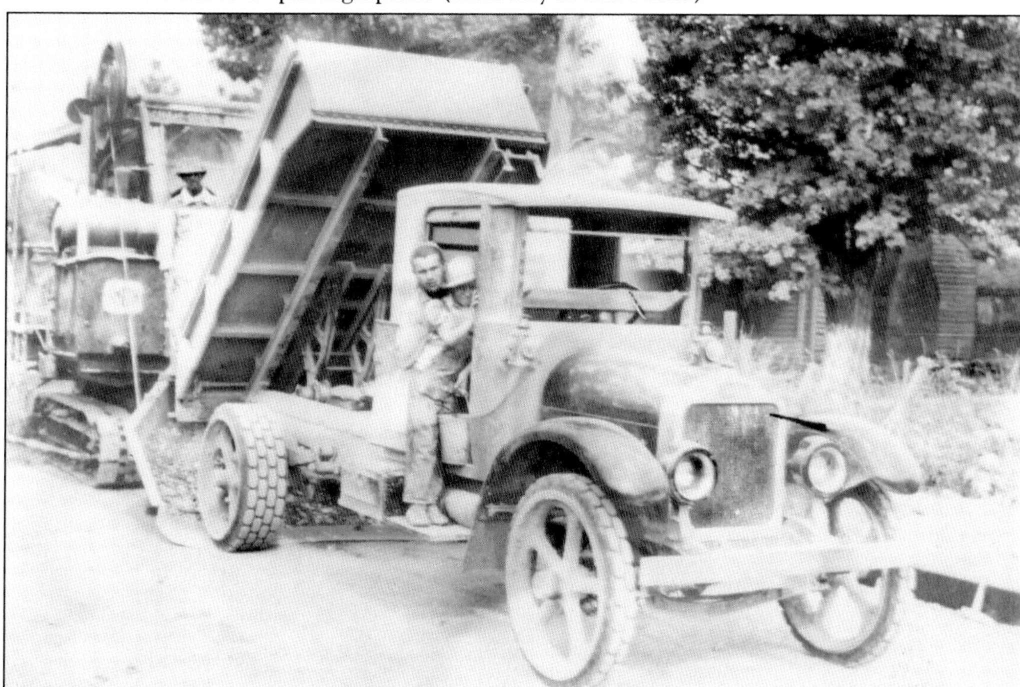

In this photograph taken in the late 1920s, three men are shown as they macadamize a roadway in the Falmouth area. Most of the roads improved in this manner were near the larger towns. Many country roads were still dirt or gravel into the early 1950s.

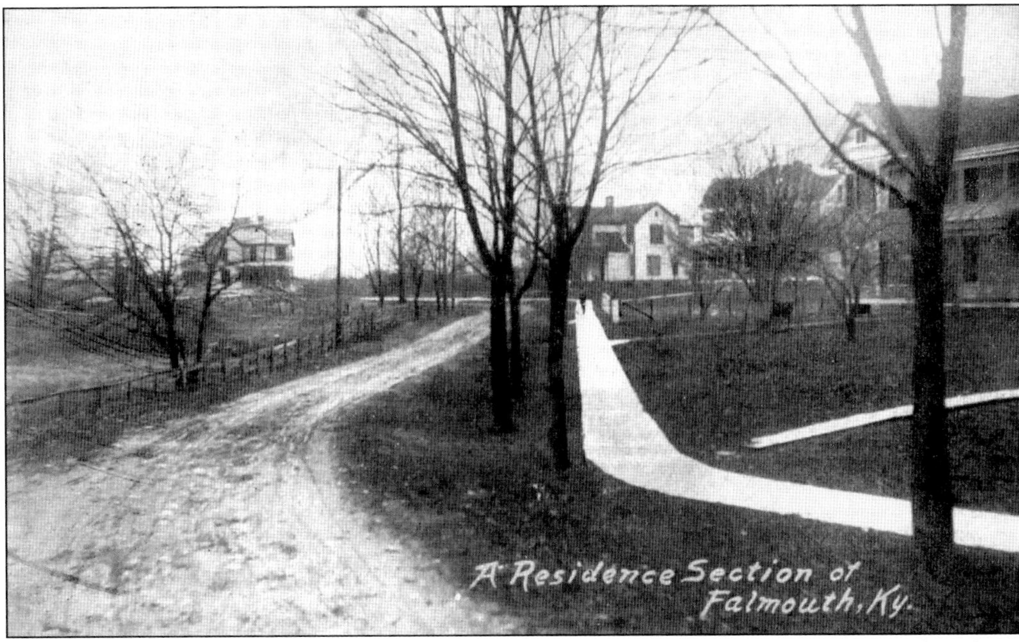

This postcard photograph of Riverside Drive (now Maple Avenue) gives a view from the edge of Falmouth looking west toward Riverside Cemetery. The house in the foreground on the right was owned by Dr. William Townsend, a local physician. Henry Browning and George House were neighbors; their homes are visible farther up the avenue. (Courtesy of Cheryl York.)

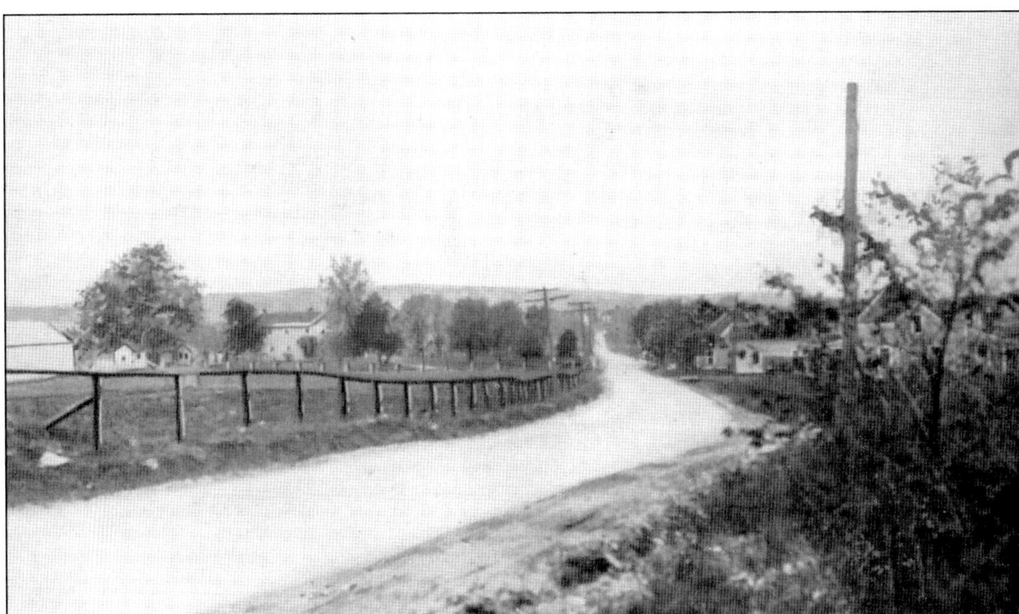

The road in this photograph follows the route taken as one comes from the south, driving into Falmouth from what is now KY22, or Main Street. On the left stands the Berger home and farm, which later was developed into the Berger Subdivision. Beech Street, Robbins Avenue, and Broad Street turn off the road to the right as one heads toward downtown Falmouth. (Courtesy of Cheryl York.)

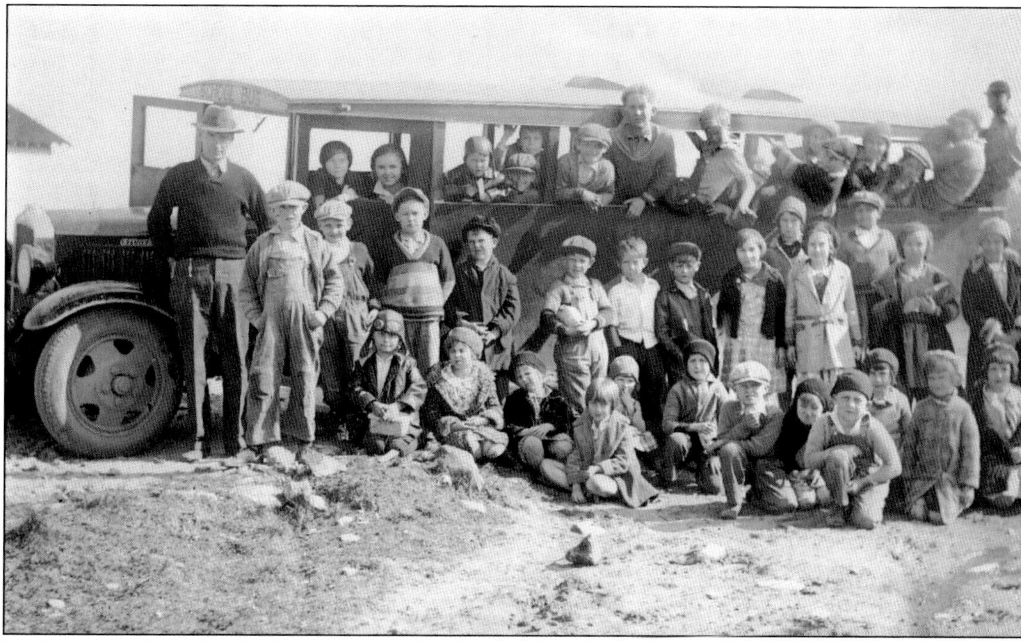

In the 1930s, Pendleton County ran a few buses transporting students to their schools. Here is a typical busload of students. The driver and students are unidentified but most likely are from the Butler area. (Courtesy of the Opal Jackson family.)

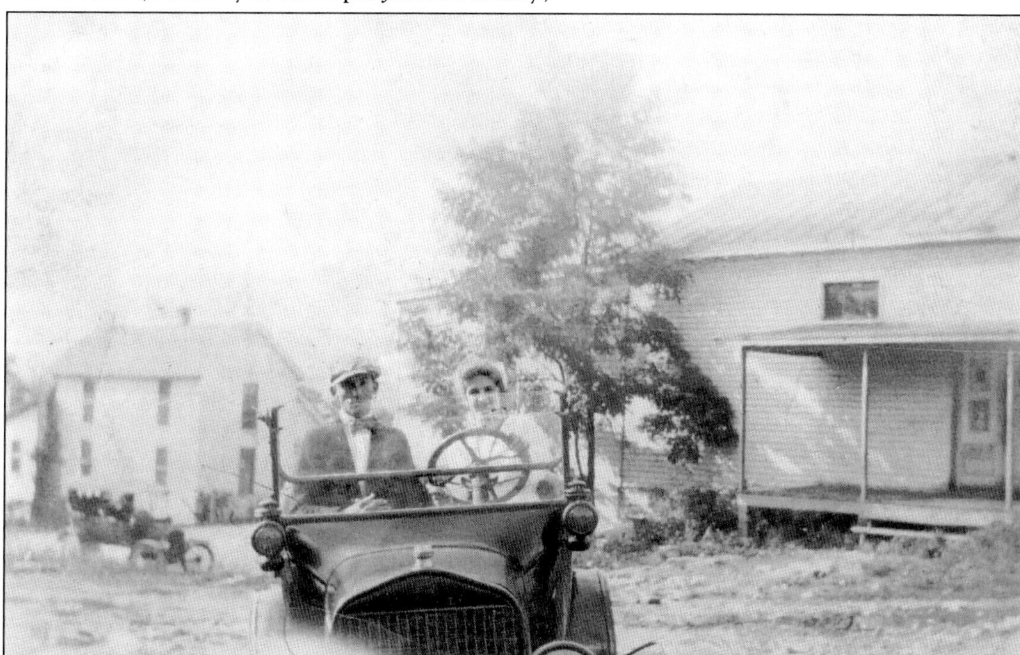

In this photograph, William Gilbert Newman and Lillian McLaughlin appear to be having a great time driving their automobile. This was taken about 1920 in Callensville, a small town near Morgan. At one time, there were several businesses and homes in this town. Years later, most families and businesses moved into Morgan, leaving few signs of Callensville's existence today. (Courtesy of Billie Newman.)

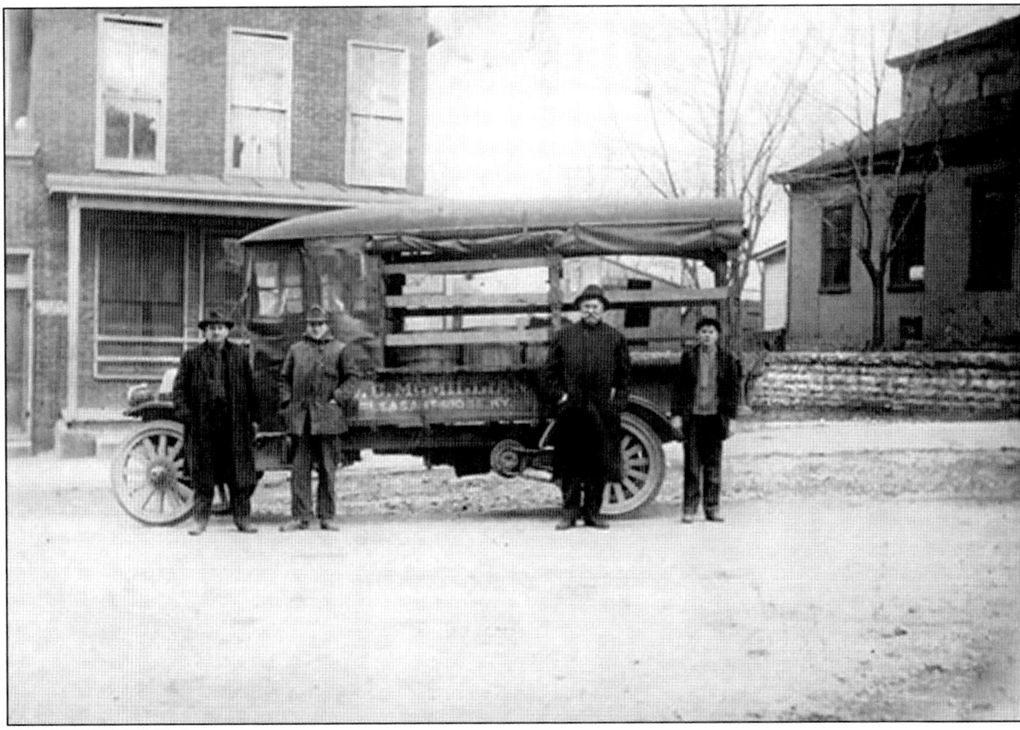

In the early 1900s, Walter Cash McMillian, second from the right, traveled to Covington to purchase goods for his huckster wagon. He would then drive back to the Foster area with the various items in hopes of reselling them to the residents there. (Courtesy of Mark Black.)

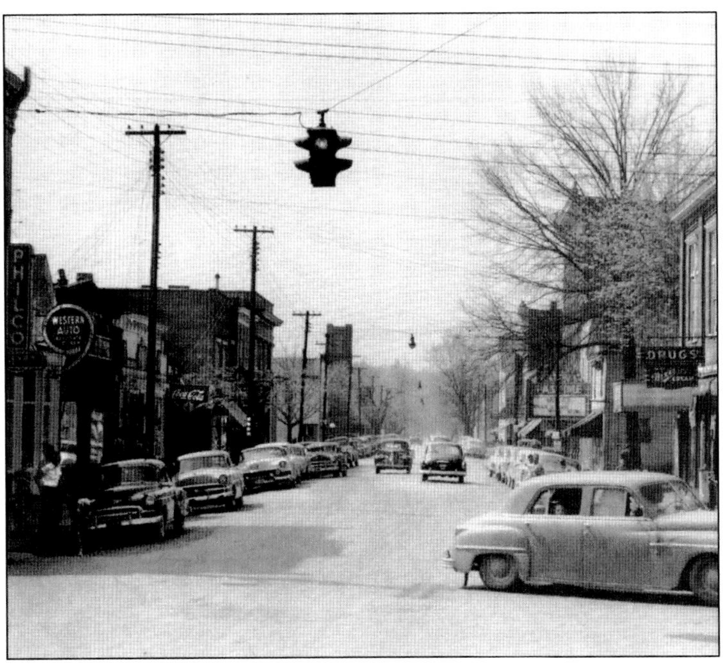

This view of Shelby Street reveals how busy downtown Falmouth was in the mid-1950s. Seen on the left is the Western Auto Store owned by Alex and Dorothy Caldwell. They bought the building and contents, adding new items over the years. On the right is Moreland Drug Store, and just down from there is the Pastime Theatre, which was the main theater in town. Of interest is the number of street lights hanging at the intersections. (Courtesy of Dixie Wyatt.)

Three

FAMILY AND FRIENDS

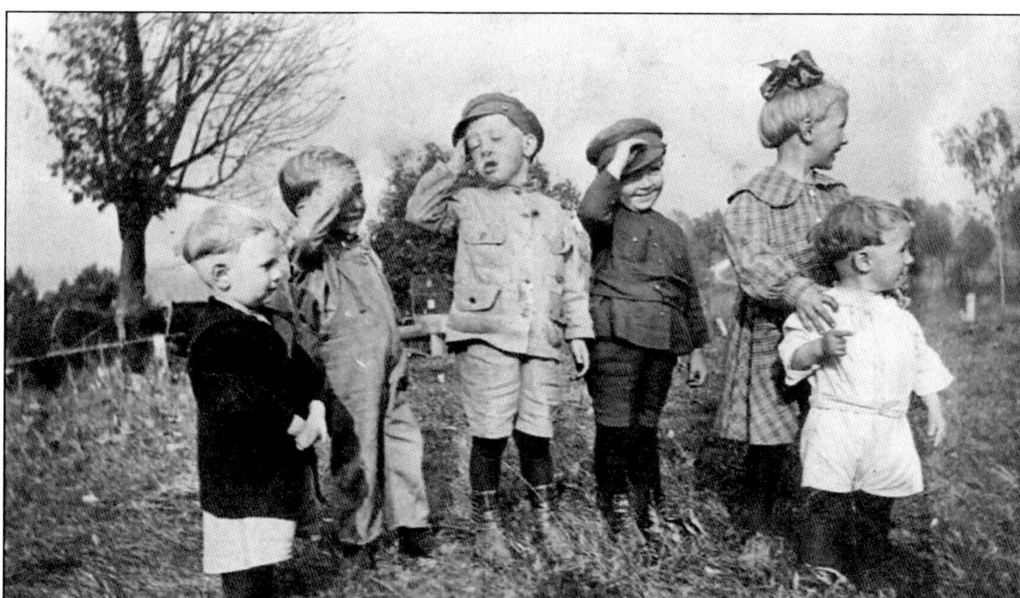

Gathered for a moment in 1917 on the front lawn of Frank and Emma Conrad's home at Short Creek, these youngsters visited often with their family. Seen from left to right are Arnold Conrad, Emmitt Conrad, Richard Gulick, Carl ?, Louise Conrad, and Chester Conrad.

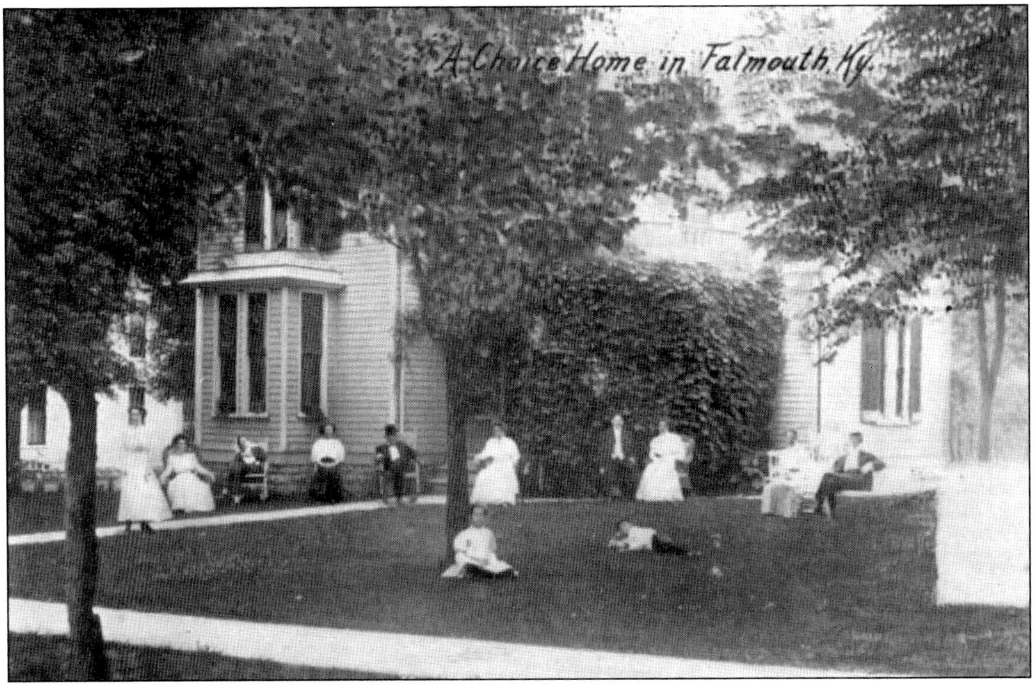

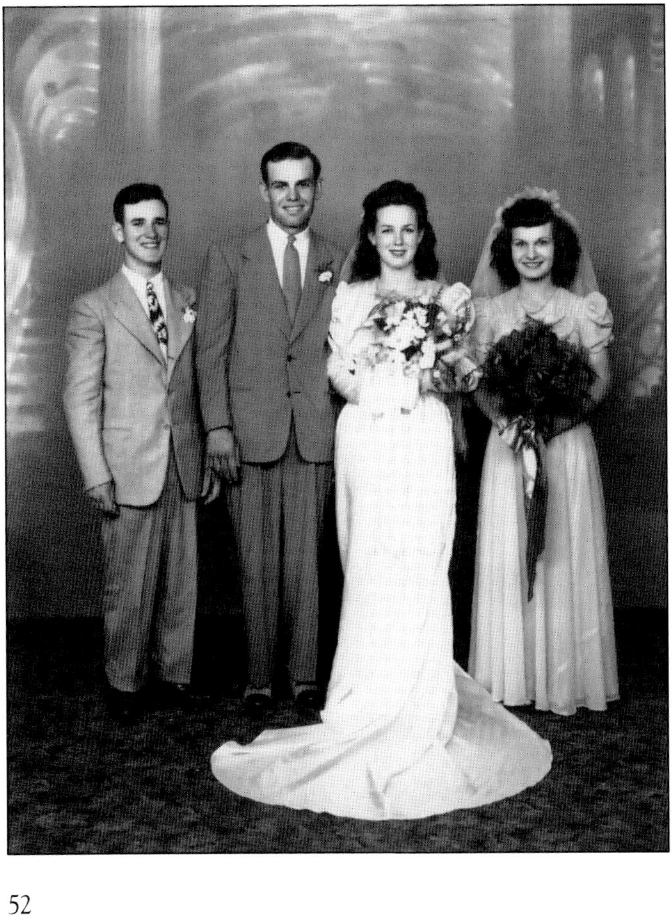

Here neighbors have met in their respective yards on Riverside Drive to share an afternoon of frolicking and talk. This street was once called Cemetery Road. Today it is Maple Avenue. Several smaller streets branched from it as one traveled to the end at Riverside Cemetery. (Courtesy of the Opal Jackson family.)

On June 28, 1947, Raymond LaFollette and Eula Caldwell were married by Rev. W. M. Lenox. Eula's brother, Jack Caldwell, was the best man, and Raymond's sister, Eula LaFollette, was the maid of honor. (Courtesy of Teresa Johnston.)

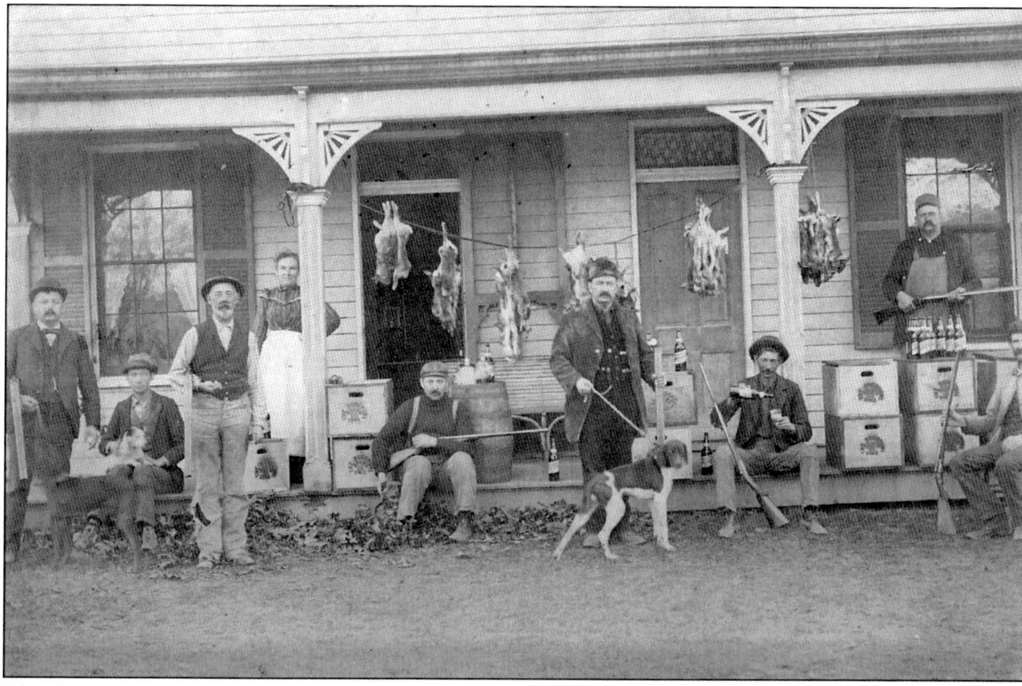

The farm property and house in this photograph were owned by Bill Ducker and located on Flour Creek Road across from the Myers Distillery. A group has gathered to relax and enjoy a bottle of Hudepohl Beer after what appears to have been a good day hunting rabbits. Seen here from left to right are an unidentified hunter, Howard Ducker Sr., Bill Ducker, Molly Ducker, two unidentified, Frank Scott, and another two unidentified. The house burned down in about 1958. The property is now owned by George Hornbeck. (Courtesy of George Hornbeck.)

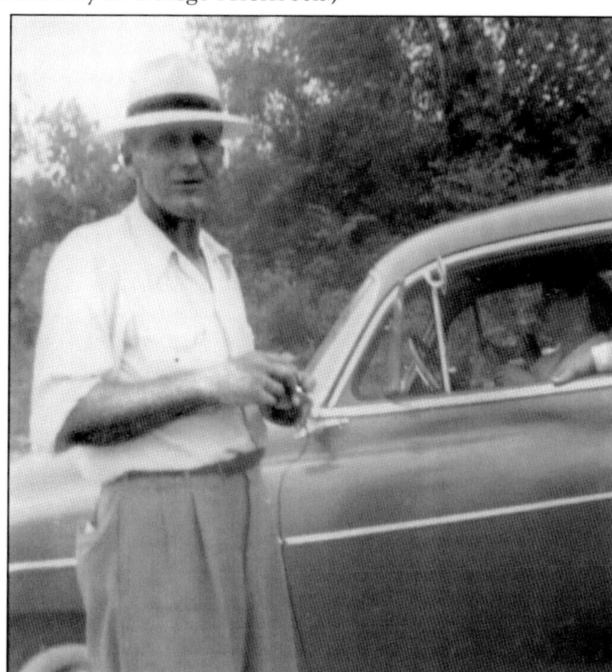

Born in 1902, William "Willie" Jacob Klaber was a farmer living on Dahms Road, off KY22 west of Falmouth. Helping in his work was his wife, Naomie McKinley. He had five siblings, Charlie, Dutch, Catherine, Francis, and Florence. (Courtesy of the Bernice Hess family.)

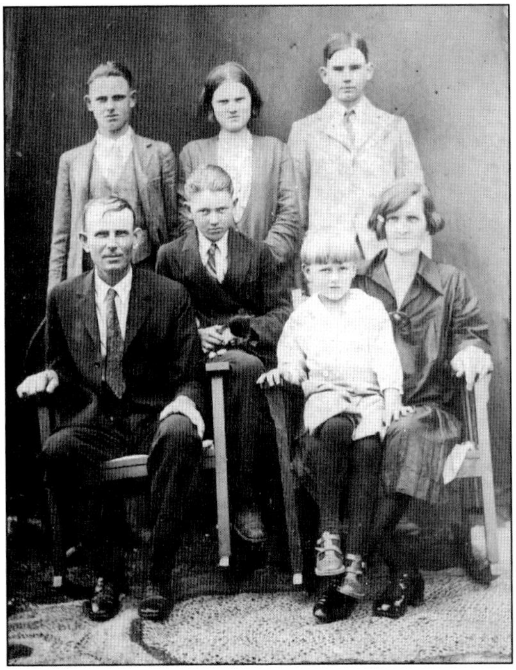

The Earl Fossitt family from near Peach Grove is shown here in a family photograph taken in the late 1920s. Seated is Earl Fossitt with his son, Albert, standing next to him. Clarence is seated on the lap of his mother, Minnie Shaver Fossitt. Standing behind their parents are their other children. From left to right, they are Lansing, Violet, and Rudolph. (Courtesy of Chris Fossitt.)

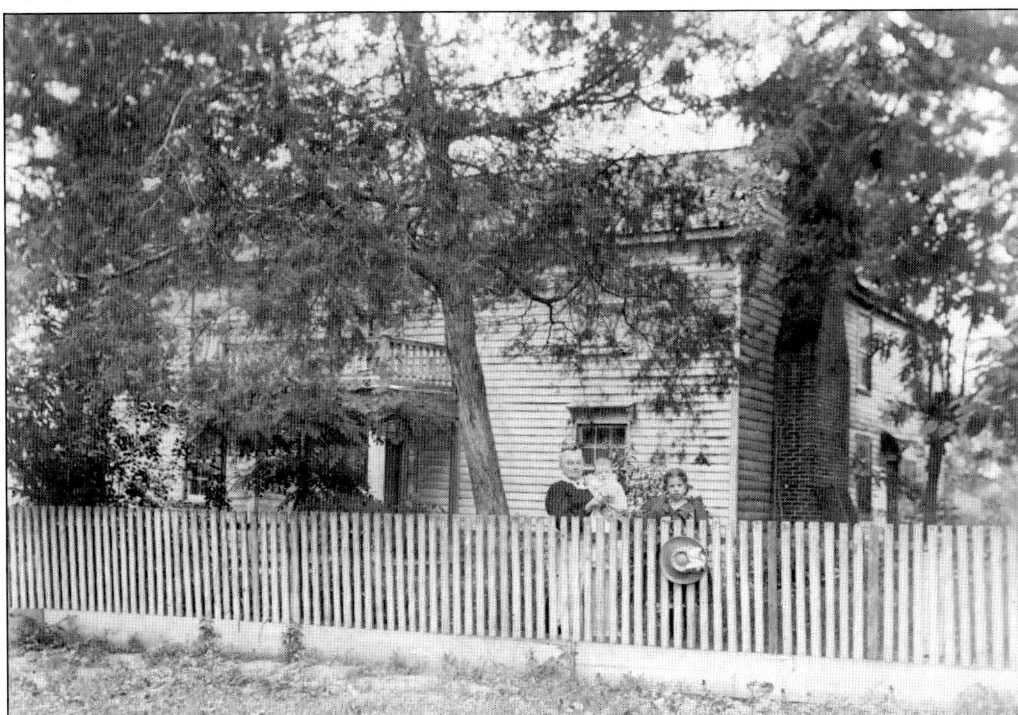

Before the days of day care, there were nannies or nurses to care for the young children in a family. Standing is Fannie Taylor holding William C. Hagemeyer, with his sister Elizabeth Hagemeyer on the right. As an adult, William owned several businesses along Mill Street in Butler with his father, C. C. Hagemeyer of Cincinnati. William died in 1987 in Monterey, California. (Courtesy of the Opal Jackson family.)

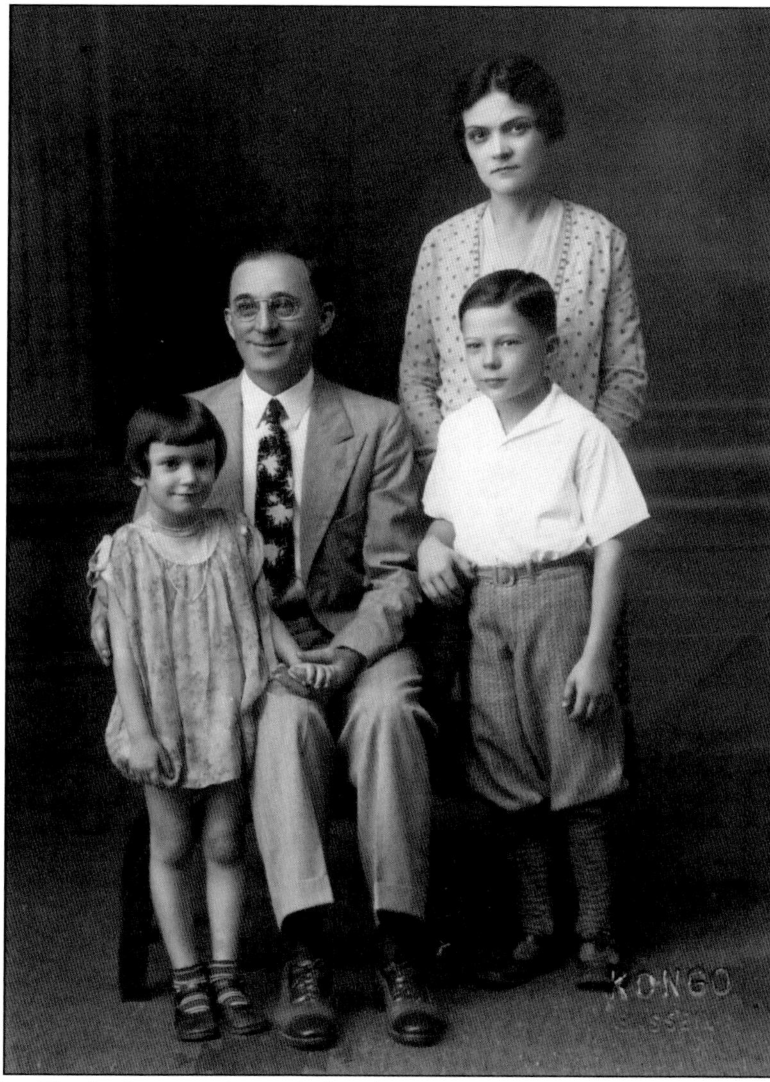

Born in 1888, Charles Lamont Conrad played an important part in a variety of world events. Early in his life, he trained for the ministry and was ordained in 1911 to preach in the Baptist Church. During World War I, he served in France on the YMCA International Committee. In 1919, he was assigned to work in Bassein, Burma with the Pwo Karen of Southeast Asia through the American Baptist Foreign Mission Society. In 1921 he married Ruth Zachary and returned to the United States soon afterwards for more training. He and Ruth went back overseas to Jamshedpur, India in the early 1940s, but were forced to evacuate or be captured by the Japanese during World War II. They returned to India a few years later but again were forced to leave or be caught up in the 1949 civil war there. In 1953 he retired from this ministry and returned to Pendleton County. He soon was in the midst of activity again. During the next few years he was elected as a state representative, played an important part in the development of Kincaid Park, was a grand mason, and a member of the Falmouth Baptist Church. During this time back home, his wife died. (Their son died tragically in 1960.) In 1963 Charles married Emmaline Arnold. Tragedy struck again when his only daughter, Florence, died during a fire at her home. Charles L. Conrad passed away in 1984 at the age of 96, after four years residing in the Louisville Retirement Home, leaving Emmaline as the only survivor of his immediate family.

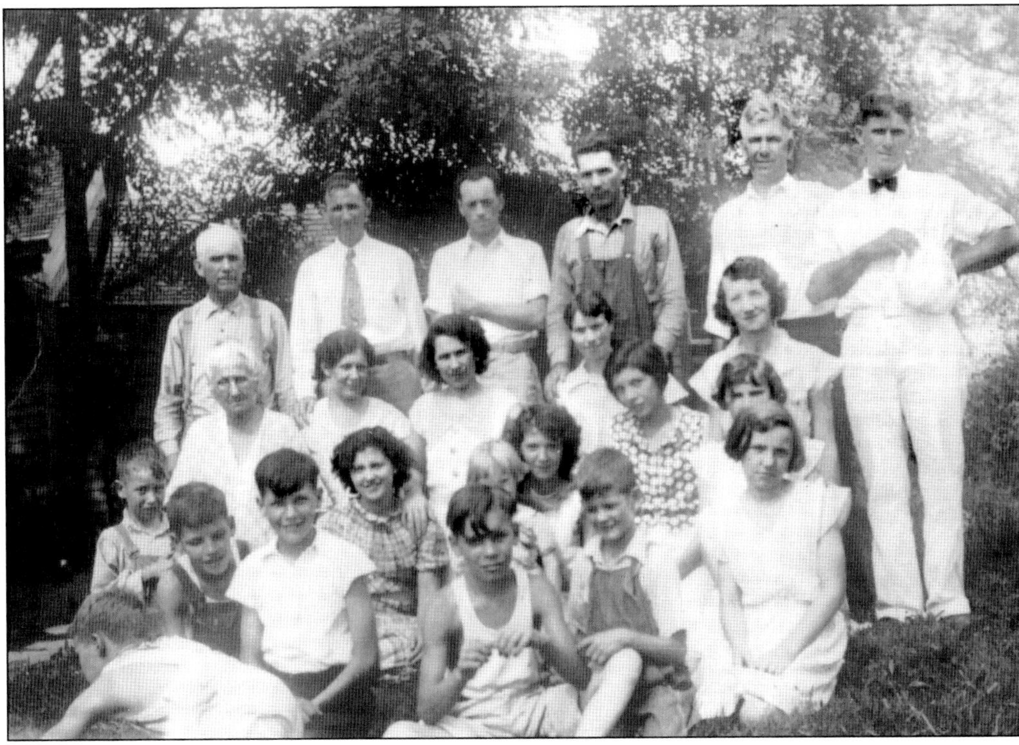

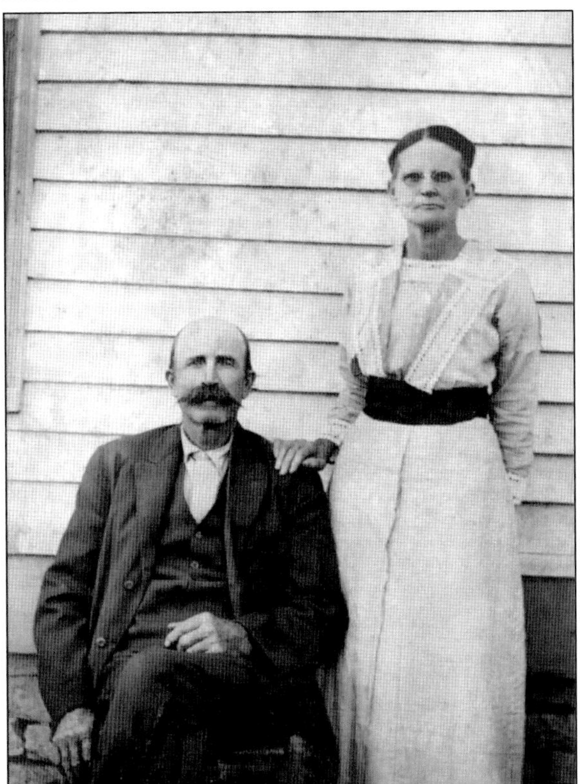

Posing for the camera is the George and Margaret Lovelace family of Caddo. Behind the grandchildren in front, the adults are, from left to right, (kneeling) Margaret, Merte C., Bertie Bush, Dola, and Cecil; (standing) George, Elmer C., Hobert Bush, Dallas L., Walter L., and Henry L. (Courtesy of Chris Fossitt.)

Bart and Florie Fossitt pose in front of their home on Flour Creek Road. Bart was born Daniel Barton Fossitt in 1850; Florie was born Flora Belle Lancaster in 1857. They married in 1877 and raised 15 children together. (Courtesy of Chris Fossitt.)

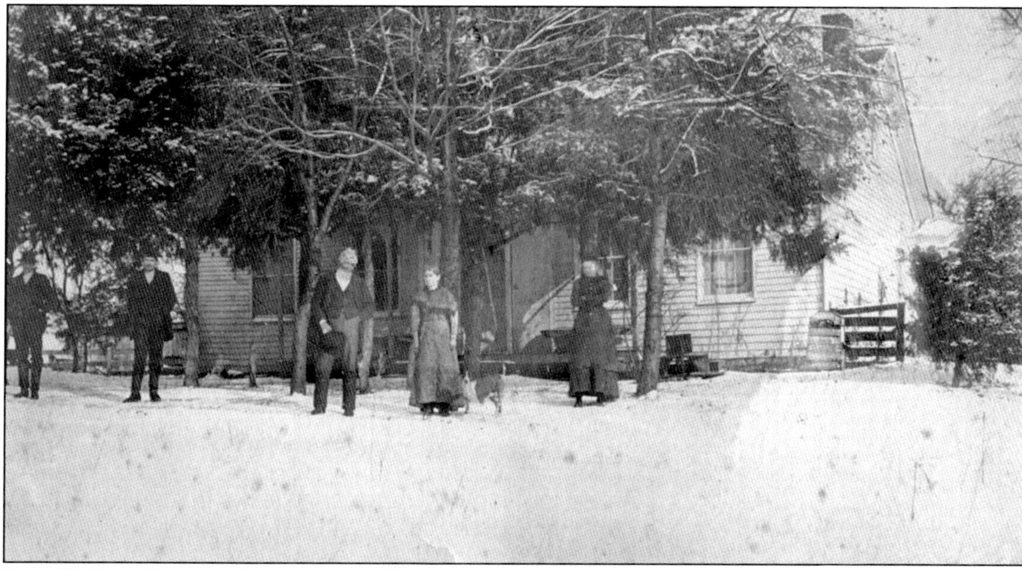

The William Barnard home in Peach Grove is shown as it looked in the late 1800s. More recent generations of this Barnard family have served the Pendleton and Campbell County area with their preaching and singing ministries. The home remains under the care of Adlyn Fossitt Cox. (Courtesy of Chris Fossitt.)

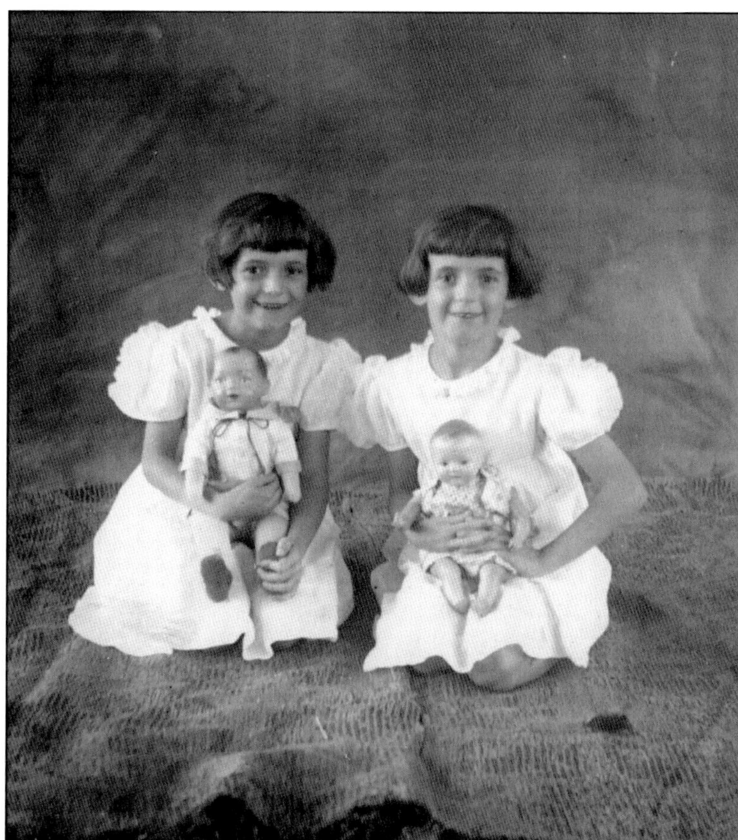

Alta Mae Fryer Johnston and Alma Faye Fryer Flairty are the twin daughters of Edward Percy Fryer and Lillie Dunaway Fryer of Flour Creek. They were the last Fryers to be born in the Fryer stone house at the intersection of US 27 and Flour Creek Road, and the sixth generation to live in Pendleton County. (Courtesy of Teresa Johnston.)

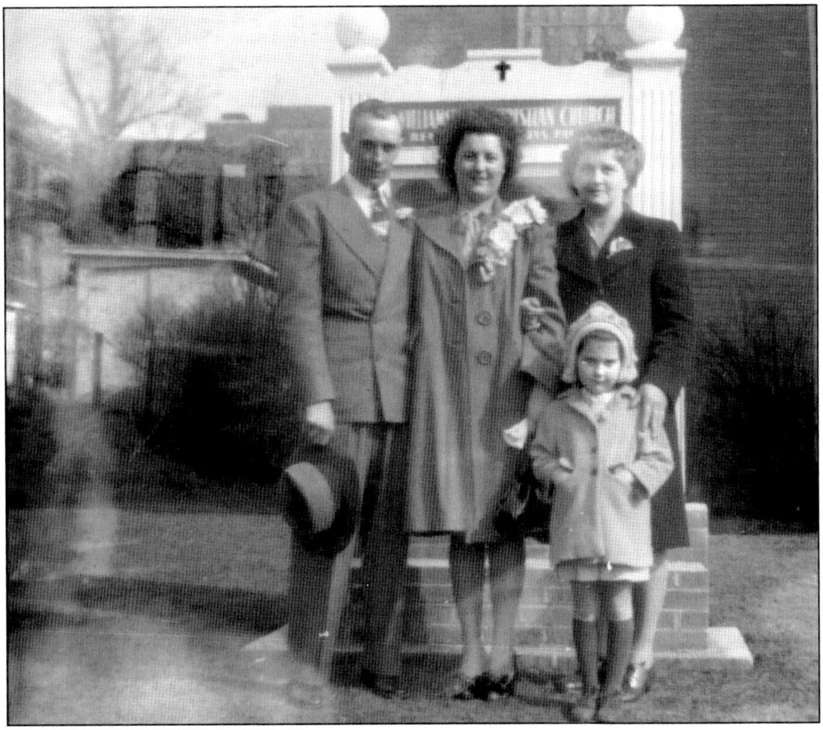

Vic Moore and Dorothy Whaley are seen standing outside of the Williamstown Baptist Church on their wedding day. Next to Dorothy is her mother, Mable Kenner Whaley, and her younger sister, Jane Whaley Stahl. (Courtesy of Jane Stahl.)

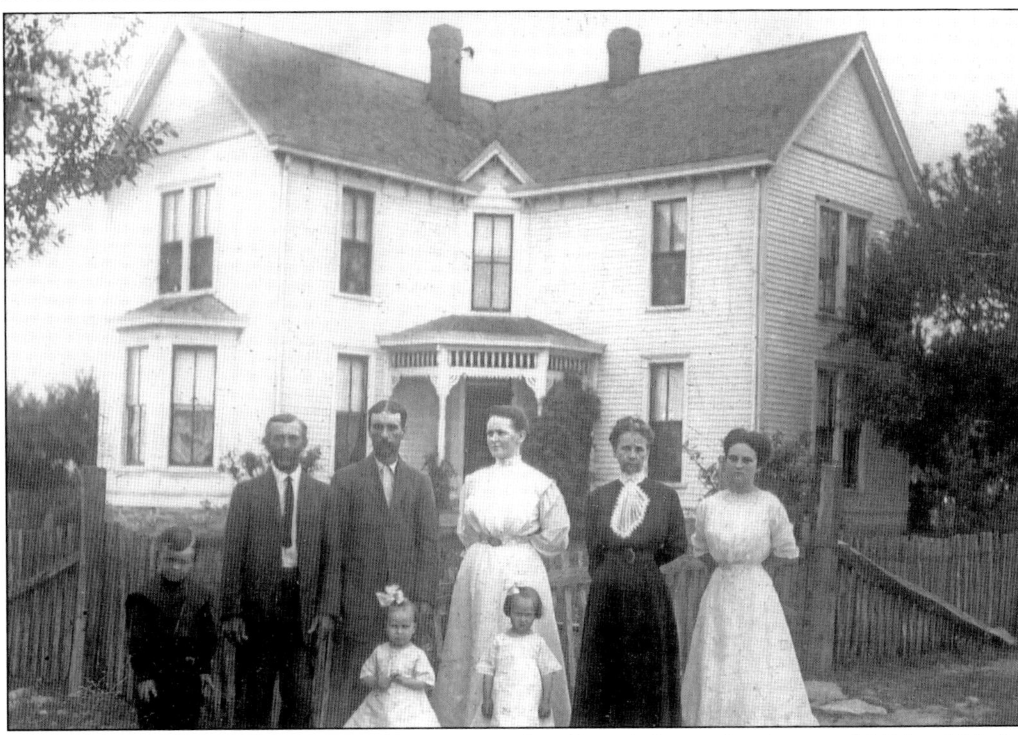

The Chiles family posed to capture this time together. From left to right, they are (children) Harley Chiles, Lucille Chiles, and Gertrude Chiles; (adults) James Mitchell Chiles, Ira Chancellor Chiles, Melinda Chiles, Aunt Pearl Chiles McNay, and Aunt Mae. (Courtesy of Becky Chiles.)

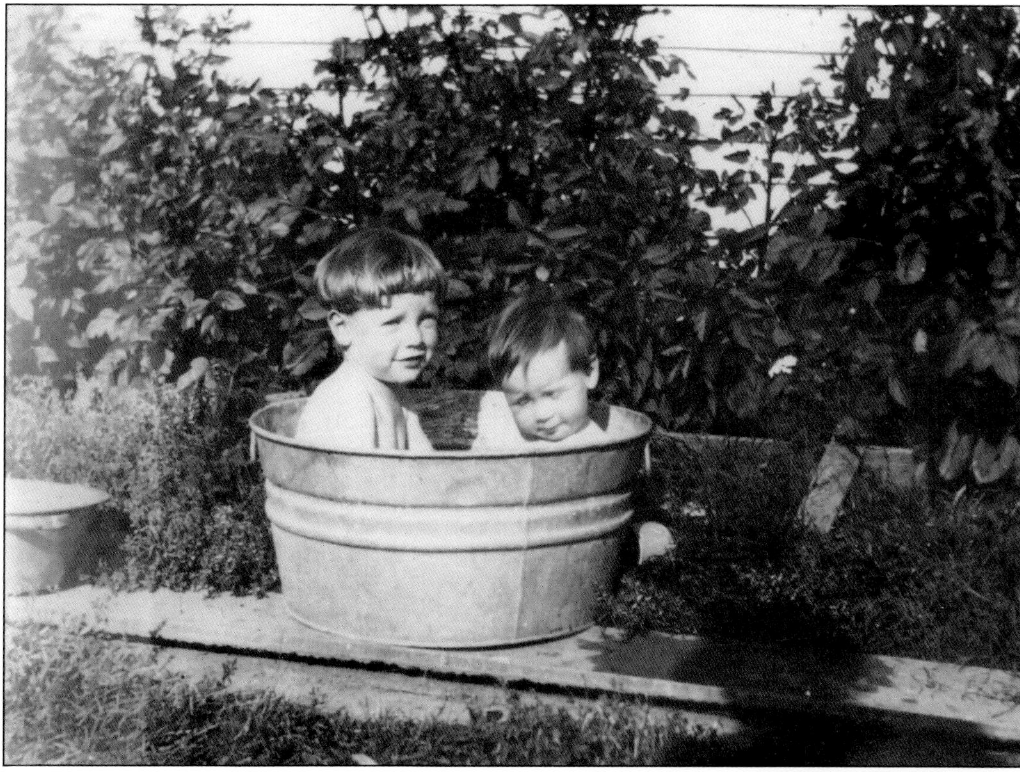

Nothing is better than cooling off on a hot summer day in a large washtub filled with water. In this photograph, Ellis Campbell (left) and his sister Lois do just that. They are the children of James Campbell of Boston Station. Their family owned what was considered by many the first dairy barn in the county. They also owned a large threshing machine used to prepare the large amount of feed needed for their cows. (Courtesy of Lois Wilson.)

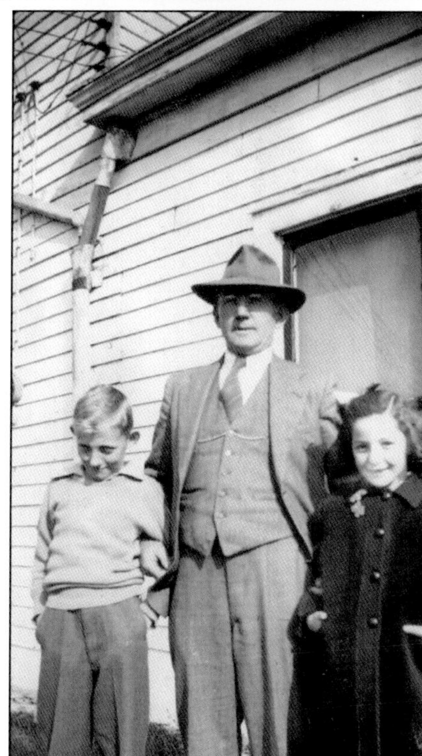

Frank G. Marquette stands between his grandchildren, Terry Cummins and Audrey Cummins. Frank was born about 1886 and died in 1961. He was a civic leader, helping to establish the rural electrification of the local area,and held the office of Kentucky State Representative for the 68th District in 1946 and 1948.

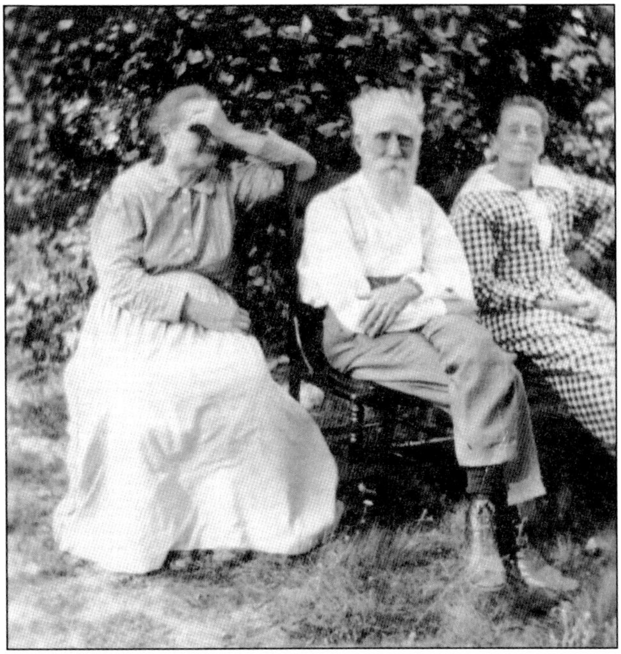

John William Alexander Monroe was the son of John Alexander Monroe, one of the early settlers of Falmouth. Born in 1837 in Callensville, he first married Rachel Ann Thompson, with whom he had five children. Rachel died in 1863, after which John William married Mary Elizabeth Bailey. From this union one son, James W., was born before Mary died in 1868. Margaret Ellen Taylor was J. W. Monroe's third wife. They had five children. In this photograph, J. W. Monroe is seated with his third wife, "Maggie," on the left and daughter Emma Monroe Conrad on the right.

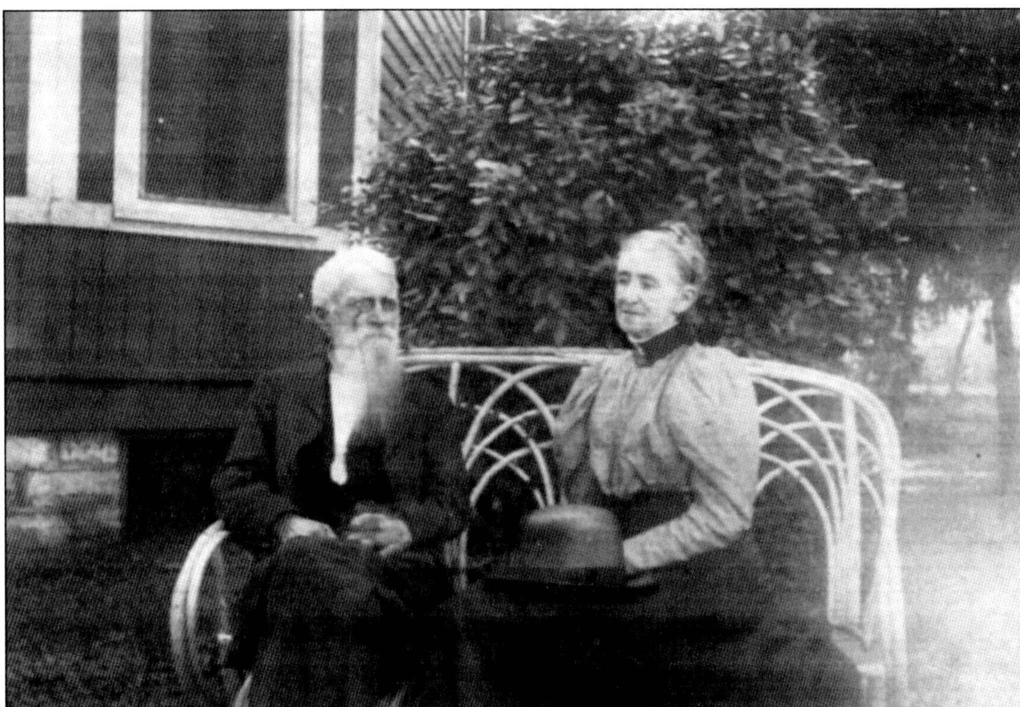

Leslie Applegate, born in 1854 and reared on the home farm southeast of Falmouth, was educated in Falmouth and then Danville, Kentucky. He studied law and began his practice in Falmouth in 1876. In 1887 he married Sally Menzies. Here they are seen sitting in the side yard of their house on Maple Avenue. The home, a Victorian dwelling with shingle siding, was built in 1884. (Courtesy of Shirley Tuemler.)

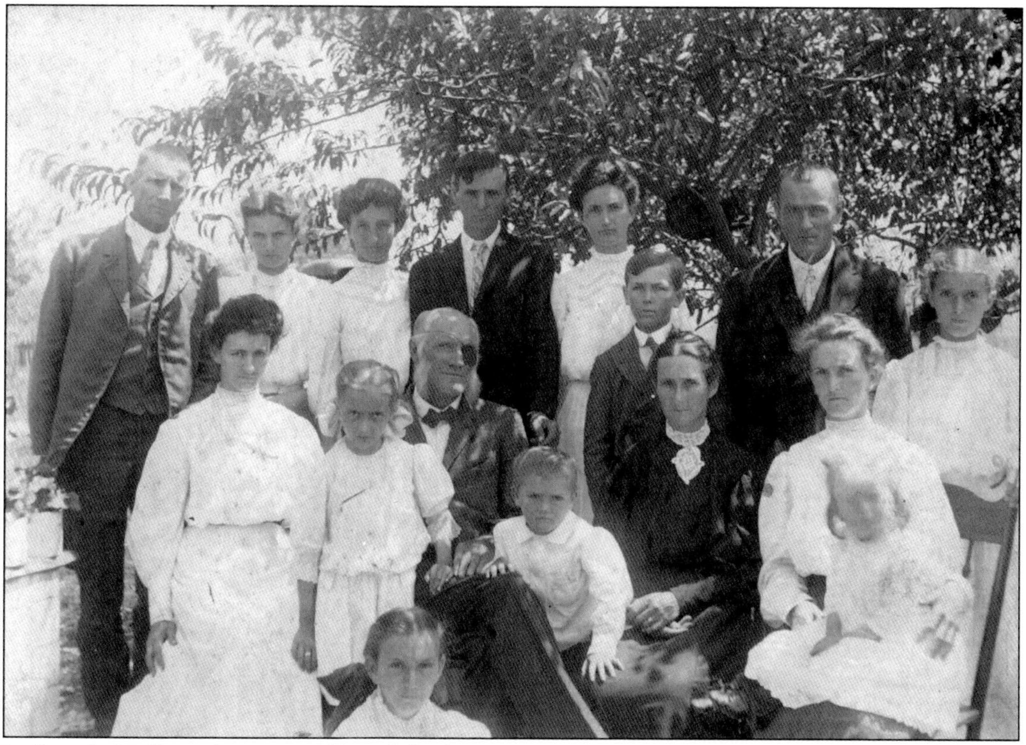

Larkin G. Hall was born in 1853 and died in 1940. He married Margaret Casey. In this 1908 photograph, his family gathers with him. Cecil Hall is in the foreground. From left to right, the others are (first row) Eve Hall Washburn, Christine Hall Woods, Grandpa Larkin Hall, Garrett Hall, Carl Hall, Grandma Martha Hall, and Grandma Bessie Hall Mains (holding Hazel Mains Jacob); (second row) Denny Washburn, Abbie Hall Courtney, Clara Hall Crawford, Charlie Hall, Ethel Hall Sharp, Garrett Hall, Grandpa Jim Willie Mains, and Dell Hall Fields. (Courtesy of Joyce Carson.)

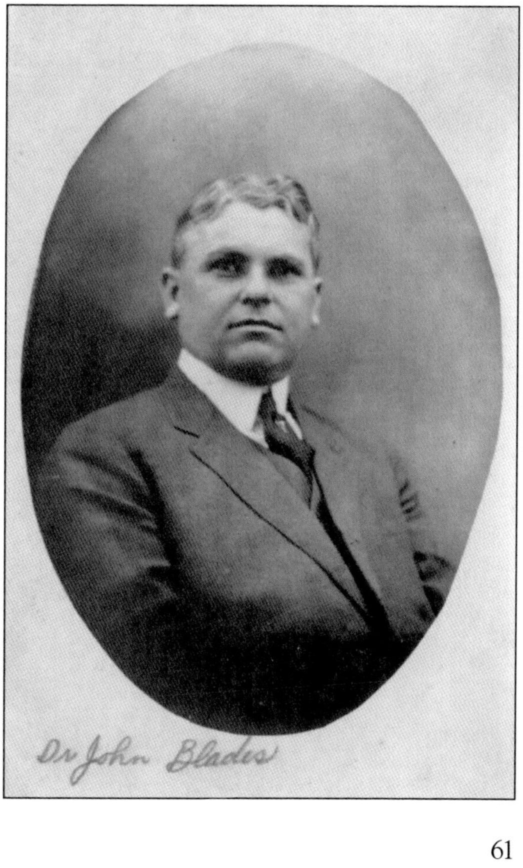

Dr. John M. Blades moved from California, Kentucky to Butler about 1916 and purchased a home on Peoples Street. He and his wife, Estelle Fairo, settled there to raise their two children, Adrienne and Hendon. John continued the practice of general medicine he had started a few years earlier. Estelle taught music in their home until her death in 1925. Sometime after 1927, Dr. Blades married Anna M. Sloan, who came to Butler to teach school. (Courtesy of Opal Jackson family.)

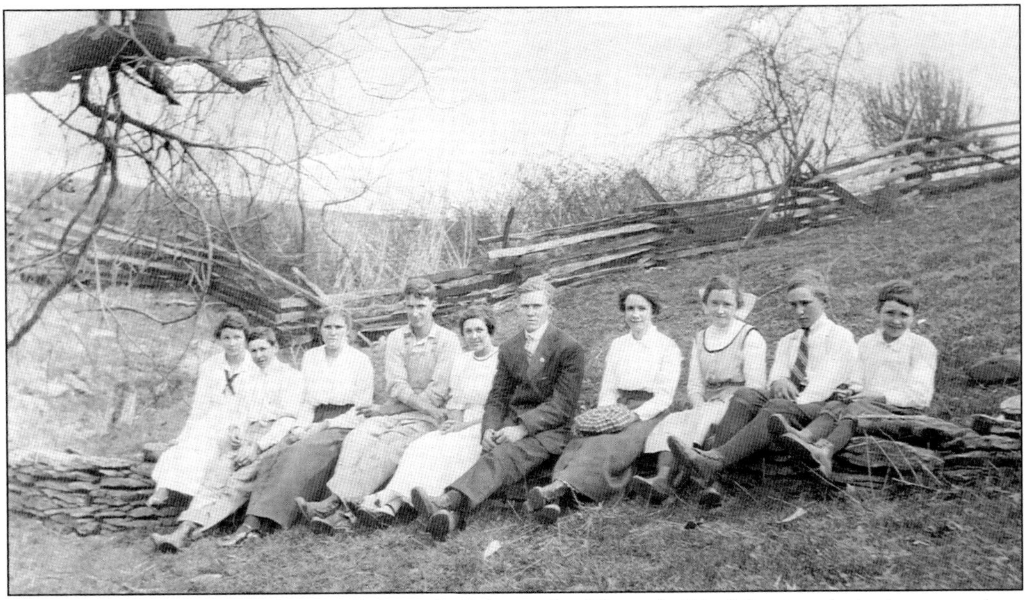

Seated on a rock wall on the Frank Campbell farm, the "Campbell kids" enjoy their time together. From left to right are Jane Tewell Dearborn, Ed Spaulding, Bertha Campbell Lightfoot, Alex Bradford, Pearl Spaulding Wolf, Dewey Campbell, Virgie Abercrombie Gosney, Cecil Abercrombie Carr, Clarence Campbell, and Ben Tewell. (Courtesy of Charlie Pyles.)

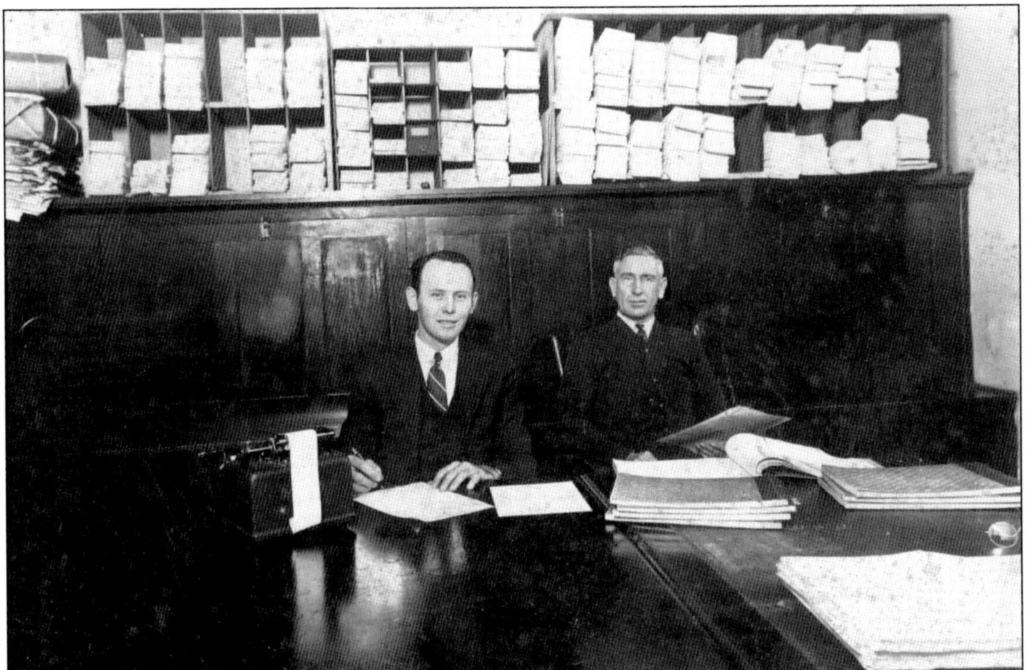

On the right is Charles Ashcraft, who served as Falmouth city clerk for approximately 25 years. He was also the Pendleton County sheriff in 1942 and the county tax commissioner in 1946. One of Ashcraft's duties as sheriff was the personal notification of a soldier's death to their family during World War II. On the left is James Leo Conroy, Ashcraft's deputy commissioner and son-in-law. (Courtesy of Pat Conroy.)

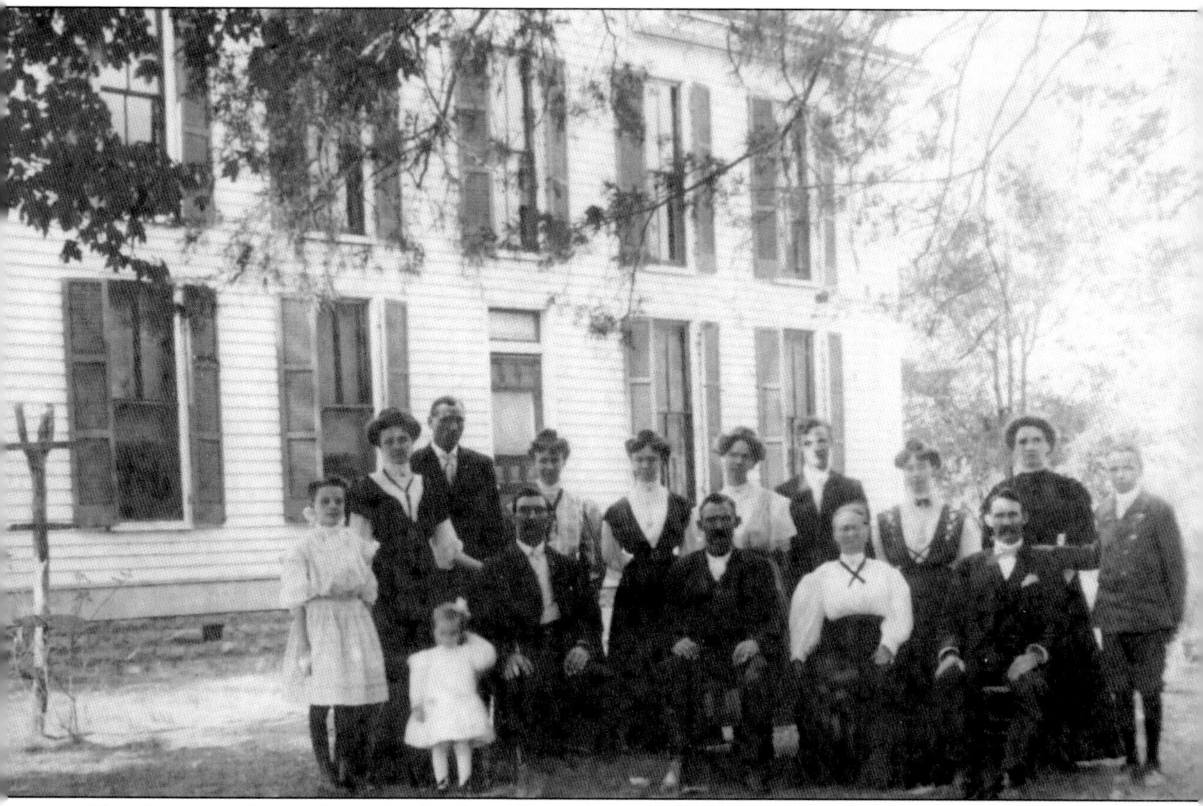

The Cummins family home looks down from the hill on which it sits. In this family photograph, William Cummins and Johanna Baush Cummins, the patriarch and matriarch, are seated in the center. William's son Lee Grand "Bee" Cummins is seated on the left, and his son Everett Cummins is on the right. Standing on the left is Bee's wife, Mary Loomis Cummins, with daughters Florence and little Lucille. Right of her, William Dahms stands beside his wife, Della Cummins Dahms. Continuing to the right are Resa Cummins, Lillie Cummins, Rob Cummins, Cora Cummins, Mary Sorrell Cummins (Everett's wife), and their son, Cecil. The Cummins home stands today near the intersection of US27 and KY22W. (Courtesy of Myron Doan.)

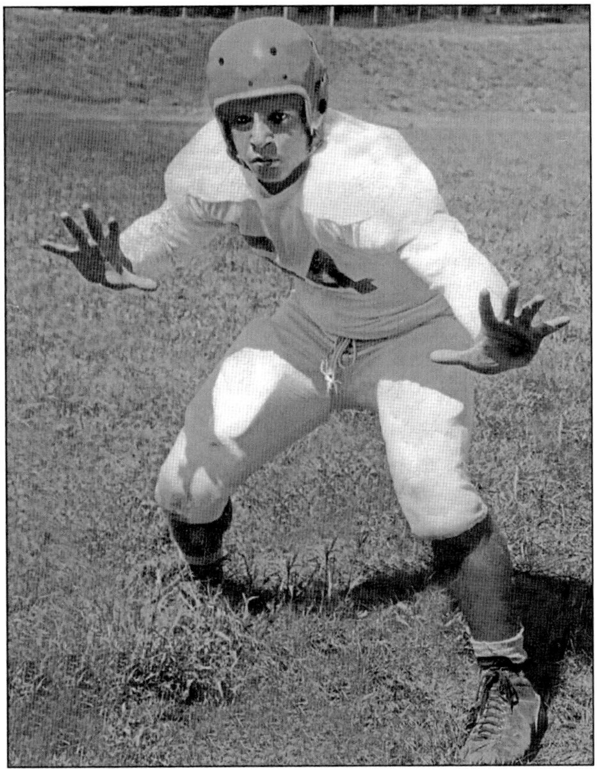

John Ayers Merritt, son of Bradley and Grace Ayers Merritt, was born in 1926 and attended school in Pendleton County before leaving for Louisville and Central High School. After high school graduation, he attended Kentucky State University on a football scholarship, playing offensive guard. Merritt went from Louisville to Tennessee State University, where he spent more than 20 years as head football coach. In the fall of 1983, he was inducted into the Tennessee State University Sports Hall of Fame. He was the second-most-winning football coach in the country at that time. (Courtesy of Ralph Taylor.)

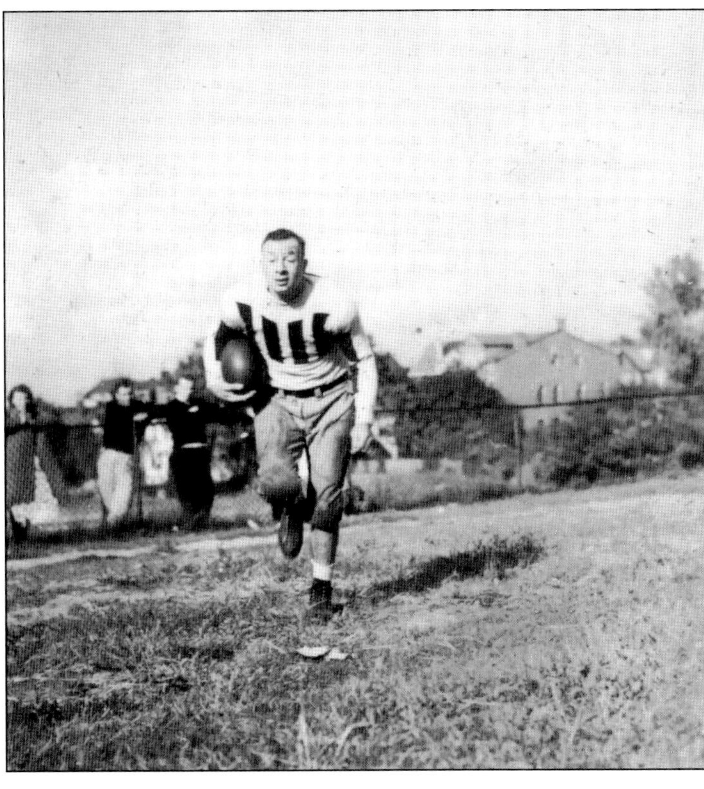

Richard Gulick was born, raised, and died in Pendleton County. He attended the University of Cincinnati as an undergraduate on a football scholarship. Upon graduation Gulick continued his education at the University of Kentucky. He then returned to Pendleton County where he taught at several of the county schools and at times also acted as principal. Gulick served as Pendleton County superintendent of schools before retiring in 1966. (Courtesy of Nancy Gulick Harville.)

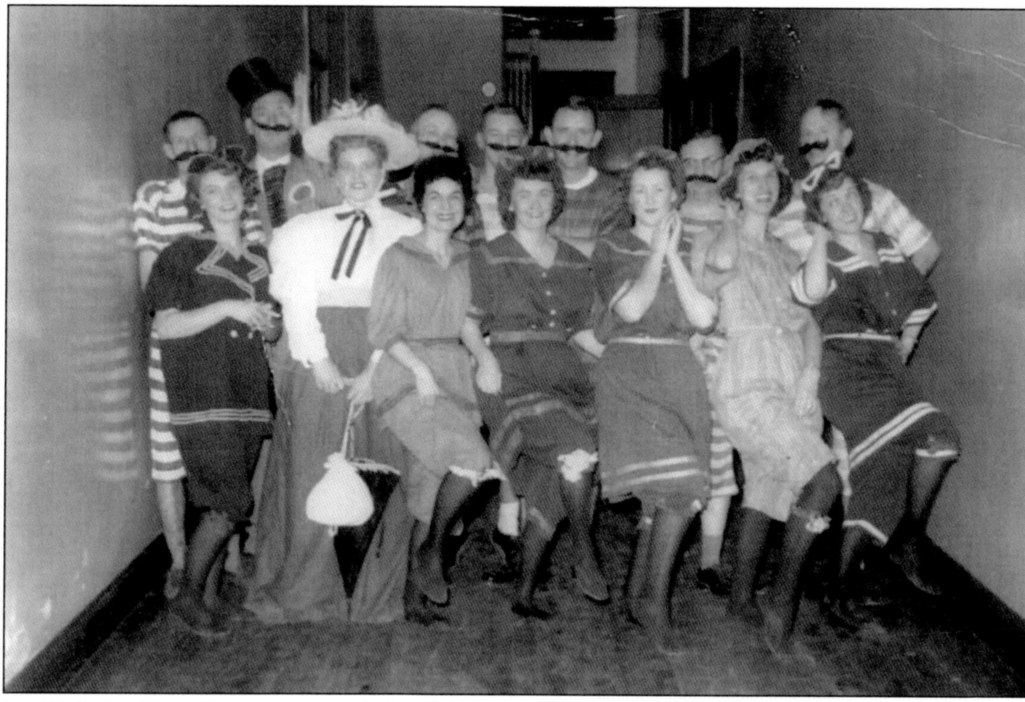

In 1957 the Kyra Department of the Falmouth Women's Club presented a special evening's entertainment when they hosted a variety show at the Falmouth School. From left to right, a few of the participants shown here are (first row) Shirley Tuemler, Wilma Hopper, Mildred Durham, Betty Singer, Icy Lucas, and Ada Beatty; (second row) Harry Gilbert, unidentified, Shelby McDowell, unidentified, Karl Hicks, unidentified, and Cecil Hellard. (Courtesy of Shirley Tuemler.)

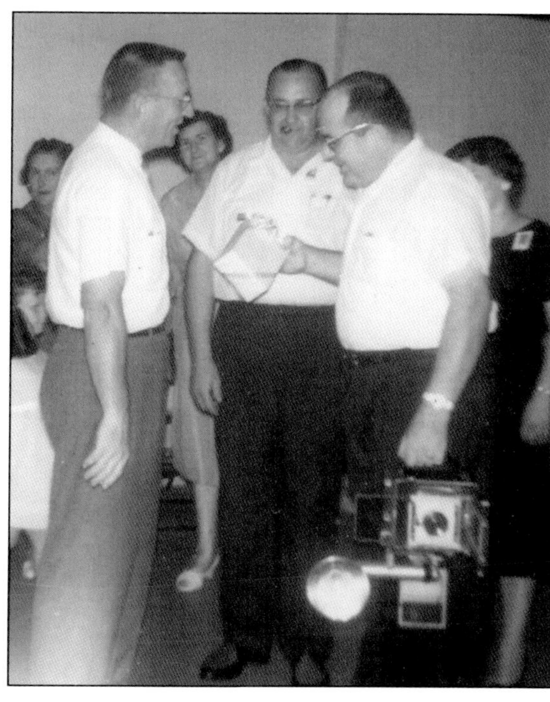

A part of being the editor of a small town newspaper is getting out and gathering pictures during community events. At a reunion of Falmouth High School graduates, Warren Shonert Jr., holding the camera, talks with Carl Frazier, a class member. Warren became the owner and editor of the *Falmouth Outlook*, Falmouth's weekly newspaper, after his father's death in 1953. The senior Warren Shonert started the paper with only nine subscribers in 1907. It grew and continued to provide news after all the other newspapers were gone. In 1986, Warren Jr. retired and sold the paper to the *Delphos Herald*, Inc. (Courtesy of Hallie Hart.)

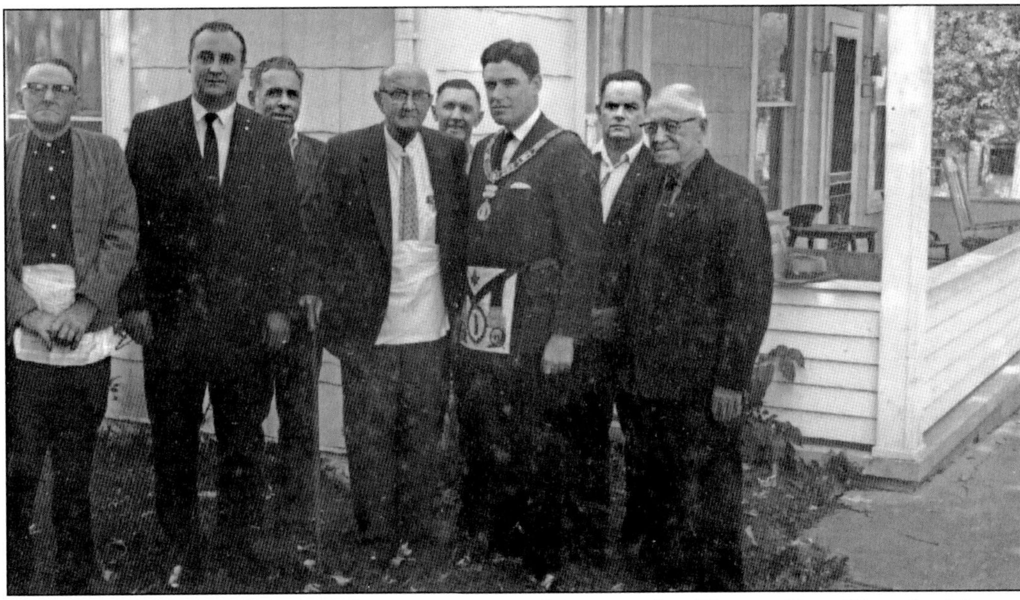

The group of men gathered in this picture are celebrating the 50 years Bert Riggs had been a member of the Milford Masonic Lodge no. 767. Bert Riggs was a retired restaurant owner. He joined the lodge in 1910. Taking part in this occasion are, from left to right, Worshipful Master C. D. LaMonda of Milford, ? Johnson from Claysville, E. T. Prince of Sunrise, Bert Riggs, Ray Jacobs of Falmouth, Carroll Curtis from the state Masonic office, Odie Pugh of Milford, and William Hamlin of Falmouth. (Courtesy of Barbara Browning.)

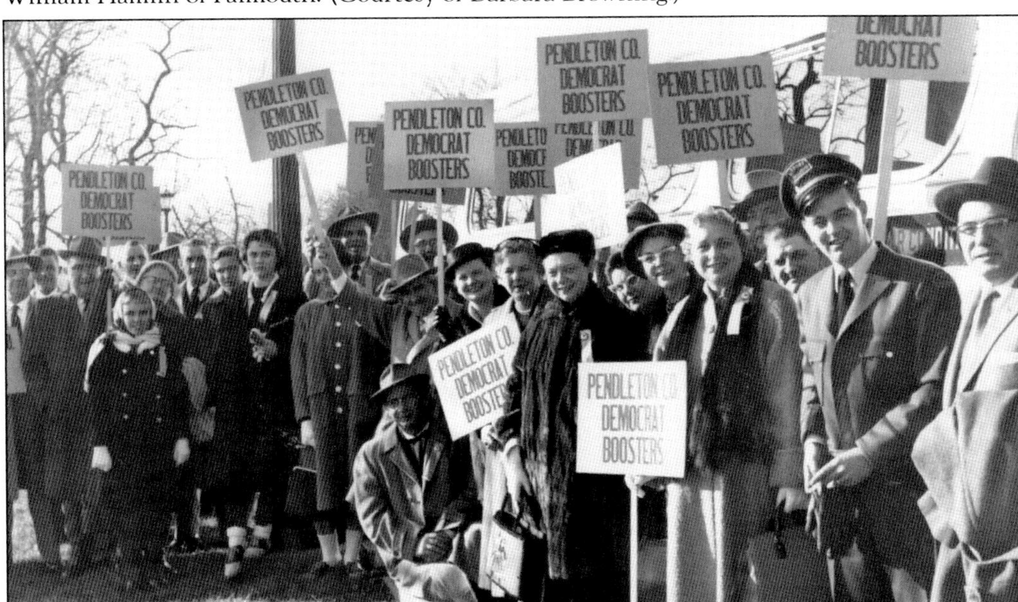

During a 1960 rally for Bert Combs, a candidate for governor of Kentucky, this group of Pendleton County Democratic Boosters met in Frankfort to show their support. Among those identified are Gene Flaugher, Sharma Flaugher, Joyce Sullivan, Melvin Hart, Hallie Hart, "Check" Tallaferro, and Juanita Craig. (Courtesy of Hallie Hart.)

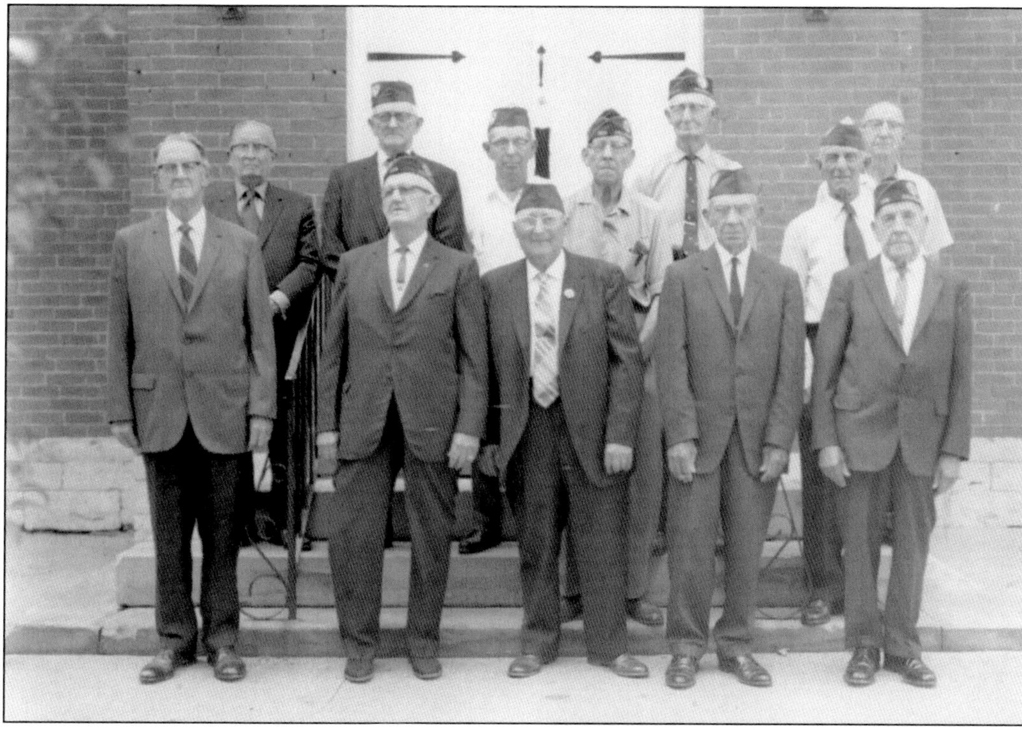

In the early 1970s, this group of World War I veterans were honored at a special recognition ceremony at the Falmouth Christian Church. From left to right, those in attendance are (first row), Colvin Wright, John C. Hamilton, A. C. Emminger, Bernard Fields, and Eugene Hancock; (second row) George Gedge, Bernard Caldwell, Carl Crecelius, Frank Race, Joe Cahill, unidentified, and Garrett Steele. (Courtesy of Pete Steele.)

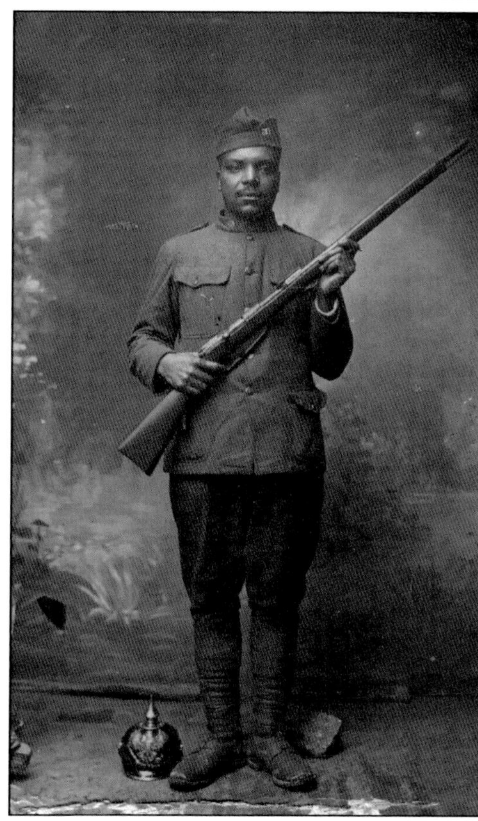

Ben Ewing, brother to William Graves of Falmouth, served in France during World War I. (Courtesy of Anne Higgins.)

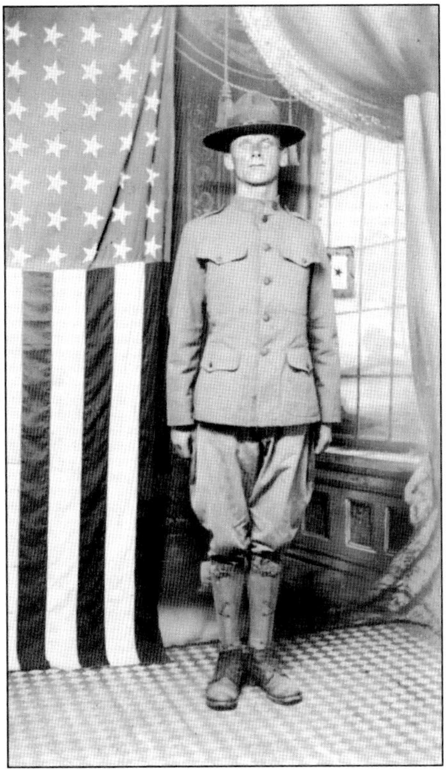

Edward M. Holmes was born in McKinneysburg in September 1893. His parents were J. R. Holmes and Amanda Provens. In 1917 he left to serve his country in World War I. He returned, married Hulda Ruth Wright in 1926, and lived to be 72 years old. Holmes died in January 1965. (Courtesy of Hallie Hart.)

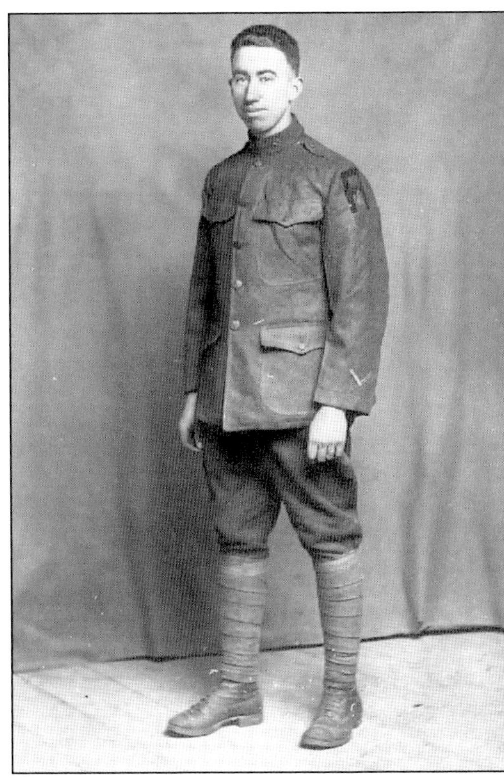

Pvt. Garrett E. Steele joined the army in 1918. He served as a cook while stationed in France. Steele returned home in 1919, passing on his sense of duty to the six sons he raised with his wife, Beulah Hitch. Of the six, two lost their lives in service to their country during World War II. Garrett and Beulah's sons were 2nd Lt. Desmond Steele, Pvt. Wayne A. Steele, Sgt. George T. Steele, Petty Officer 3rd Class Ray O. Steele, Spc. 3 Donald Steele, and Spc. 4 Floyd E. Steele. (Courtesy of Pete Steele.)

2nd Lt. Desmond Steele flew a B-24 in France during World War II. When bombing was temporarily halted, he and others made flights with food supplies to French civilians, which came to be known as the "Brogger's Grocery Run." He was killed in a bombing mission over Germany in November 1944. (Courtesy of Pete Steele.)

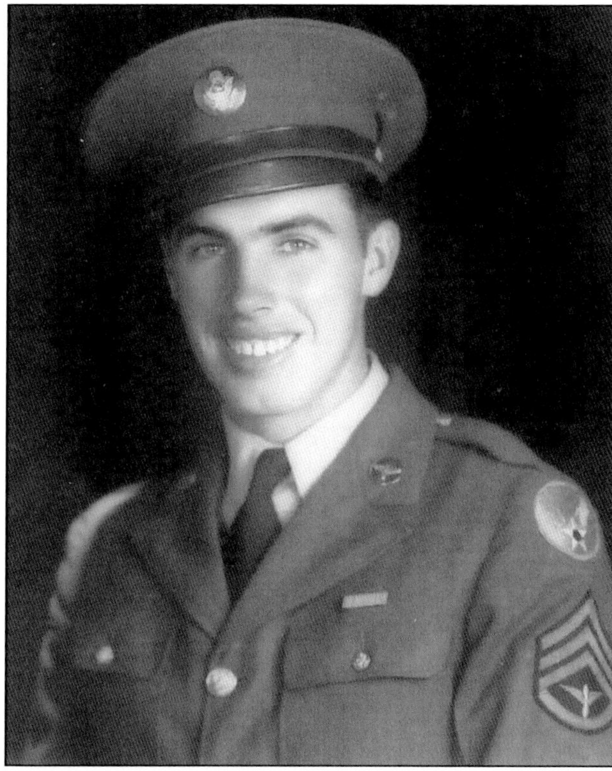

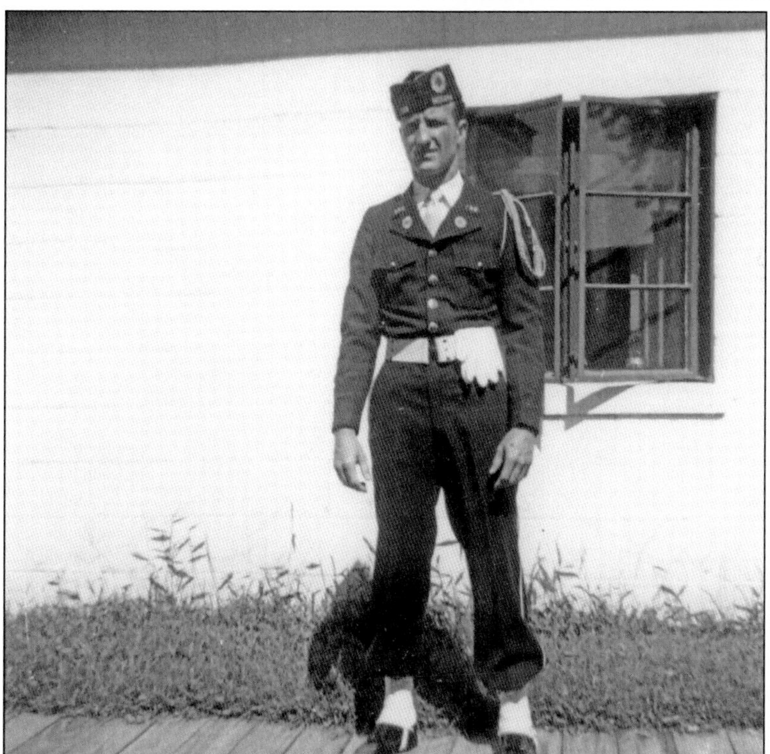

Paul E. Thornberry is shown here in his dress uniform. He attained the rank of corporal during World War II, flying with the Air Force in a B-24 as a tail-gunner and radio operator. Thornberry spent seven months flying missions over Italy and received four Bronze Stars with oak leaves. (Courtesy of Fern Thornberry.)

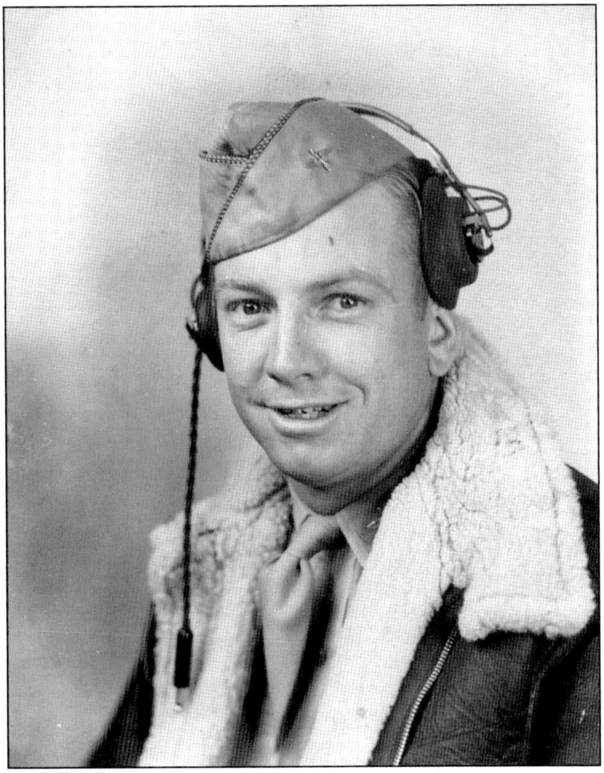

Lt. Ralph P. Bowling enlisted in the Army Air Forces Bombardment School in 1941 at the beginning of World War II. In April 1944, while flying a mission, he was shot down over Berlin and captured by the Germans. Bowling was taken to Stalag Luft 1 in Barth, Germany. There he was imprisoned with other officers until their release in May 1945 at the end of the war. In 1957 Ralph was elected to serve as Pendleton County sheriff. (Courtesy of Nancy Bowling Adams.)

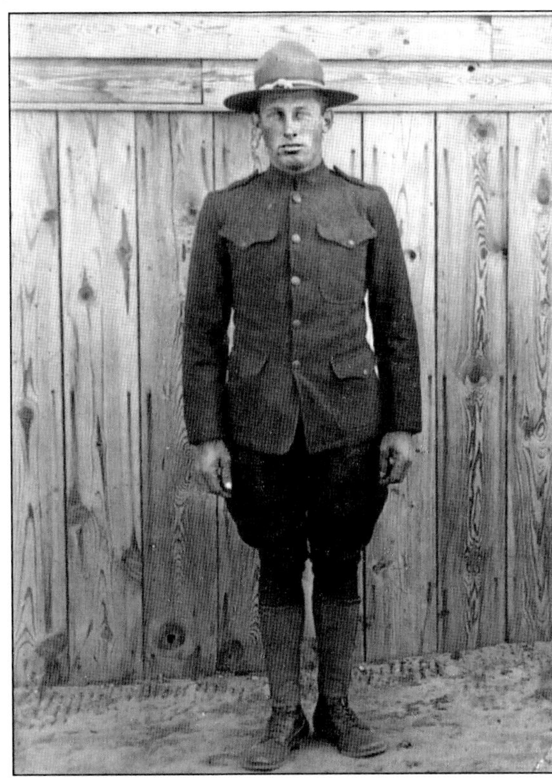

Born in 1896, Floyd Wright served his country during World War I. This photograph was taken about the time he left for service in 1917. His parents were Albert Herbert "Bert" Wright and Ora Mae McClanahan Wright. After returning from duty, Wright married Flora Cason on March 27, 1920, in Harrison County. They raised 14 children. (Courtesy of Teresa Johnston.)

Clarence Fossitt was born in September 1923 to Earl W. Fossitt and Minnie Shaver. He was one of six children. Clarence served in World War II with the 3rd Battalion under General Patton, fighting with Company L 301st Infantry Regiment, 94th Infantry Division. For services rendered he was awarded the Bronze Star. (Courtesy of Chris Fossitt.)

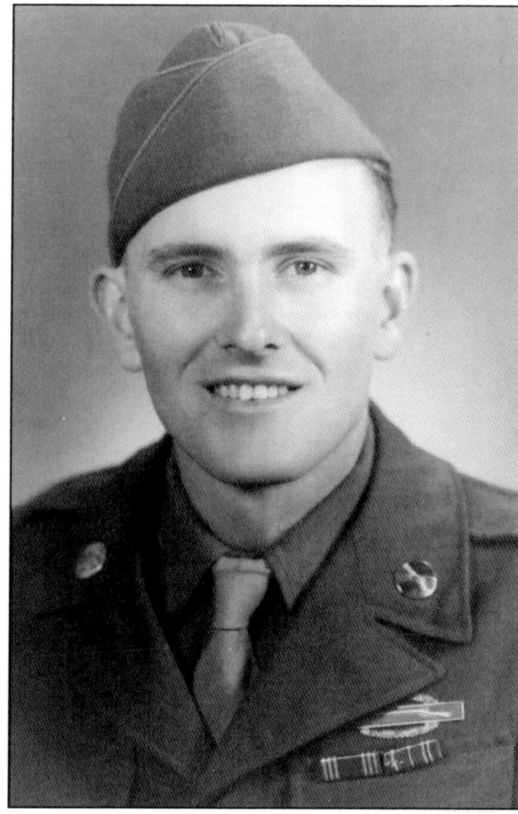

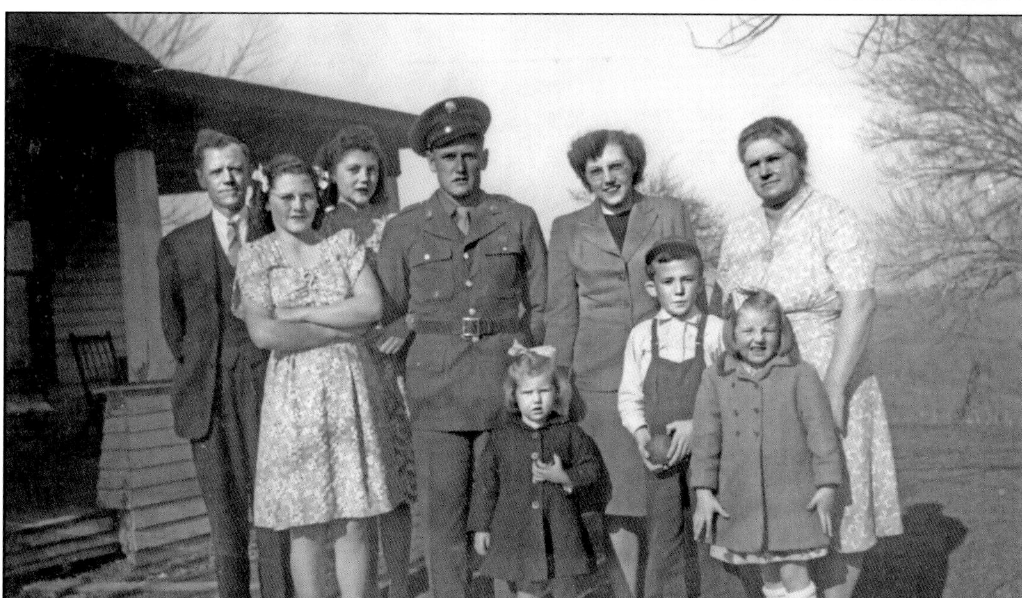

The Sherman Allender family gathers in November 1945 just before Clyde Allender heads overseas. From left to right are (children) Sue Ann, Arvel (Sonny), and Ruby Nell; (adults) Sherman Allender, Geneva Allender, Alice Allender, Clyde Allender, Velda Allender, and Loula (Mama) Allender. (Courtesy of Alice Allender Conrad.)

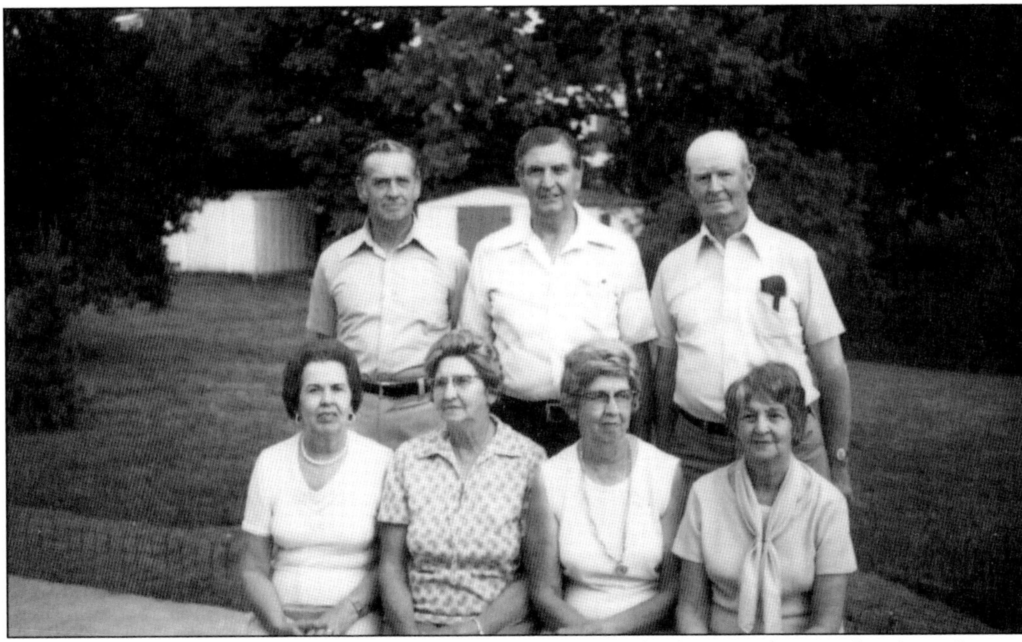

The children of Charles and Grace Wilson were photographed at a mid-1970s family gathering. Pictured from left to right are (first row) Dorothy W. Thompson, Mabel W. Carr, Mildred W. Carr, and Thelma W.; (second row) Kenzie Wilson, Harold Wilson, and Ray Wilson. (Courtesy of Fern Thornberry.)

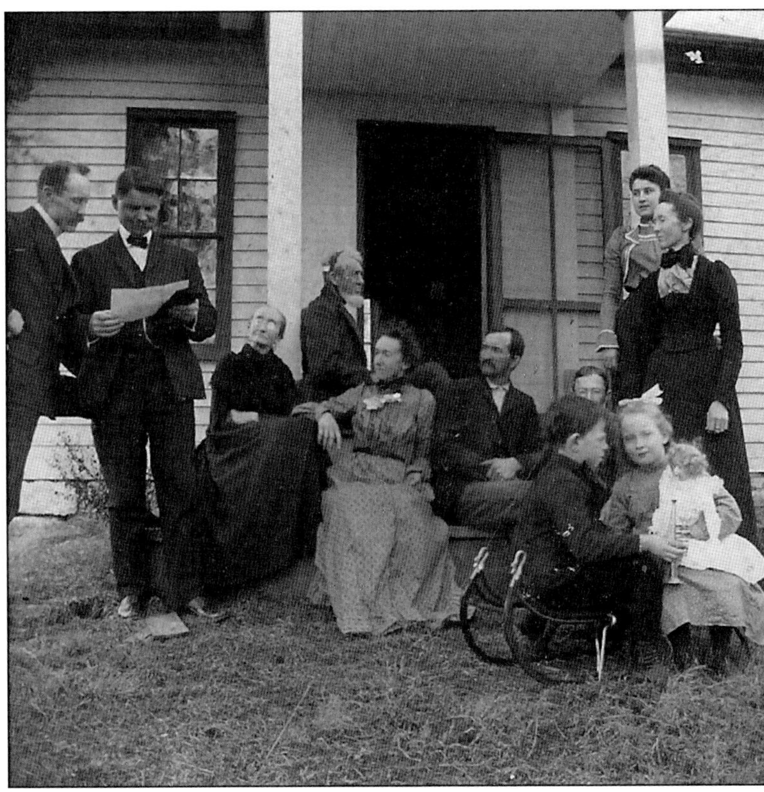

The Colvin family from Four Oaks looks on as John Colvin reads a note. From left to right are Bev Colvin, John Colvin, Sally Colvin, Berkett L. Colvin, Nancy Colvin, Alvin N. Wiggins, Vernon Colvin (with only his head visible), and Susan Wright. Colvin Wright and Florence are seated on the sled. The young woman standing just in front of the post is unidentified. (Courtesy of Carol Kirkland.)

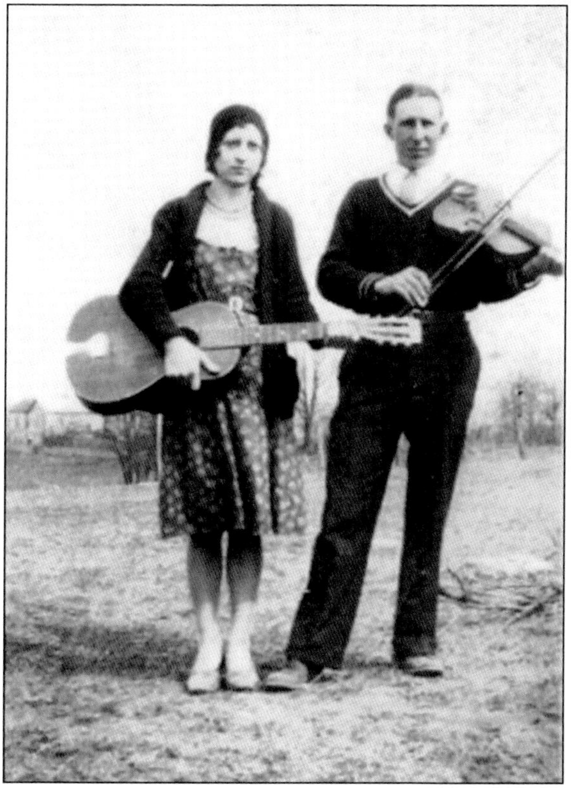

On the last day of school for students of Unity School, Joan McMillian and her brother, James, share their talents with a musical program. Both began playing instruments when they were very young. (Courtesy of Mark Black.)

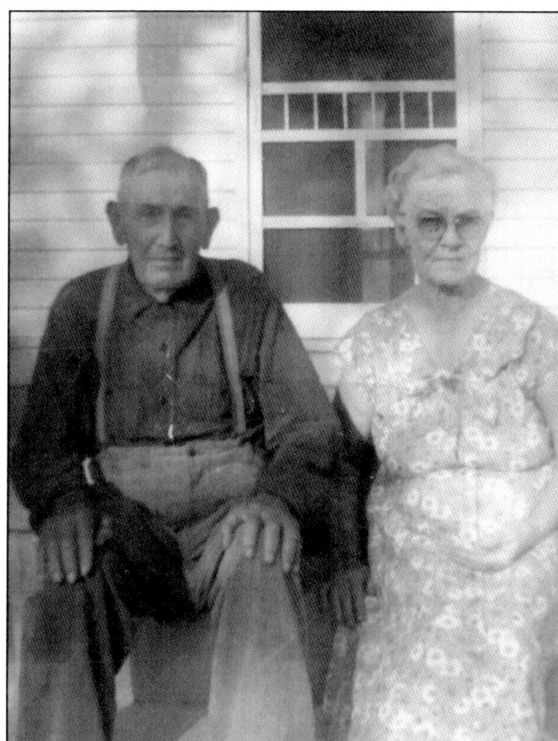

On September 23, 1959, Charles and Resa Cummins LaFollette celebrated their golden wedding anniversary. This photograph of them was taken on that day. Charles was 80 years old and Resa was 72 at the time. (Courtesy of Teresa Johnston.)

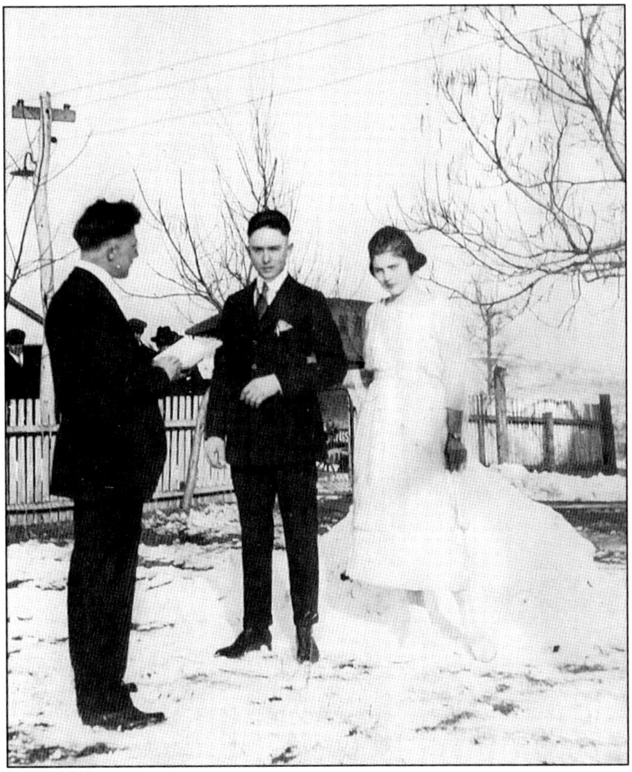

Mable Kenner became the bride of Floyd Whaley on January 27, 1921. Mable was the daughter of Joseph and Elizabeth Jane Moore Kenner. Floyd was the son of Arch and Carrie Mae Chalfant Whaley. Mable's uncle, Rev. Alexander Kenner of Wilmore, Kentucky, married them at the Kenner home off KY1054. (Courtesy of Jane Stahl.)

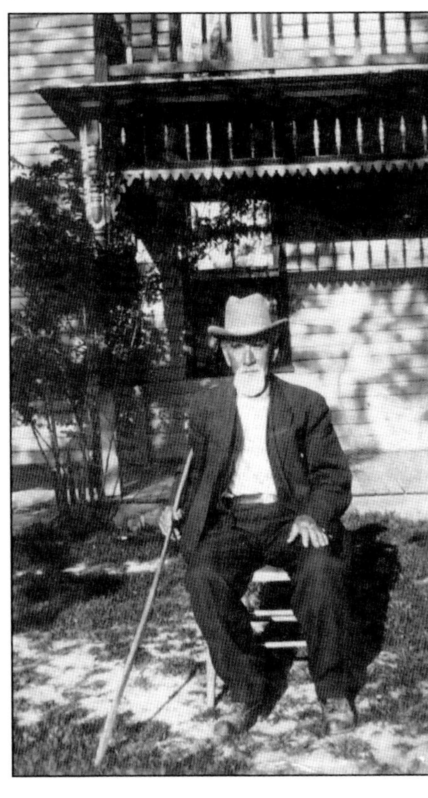

William Kidwell sits in front of the home he resided in for 50 years. The cabin was built on land first settled by pioneers of Pendleton County. It sits just outside Kincaid State Park but is not easily recognizable due to remodeling. It is now the residence of David and Ginny Pribble. (Courtesy of Alice Conrad.)

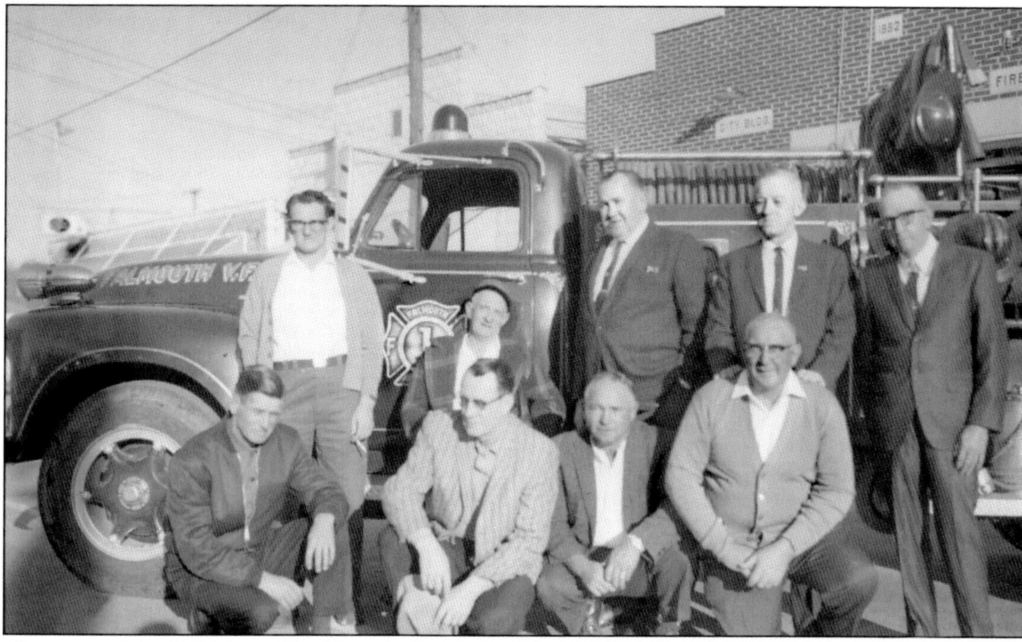

The men of the Falmouth Fire Department were always pleased to have a new truck to strengthen the service they provide. Here with their most recent truck acquisition are, from left to right; (first row) Frank Lawson, Alex Caldwell, George "Buck" Piercefield, and Virgil Florence; (second row) Jim Spencer, James "Shorty" Taylor, Melvin Hart, Earl Weaver, and Shelby McDowell. (Courtesy of Hallie Hart.)

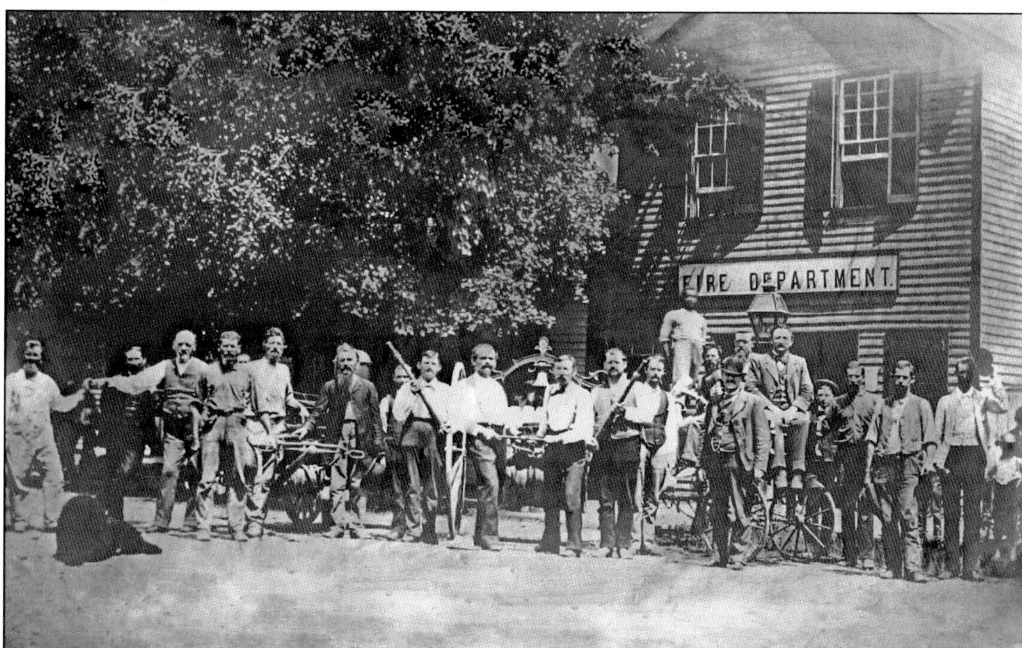

In the early 1900s, the Falmouth Fire Department was manned by volunteers who hurried to the scene of a fire at the call of a bell. They are seen here with typical equipment used for fighting fires at that time. (Courtesy of Lisa Hart.)

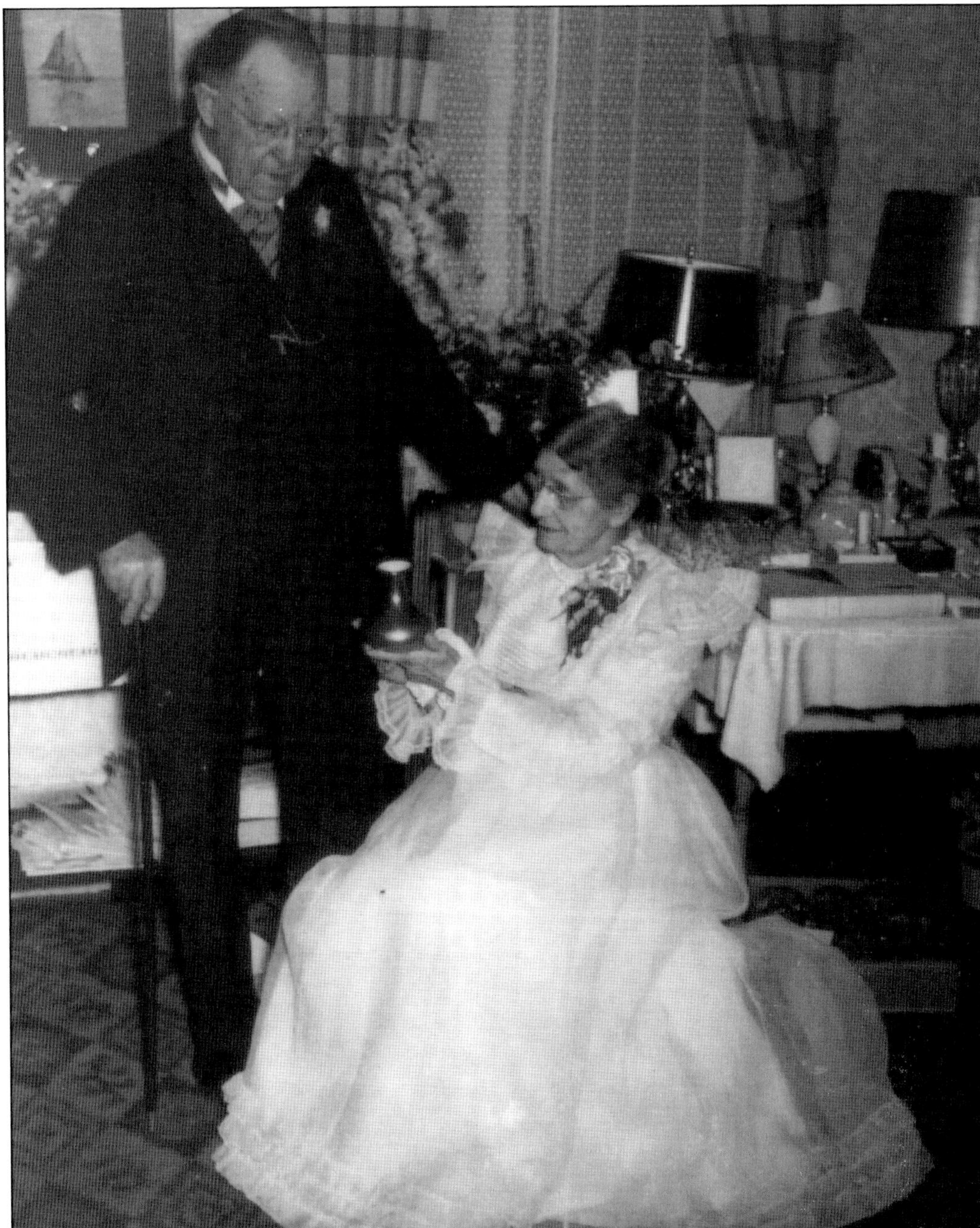

Captured for history, Dr. James E. Wilson and Fannie Lee Wilson are admiring the gifts received at the celebration of their 50th wedding anniversary. They are wearing the same clothing they wore on their wedding day. Besides being a physician, Dr. Wilson was mayor of Falmouth at one time. He was also the oldest practicing physician in the community at the time of his death in 1948. Fannie was a founding member of the Falmouth Women's Club. (Courtesy of the Falmouth Women's Club.)

Earl "Abe" and Ruby Browning Wyatt were a solid fixture in the Falmouth community. Together they owned and operated Wyatt's Grocery. Earl served the community as a member of the Falmouth City Council and as mayor. Both were members of the Falmouth Baptist Church. Ruby was an important member of the Falmouth Women's Club. (Courtesy of Dixie Wyatt Owen.)

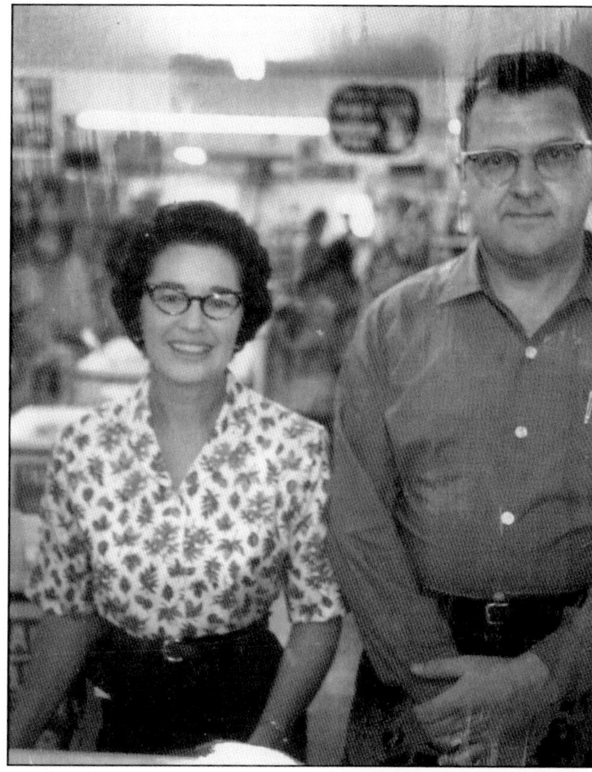

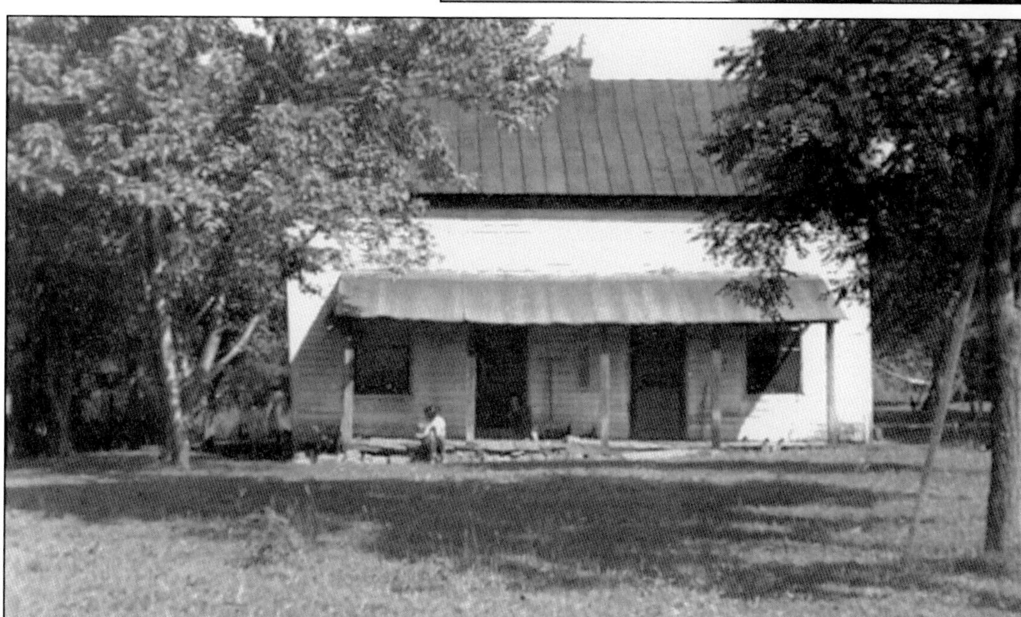

The Steele log cabin was built by Boston Steele in 1774. It is held together with wooden pegs and dovetail joints, a more expensive way of building a home even at that time. Heirs of Boston and his son, George Wesley, later sold the land for the development of Kincaid State Park, where a cabin now resides. Some believe this to be the second-oldest cabin in Pendleton County (Courtesy of Lois Gosney.)

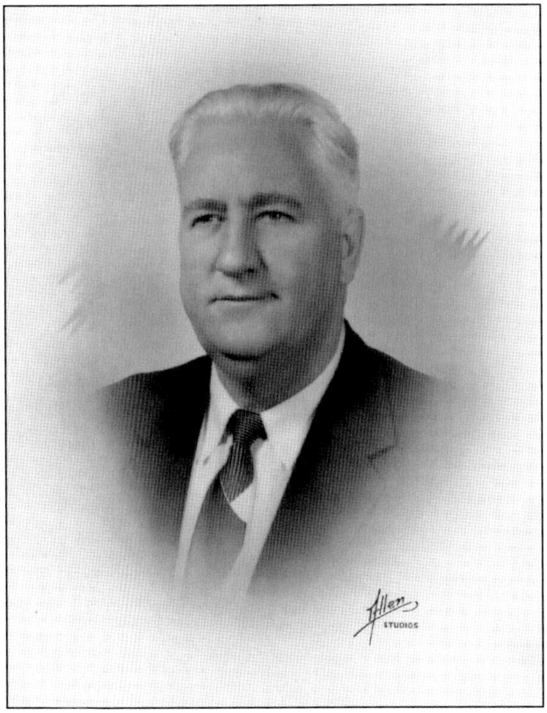

Hoyt Best was born in 1900 in South Carolina. In 1924 he came to Falmouth to practice law and later was a state senator. Shortly after 1945, he purchased the Falmouth Fairgrounds and conducted successful fairs there every summer. Hoyt was only 63 years old when he died in 1964, but he was the oldest practicing attorney in Pendleton County at the time. (Courtesy of Robert Best.)

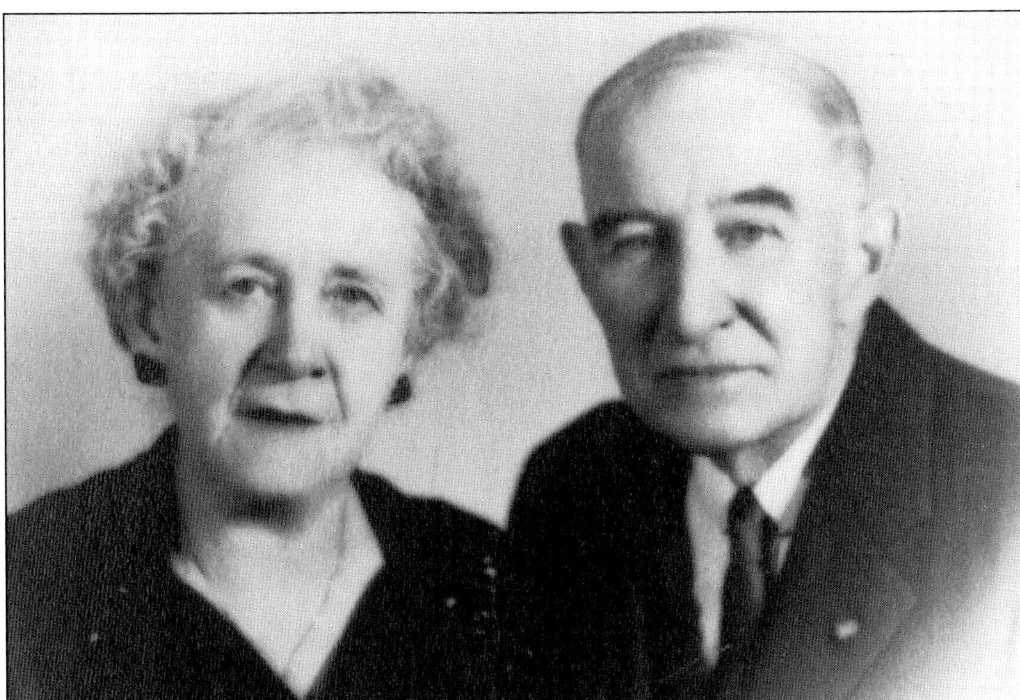

Like many others who came to settle in Pendleton County, Charles Trost was born in Germany. After living much of his adult life in Pendleton County, he died in 1913 at the age of 84. He married Gusta Marquardt, who was also born in Germany. He was a farmer and beekeeper, selling honey as a part of his livelihood. (Courtesy of Cheryl York.)

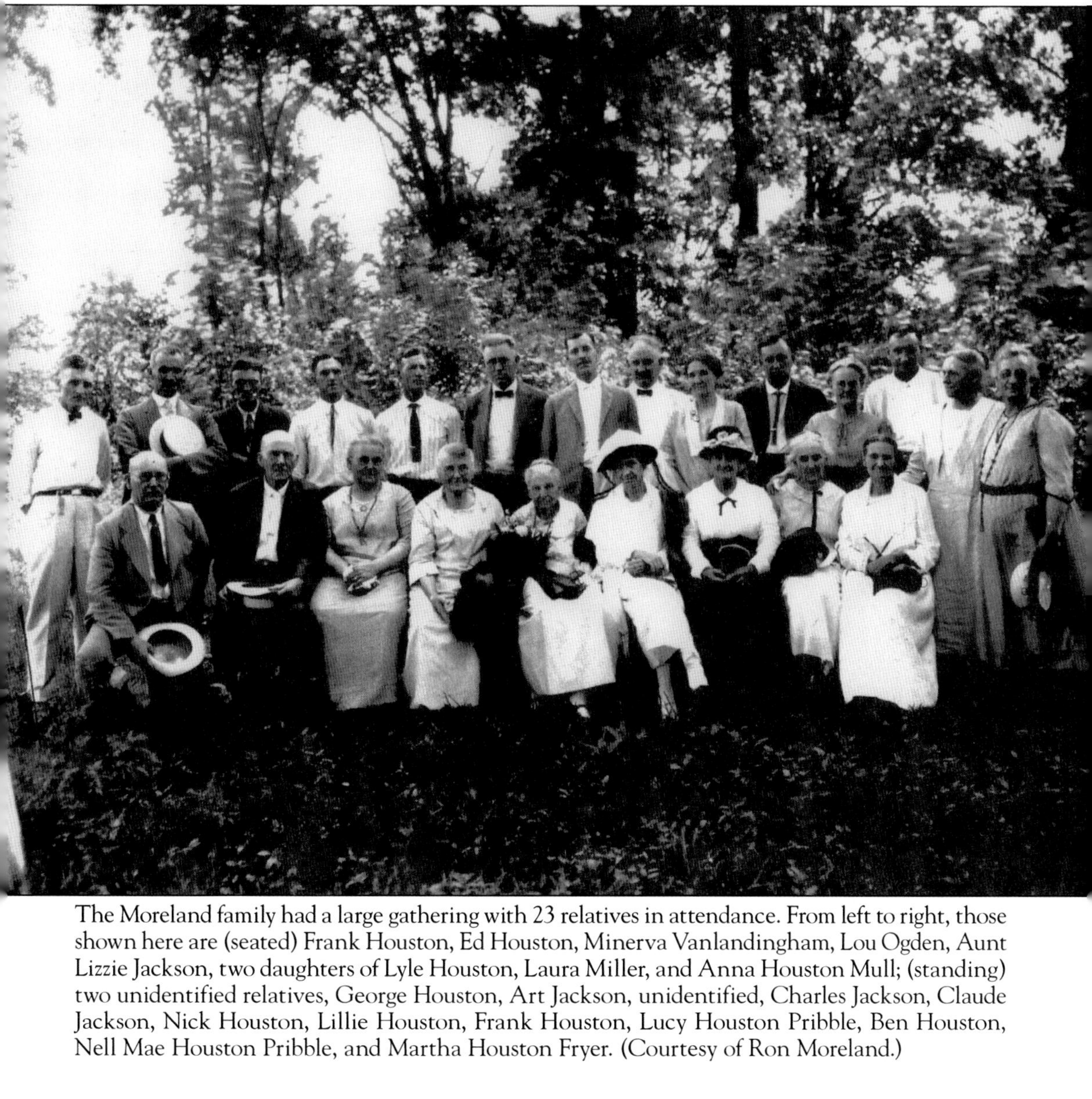

The Moreland family had a large gathering with 23 relatives in attendance. From left to right, those shown here are (seated) Frank Houston, Ed Houston, Minerva Vanlandingham, Lou Ogden, Aunt Lizzie Jackson, two daughters of Lyle Houston, Laura Miller, and Anna Houston Mull; (standing) two unidentified relatives, George Houston, Art Jackson, unidentified, Charles Jackson, Claude Jackson, Nick Houston, Lillie Houston, Frank Houston, Lucy Houston Pribble, Ben Houston, Nell Mae Houston Pribble, and Martha Houston Fryer. (Courtesy of Ron Moreland.)

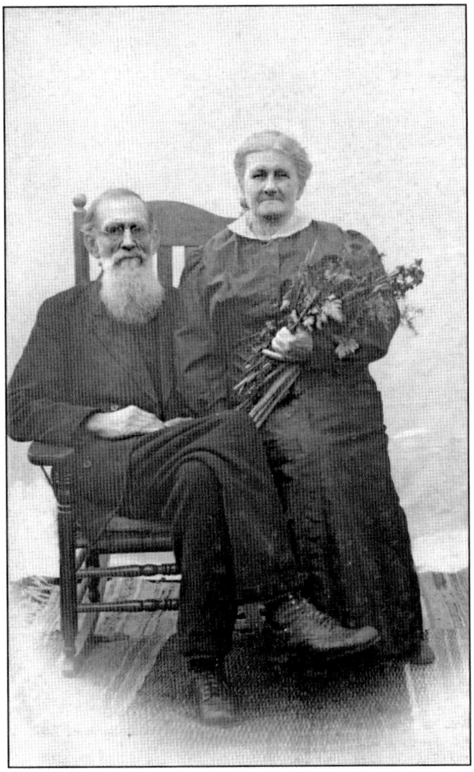

Robert C. Taylor and his wife, Harriett Gedge Taylor, are shown here in 1917 on their golden wedding anniversary. They married in December 1867. He was a farmer and a justice of the peace and also became a deacon of the Flour Creek Christian Church in 1890. Ferdinand and Sarah Kirby Taylor were the parents of Robert C. Taylor. Christian and Sarah Rich Gedge were the parents of Harriett. (Courtesy of the Opal Jackson family.)

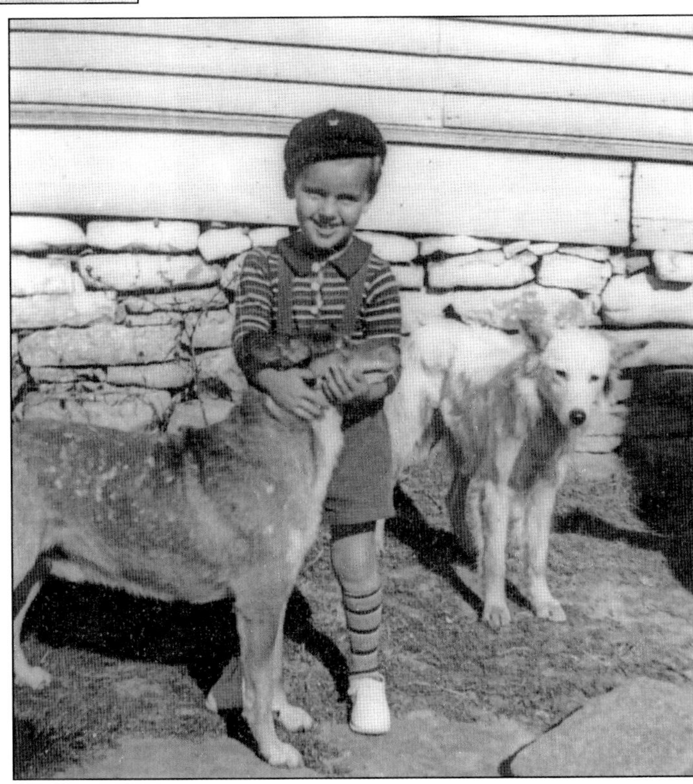

What better friends could a young boy have than his two dogs? Such was the case with Lonnie Browning, seen here with dogs Jack and Juzzie. Browning married Barbara Rigg and they made their home just behind Oakland Church in Brownings Corner. To this union, two sons were born. Browning retired from a teaching career in 2004. (Courtesy of Barbara Browning.)

Four

BUSINESSES AND TRADES

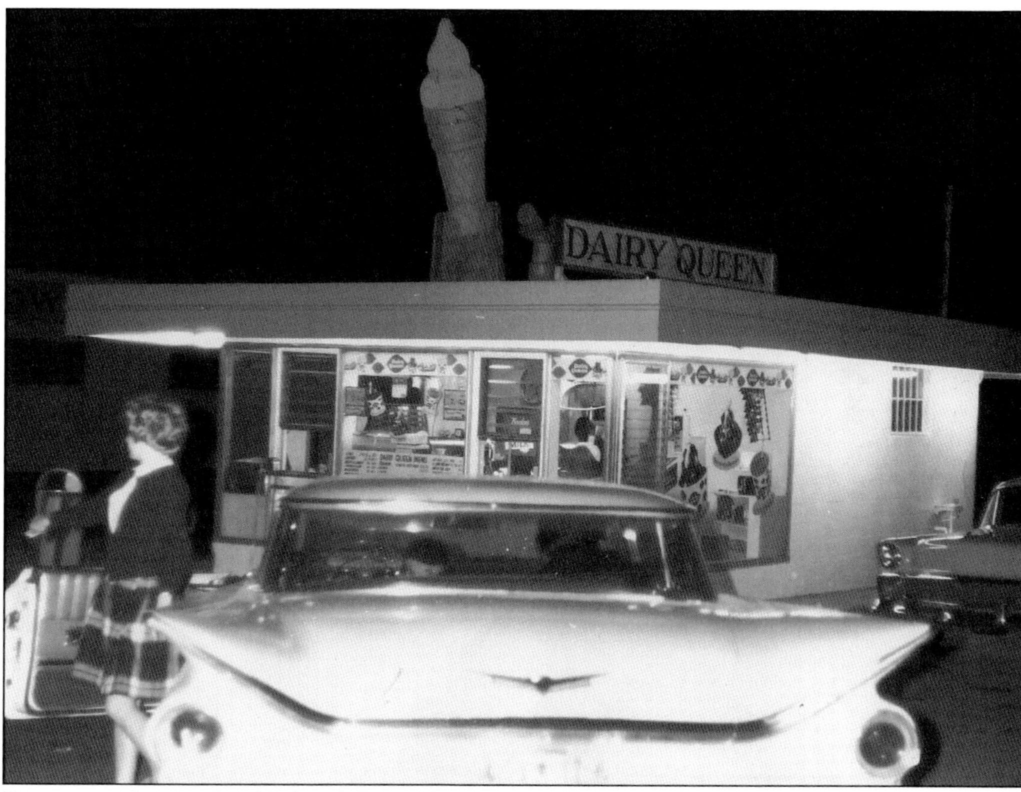

From as early as 1951, the local Dairy Queen was a small walk-up soft serve ice cream shop. It did not take long for it to become the gathering place for the local teens. Over the next several years, it changed ownership and expanded when enclosed seating was added around the old block building. In 1986, Howard Hoess purchased the facility and continued to run it as a Diary Queen. The flood of 1997 put water to the rooftop, but the building was cleaned and reopened. Disaster struck again in 2004 when a fire destroyed the building. At that time Hoess decided to rebuild and open a local restaurant under his own name: Howard's Place. (Courtesy of Jerry Conrad.)

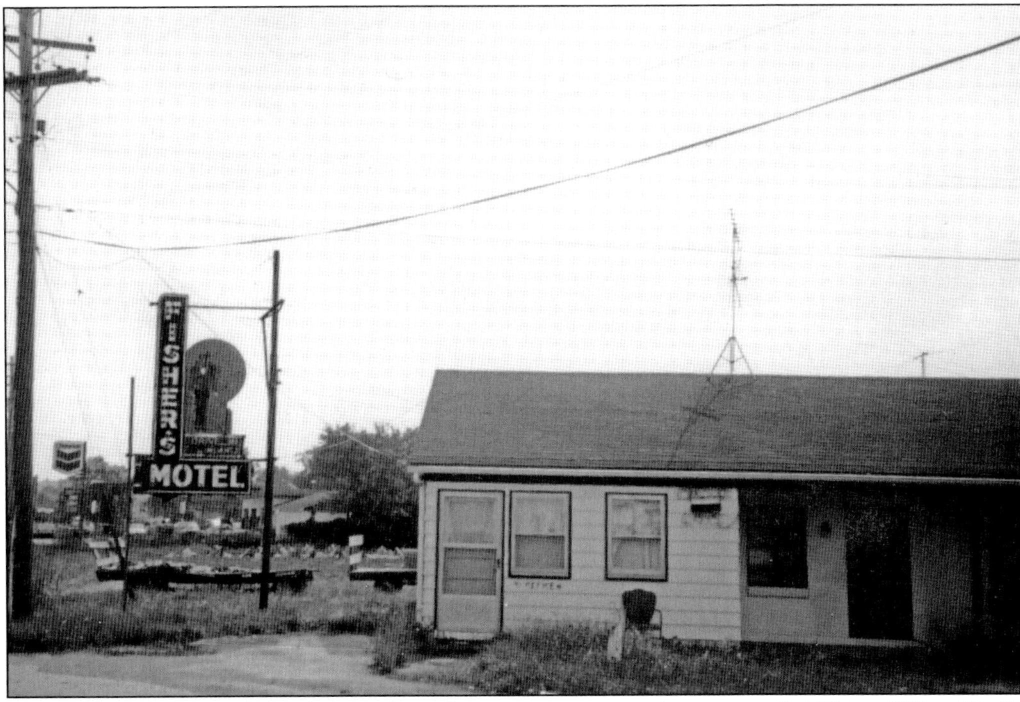

The Fisher family of Falmouth owned two large properties on the corner of US27 and West Shelby Street. They were the first businesses visitors saw as they entered Falmouth from the north. On the right side of the highway was the Fisher's Motel, which also had an apartment section. Its restaurant served breakfast, lunch, and dinner. (Both courtesy of George Lach.)

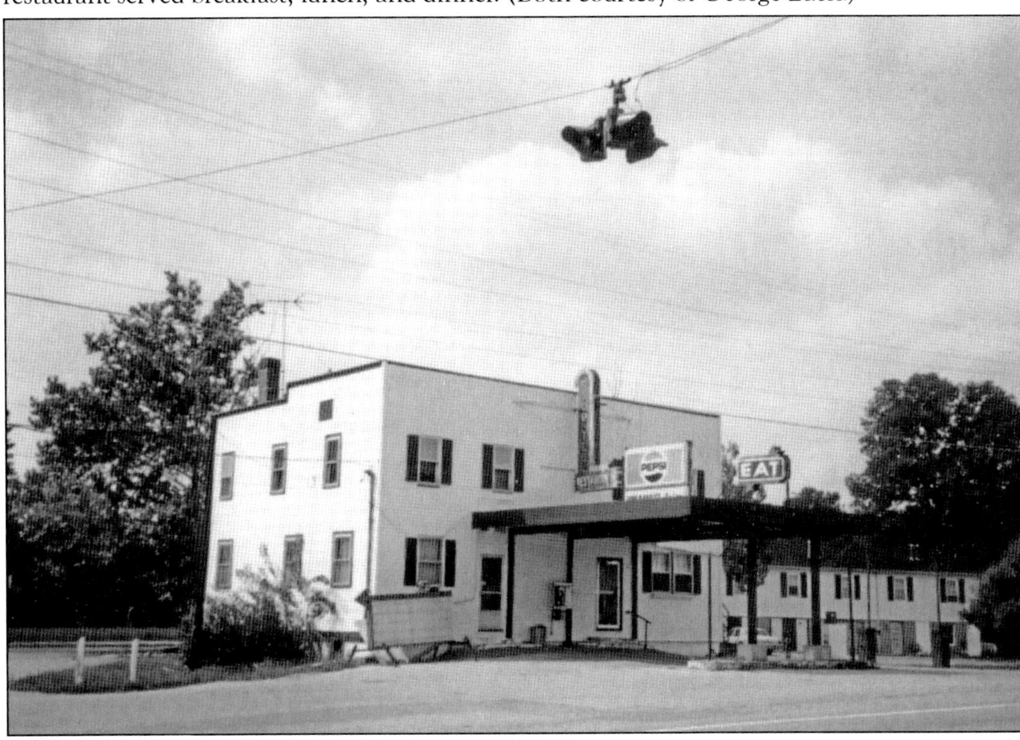

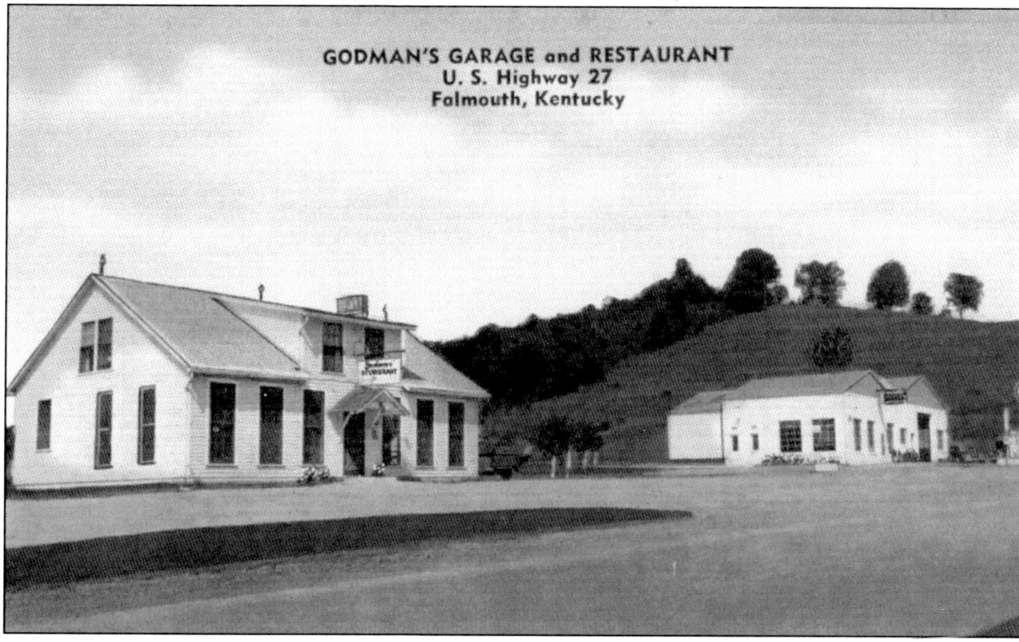

In about 1947, the restaurant known as Lakeview was raised up on a flatbed and moved from its old location at the curve on Shelby Street near Pike Street, and planted on a new foundation on US27. This was just after crossing the concrete bridge of the South Fork of the Licking River and beside Godman's Garage. The restaurant was given a new name: Godman's. In its original location, a small lake could be viewed across the road—hence the name Lakeview. From its new home, an expansive view of the Licking River was visible from the windows. About 1978 it became a Pasquale's franchise, which was the first Italian-only restaurant in town. (Both courtesy of Sandy Craddock.)

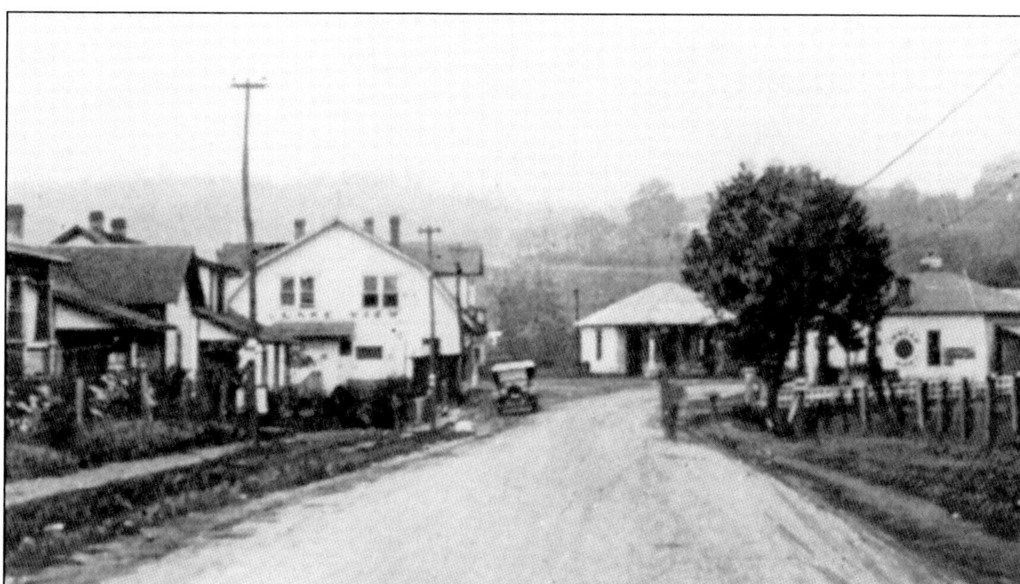

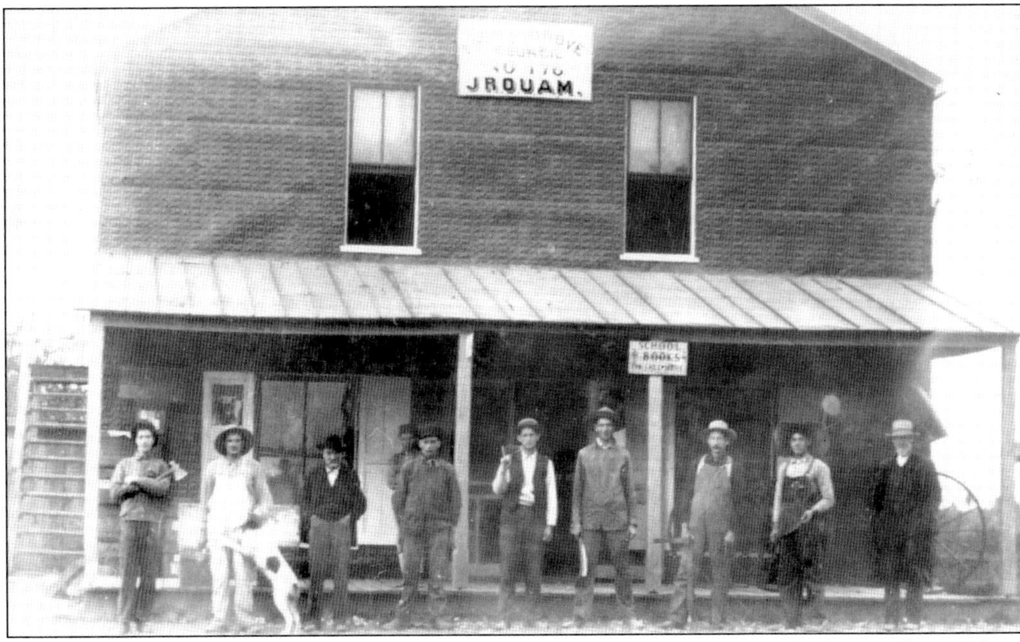

A building erected in 1908 by H. J. Poor, Horizon Jewett Poor, Newt Whaley, Walter Wilson, and Richard Jones was home to the Locust Grove General Store, which operated out of the first floor. The upstairs was used by the Junior Order of United Mechanics, an 1840s anti-immigration society. The Daughters of the American Revolution also used the upstairs for occasional meetings. Standing on the store porch are an unidentified man, George Ammerman, Horace J. Poor Sr., ? Kells, Luther Ruby, Jabez Poor (father of Helen Poor Ammerman and holding a corn knife), ? Shoemaker, Alvin Wilson, and Bill Ruby. (Courtesy of Billie Newman.)

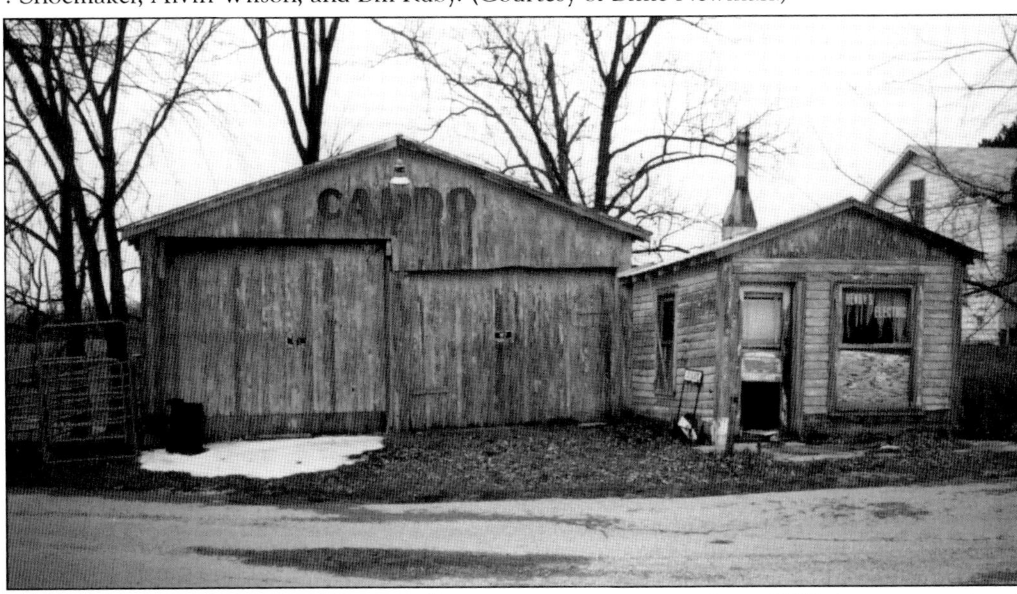

This grocery store and garage has not been in operation since about 1950, but at one time it served the needs of the small Caddo population well. Located at the junction of US10 and the Concord-Caddo Road, the George Morris family ran the store and operated a hauling service dealing in livestock, tobacco, and water. (Courtesy of Billie Newman.)

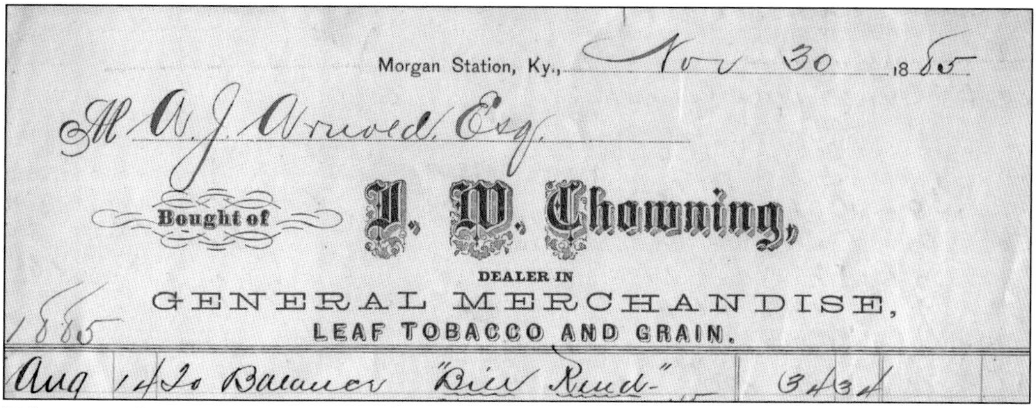

Morgan Station, Ky., Nov 30 1885

Bought of D. W. Chowning,

DEALER IN

GENERAL MERCHANDISE,

LEAF TOBACCO AND GRAIN.

Tobacco and grain were grown on large parcels of land in the rich bottomland near Morgan, or Morgan Station as it was called in the mid-1800s. The receipt here, dated November 30, 1885, indicates payment was made to D. W. Chowning, who dealt in sales related to tobacco and grains.

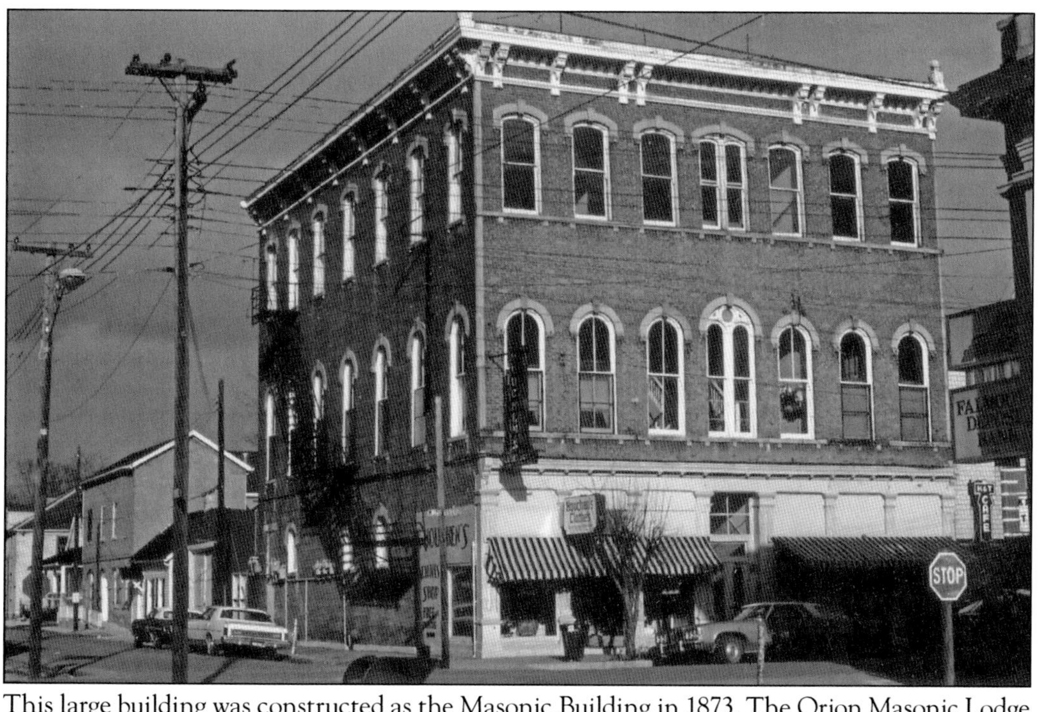

This large building was constructed as the Masonic Building in 1873. The Orion Masonic Lodge sold stock in order to add the third floor. It was on this floor that the Masons held their meetings until 1932, when they purchased the Presbyterian church building on Chapel Street and moved there. Over the years, this building has housed offices, a millinery shop, meetings of the Odd Fellows, and even the KKK. Houchen's Clothing and Shoe Store occupied the first floor at this location until 1997, when it moved to a new building on US27 South. (Courtesy of George Lach.)

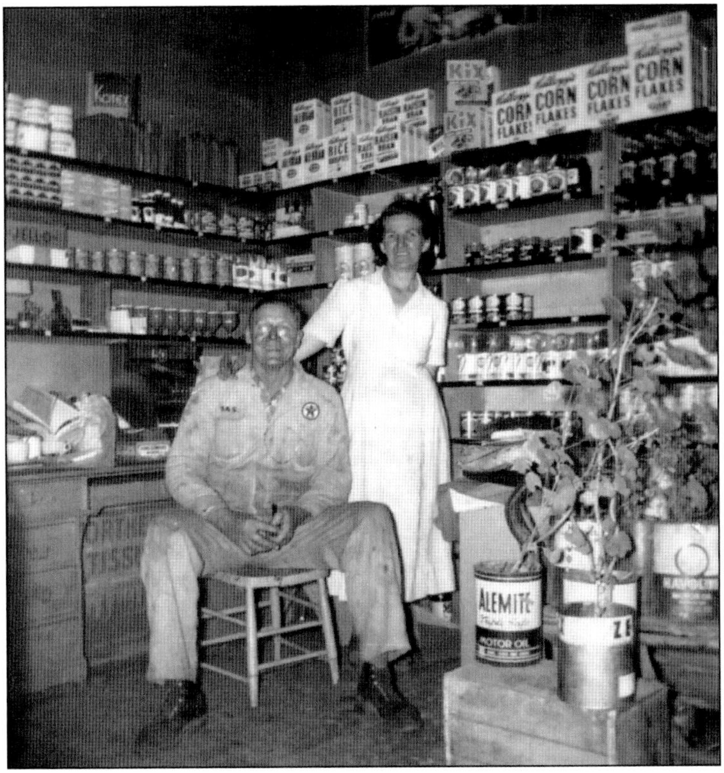

"Pop" Warner's Grocery sat on US27 for many years. It carried the usual items of a small town "quick" shop. Warner ran this store and a car-repair shop next door. (Courtesy of Terry Price.)

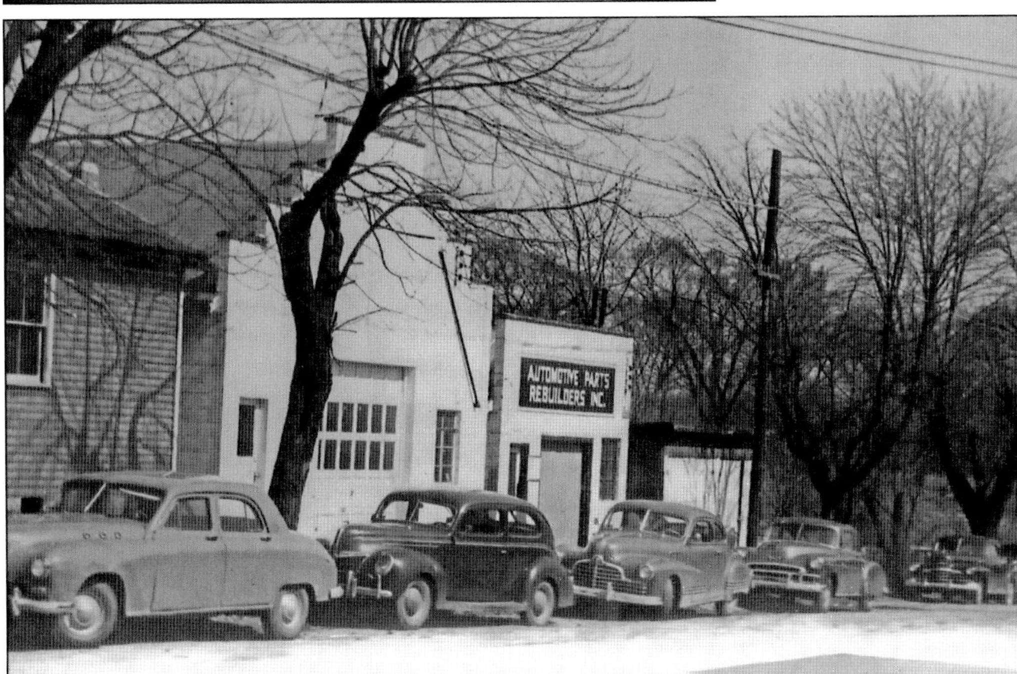

Located on East Shelby Street, the Automotive Parts Rebuilders, Inc. building was owned and operated by Alex Caldwell. He rebuilt and restored Model T and Model A Fords. (Courtesy of Dora Helen Fields.)

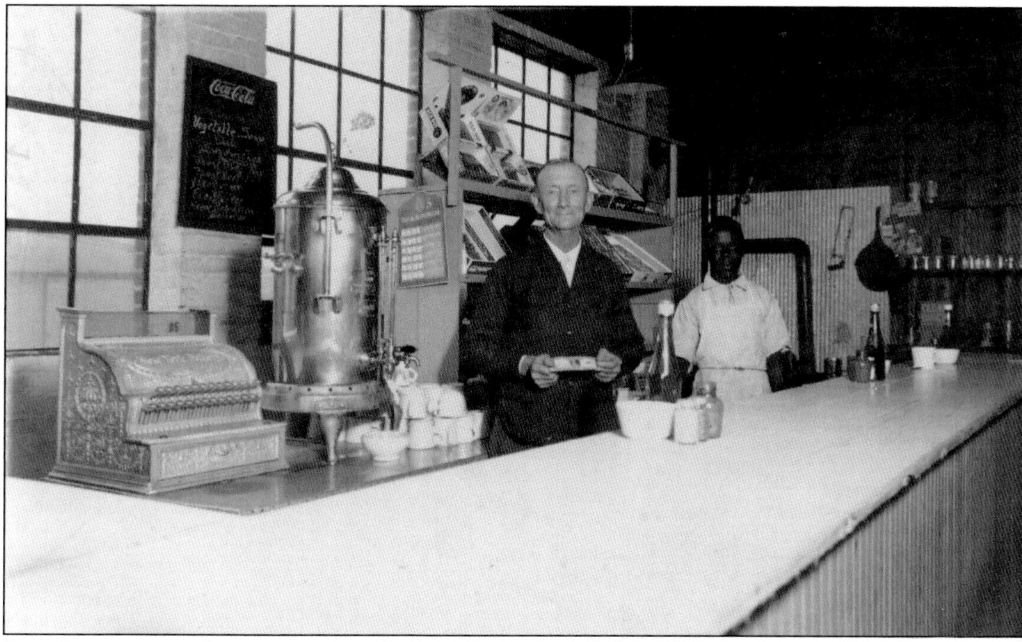

Bert Riggs operated a restaurant on Main Street next to the old Kennett Tavern building. In this picture, Riggs is standing near the cash register, and an unidentified man is standing down the counter. (Courtesy of Barbara Browning.)

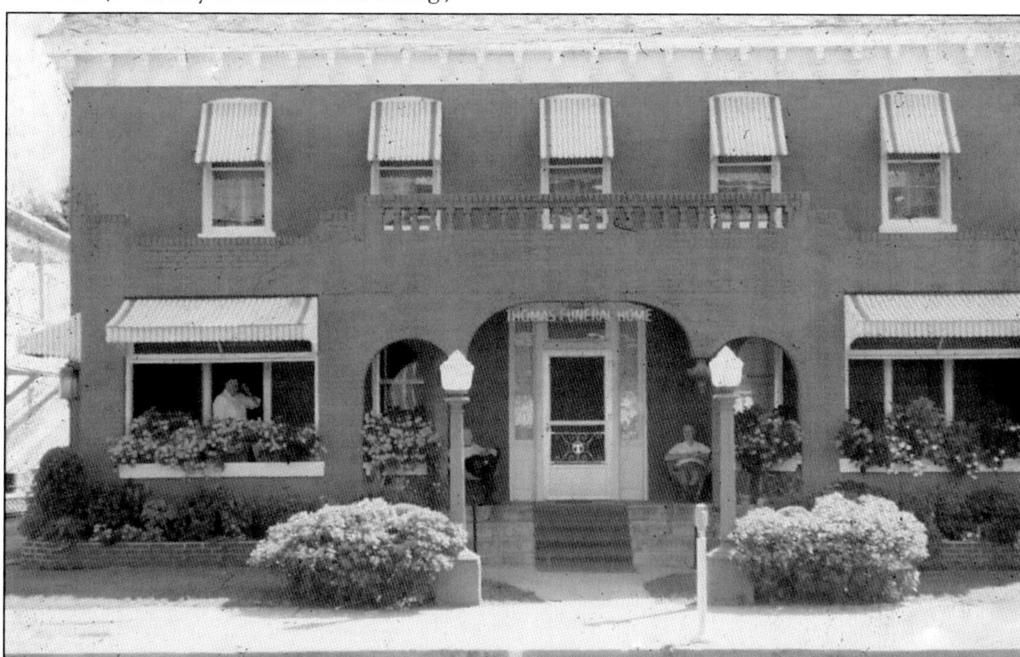

The Thomas Funeral Home, located on West Shelby Street, managed its business from 1945 until 1965, operating with several partners over the years. In 1965 Peoples Funeral Home purchased the building with the intention of expanding their funeral business. Instead, the building served as doctor's offices for Dr. Robert McKinney and a dental office for Dr. Paul Williams. It now houses the dental office of Dr. William Verax. (Courtesy of Jerry Conrad.)

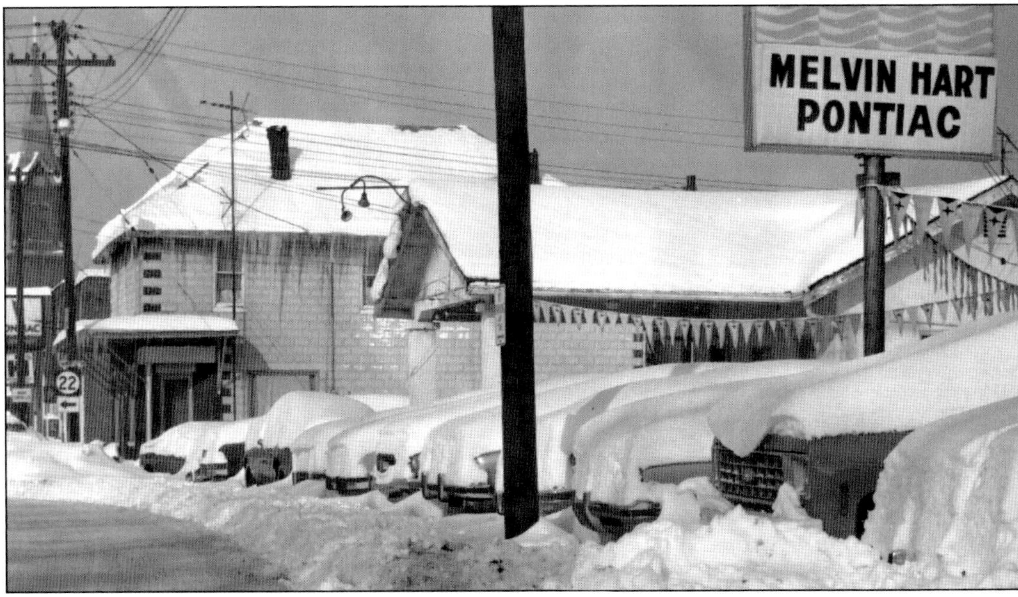

Melvin Hart's Pontiac car sales lot sat where, in early years, Bob's Gas Station could be found. This prime spot was at the intersection of Main and Second Streets with the Shoemaker Bridge nearby. In this picture, the office is where the former gas station stood. The building was torn down in 1980. (Courtesy of Hallie Hart.)

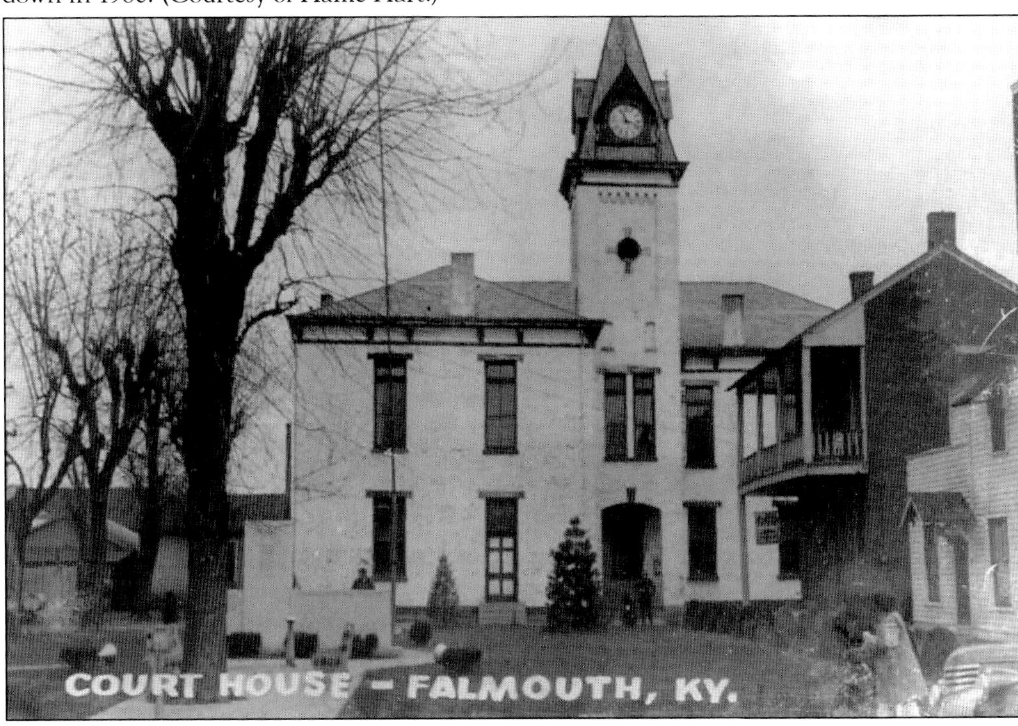

This view of the courthouse looking from Shelby Street was taken during the time it was painted white. The Veterans Memorial Monument sits in the center of the courthouse yard. This was taken before an addition was made on the left side of the building. (Courtesy of the Opal Jackson Family.)

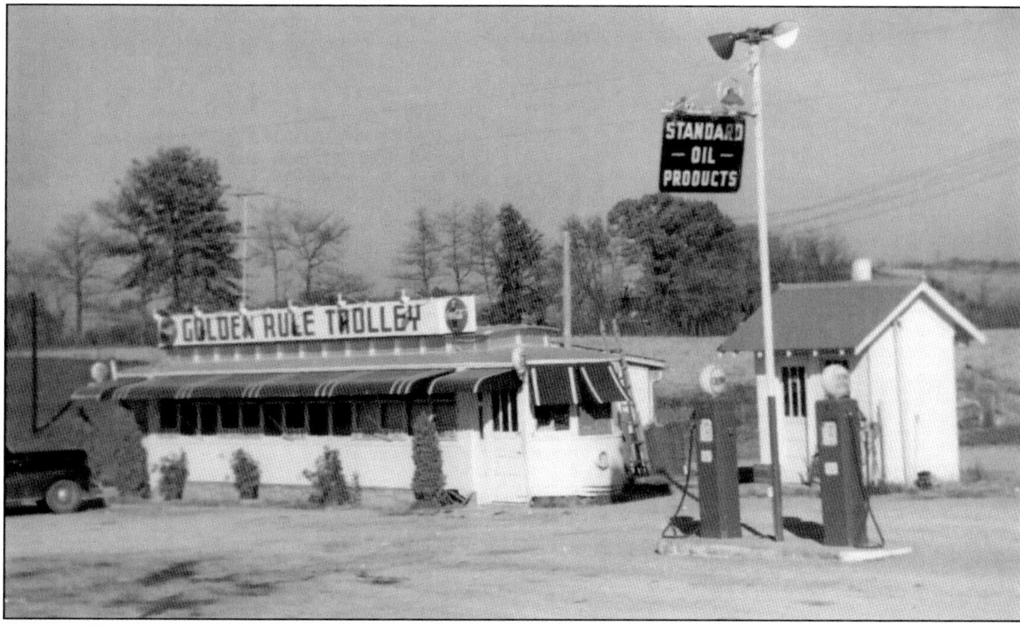

The Golden Rule Trolley was about 4 miles south of Falmouth on US27 at the intersection of the old LLL Highway. Breakfast, lunch, and dinner were served in the main area seven days a week. An extension off the back of the restaurant allowed for small church or club groups to meet for parties.

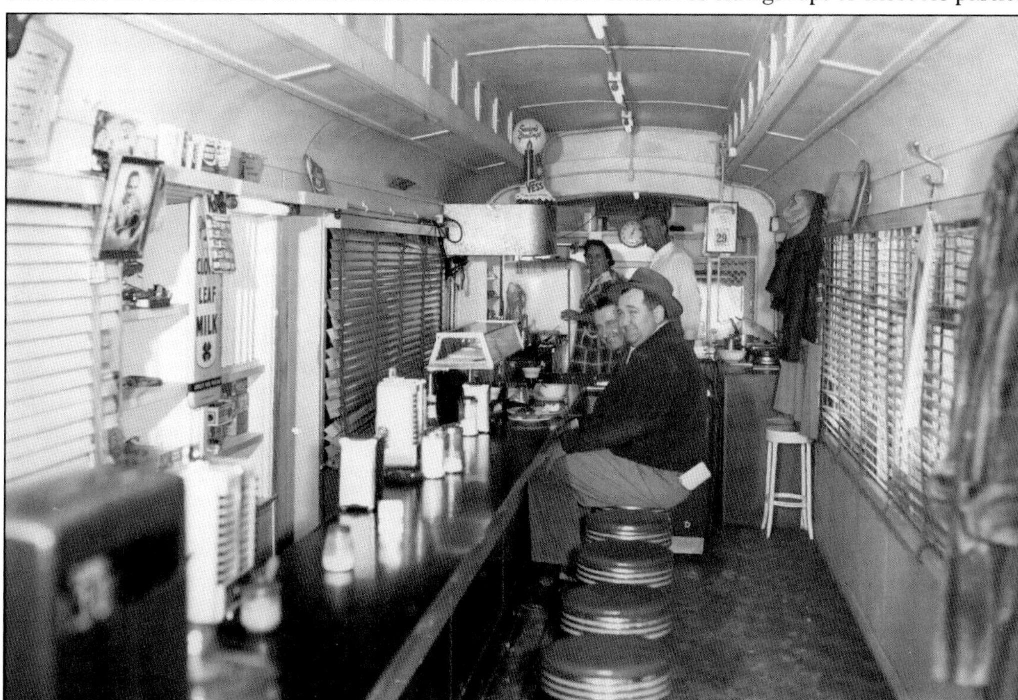

Taken at Christmas in 1953, this photograph gives a look inside the local eatery called the Golden Rule Trolley. In this picture, customers Melvin Hart and Morgan Johnston enjoy food and conversation with owners Goldie and Eness McKinley. They owned the smoke-free restaurant for 24 years, closing it in the late 1960s. (Courtesy of Hallie Hart.)

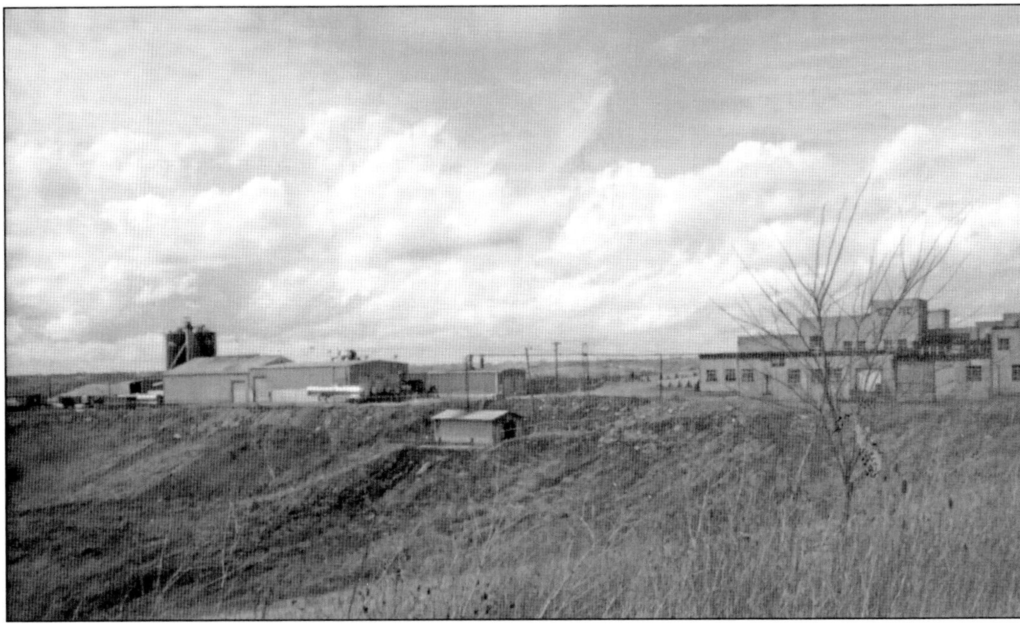

Griffin Industries was founded in 1947 by John L. Griffin under the name Falmouth Fertilizer Company. The name changed in 1966 to Griffin Industries, and shortly after that it became Griffin Industries, Inc. Griffin was only 19 years old when he began collecting dead animals and taking them to a rendering plant in Reading, Ohio, and later Germantown, Ohio. This was a job few people were interested in doing. In 1942 John L. and Rosellen Griffin were married in Ohio, and in 1943 they moved to Falmouth, Kentucky to begin an odyssey that continues today. In 1947 Griffin built his own rendering plant 2 miles off KY17 in order to reduce his time spent driving. Today Griffin Industries, Inc. is an international business that continues to expand its programs to meet the company's needs and those of the world. The photograph above shows the old plant and the new plant building in the early 1980s. Below, John L. Griffin (right) and his cousin Larry Wys stand next to the second truck purchased and used by Griffin for transporting carcasses to the plant for processing. (Both courtesy of Teresa Johnston.)

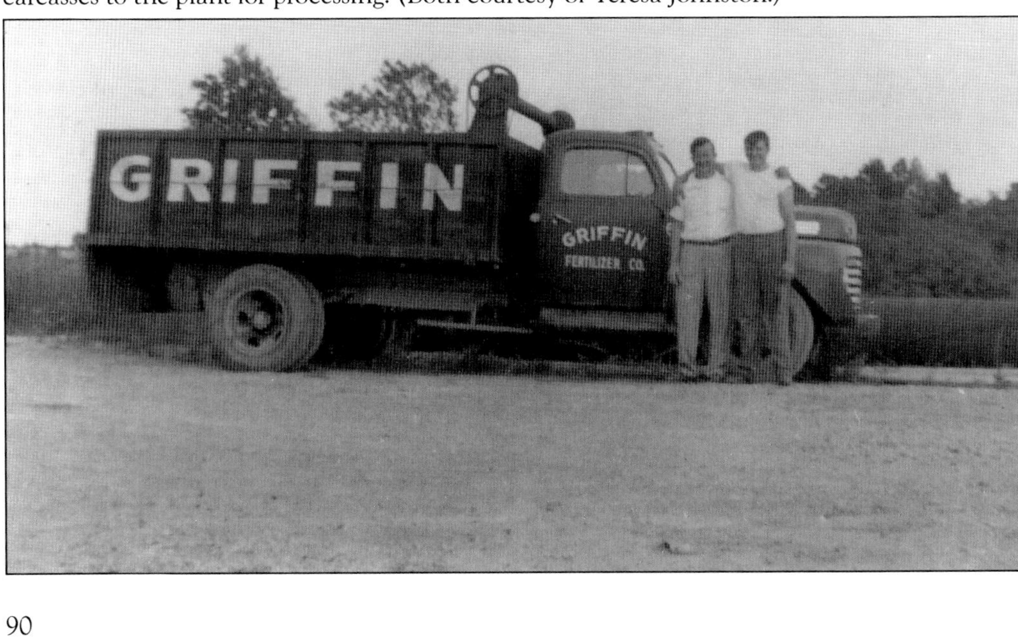

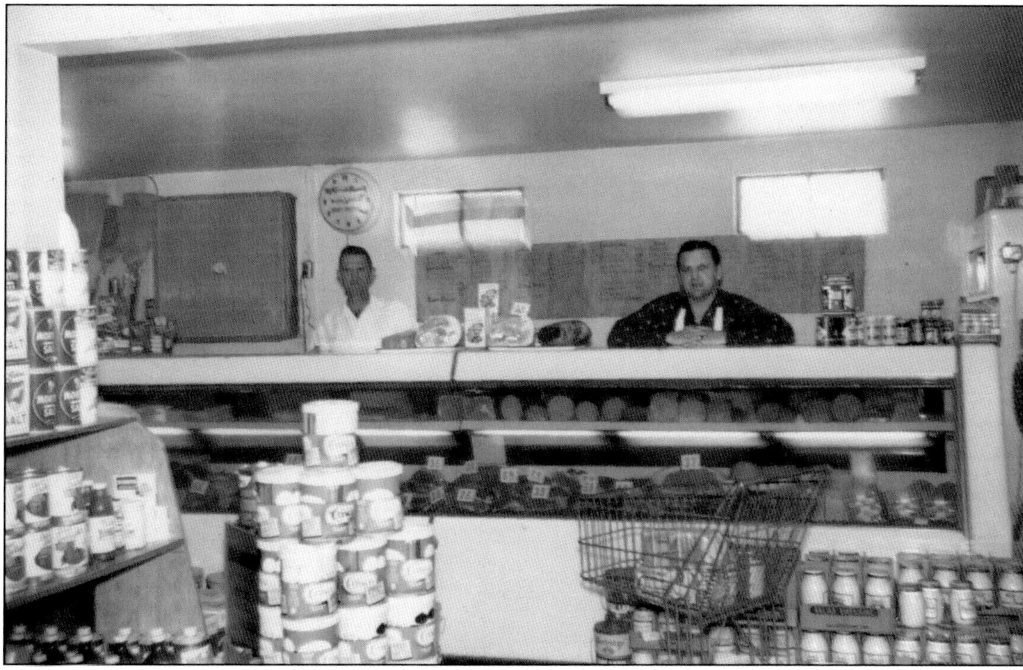

In 1945, Earl and Ruby Browning Wyatt began their family grocery business selling products out of a Studebaker wagon that traveled around the community. Later they built their first store, which included a second story for living quarters. Business increased, and the need for a larger store led to a modern new building in about 1995. Today the family business continues under the direction of their daughter, Dixie Wyatt Owen. (Courtesy of Dixie Wyatt Owen.)

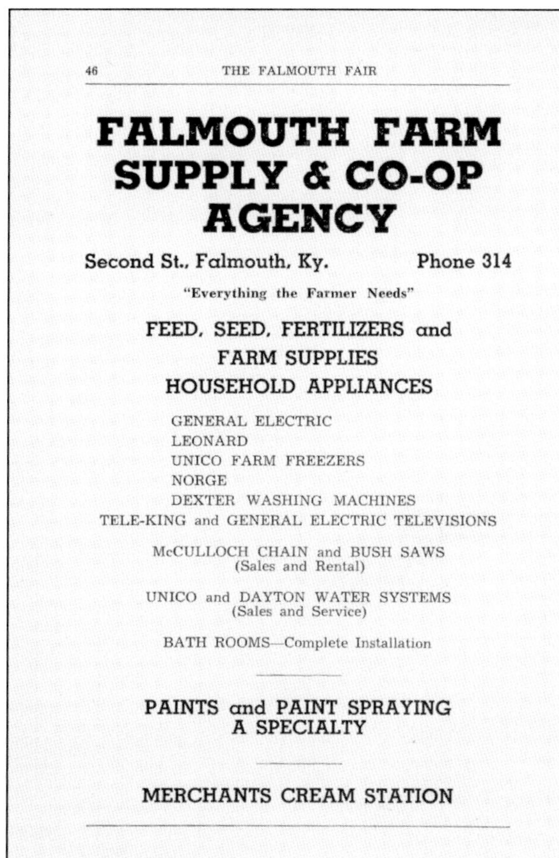

46 THE FALMOUTH FAIR

FALMOUTH FARM SUPPLY & CO-OP AGENCY

Second St., Falmouth, Ky. Phone 314

"Everything the Farmer Needs"

FEED, SEED, FERTILIZERS and FARM SUPPLIES

HOUSEHOLD APPLIANCES

GENERAL ELECTRIC
LEONARD
UNICO FARM FREEZERS
NORGE
DEXTER WASHING MACHINES
TELE-KING and GENERAL ELECTRIC TELEVISIONS

McCULLOCH CHAIN and BUSH SAWS (Sales and Rental)

UNICO and DAYTON WATER SYSTEMS (Sales and Service)

BATH ROOMS—Complete Installation

PAINTS and PAINT SPRAYING A SPECIALTY

MERCHANTS CREAM STATION

In the early 1950s, the Falmouth Fair gave space for the local merchants to advertise their wares to a large audience. In this ad, the Falmouth Farm Supply and Co-Op Agency lists "Everything a Farmer Needs." This includes items from seed to bathroom fixtures.

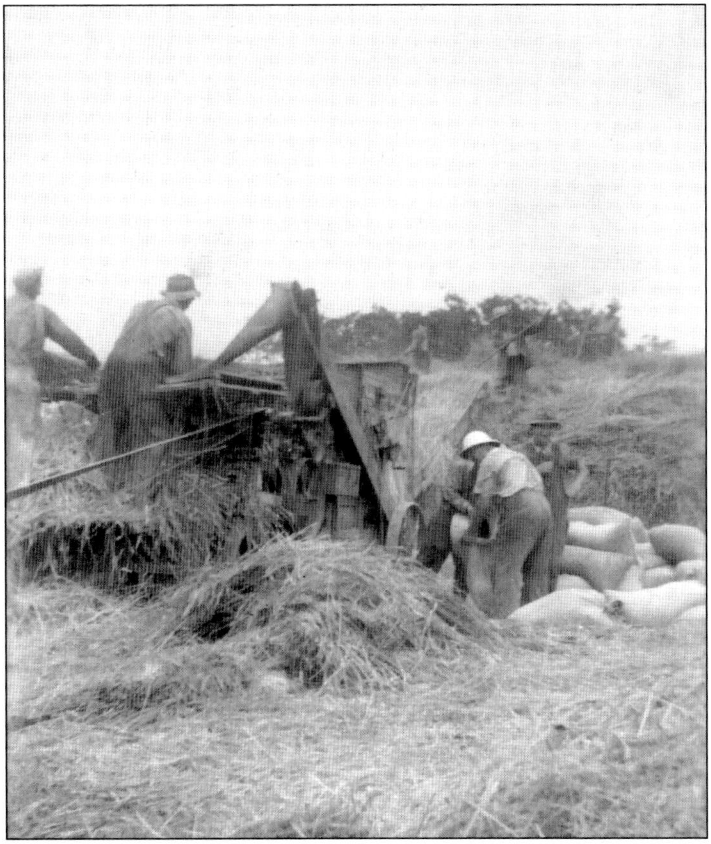

When running a dairy farm, much grain is needed for cattle feed and also for selling at the local mill. This photograph shows how the Campbell men would thresh the grain and bag it for later use. (Courtesy of Lois Wilson.)

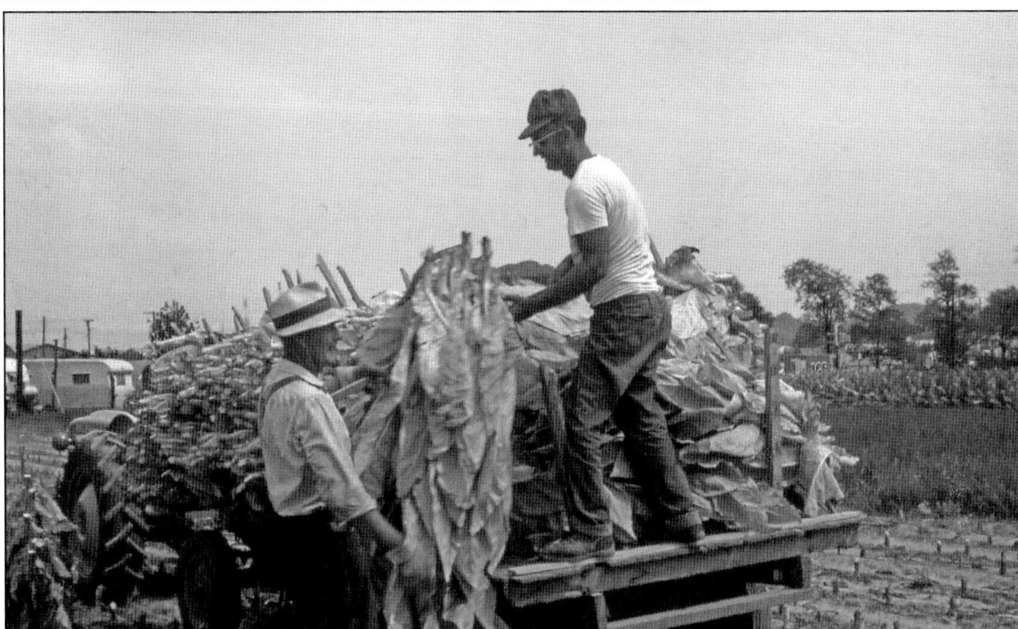

Pendleton County was a large tobacco-growing area from its earliest years. In this photograph Jimmy Klee is loading a stick of tobacco on his wagon. (Courtesy of George Lach.)

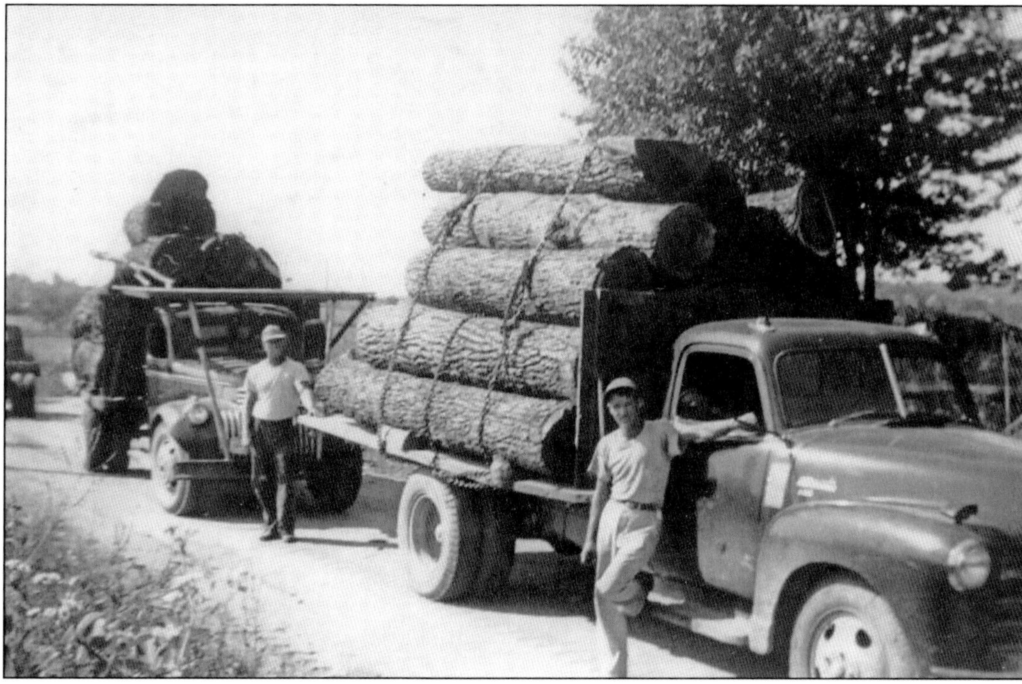

Pendleton County began as a land of primeval forests, and even into the mid-1950s there were large trees to cut. Harold Wright and his fellow worker are shown here with their two trucks loaded with large logs heading to Lawrenceburg, Indiana. (Courtesy of Gary Wright.)

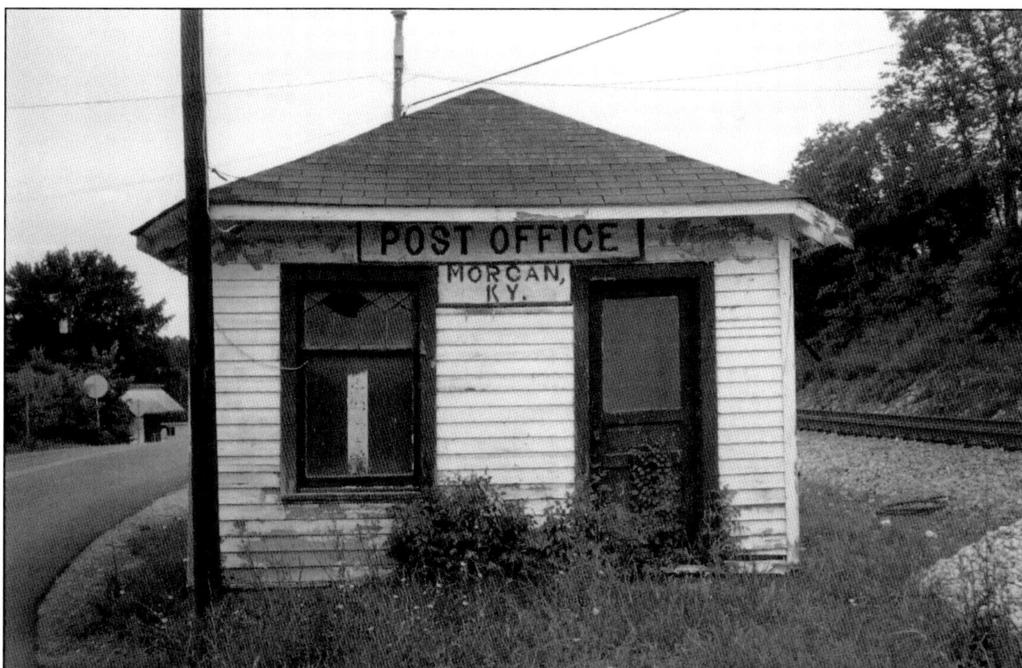

Morgan's Post Office was located near the right-of-way for the Louisville and Nashville Railroad. It stood across from the Ewing General Store. It closed around 1958 and stood empty until it was bulldozed in 2008. (Courtesy of Nancy Bray.)

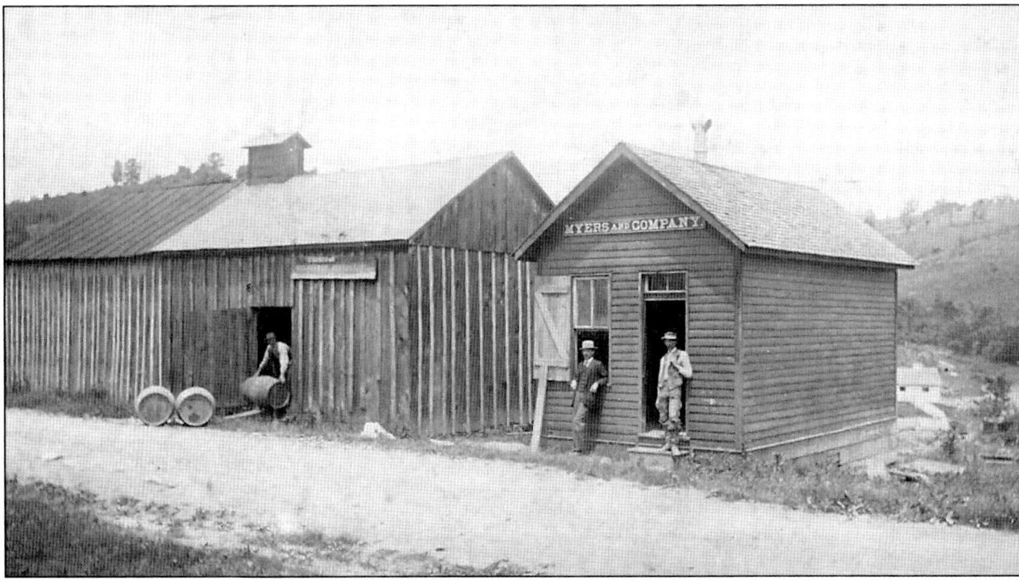

In this photograph of the Myers and Company Distillery, the large storage building and the smaller gauger building are seen. The gauger building was where the whiskey was tested for quality and taste. The road in front is Flour Creek Road. Frank Scott is seen standing in the doorway. The land where the distillery stood in the early 1900s was owned by the Ducker family. In later years the two buildings were moved to the Frank Scott property about a quarter of a mile up the road. (Courtesy of Mary Ann Hornbeek.)

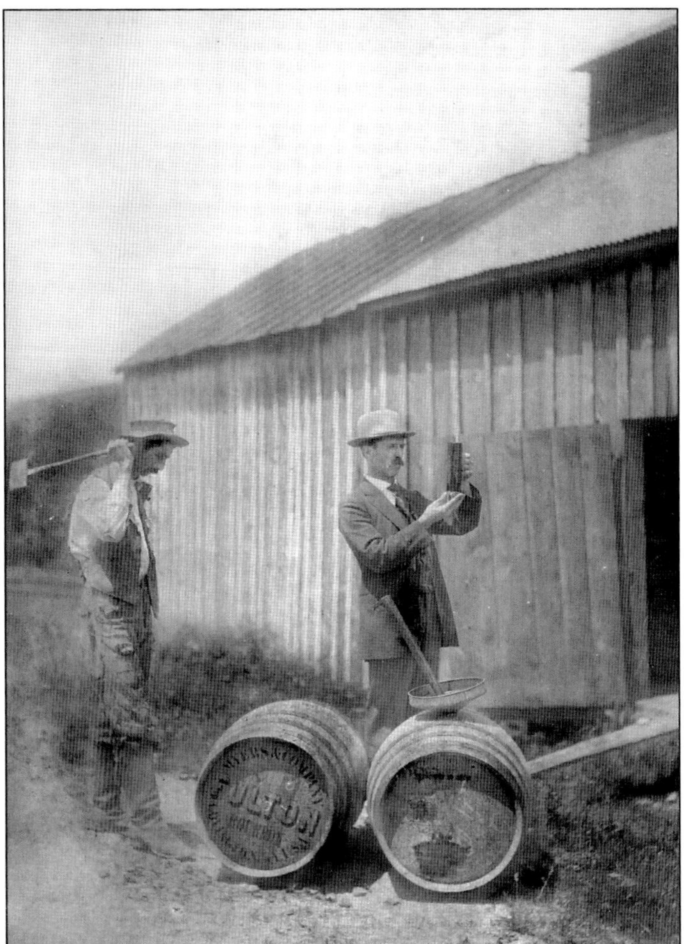

Frank Scott (left) watches as a gauger tests Fulton bourbon from the Myers and Company distillery for quality. (Courtesy of Mary Ann Hornbeek.)

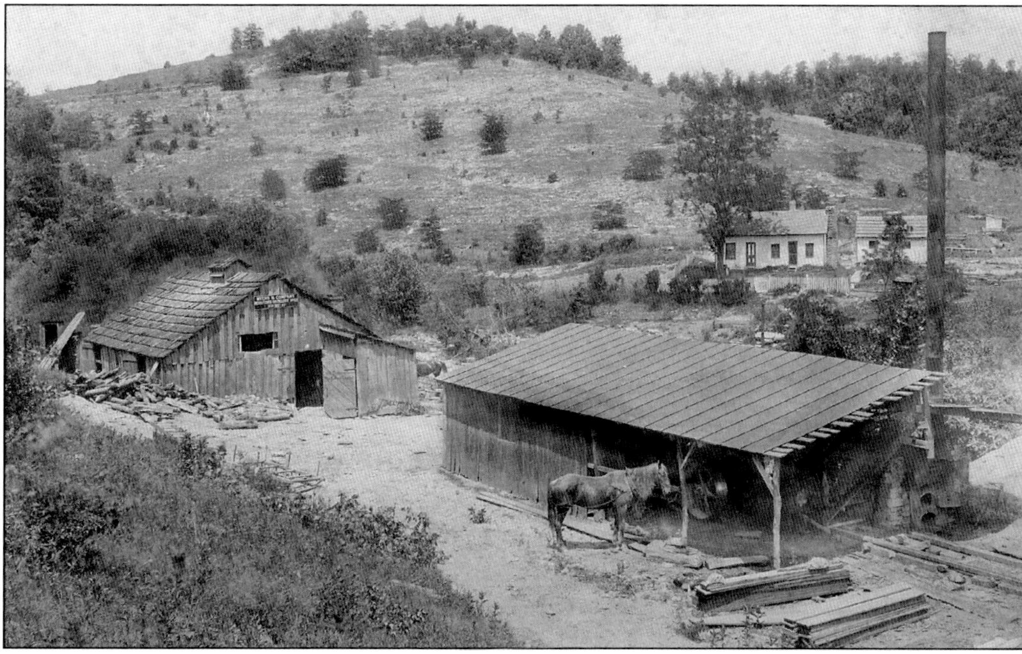

The building in the background was the distillery owned by Myers and Company in the 1900s. It was located on Flour Creek Road, about a mile from the present-day intersection of Flour Creek Road and KY177. The Ducker family owned the property where this distillery and a sawmill stood. (Courtesy of Mary Ann Hornbeck.)

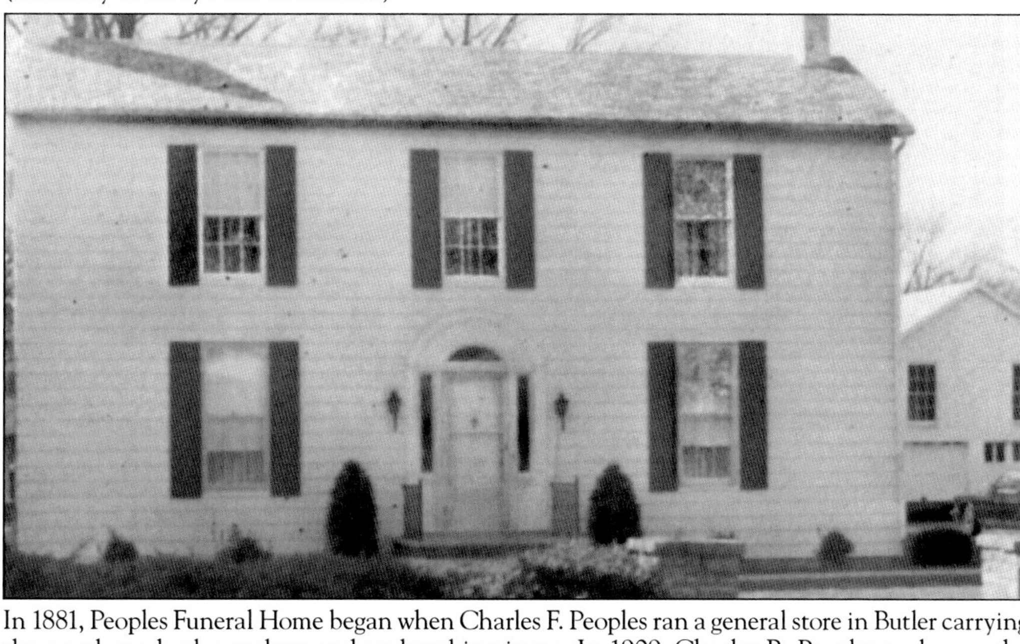

In 1881, Peoples Funeral Home began when Charles F. Peoples ran a general store in Butler carrying the usual goods plus caskets and undertaking items. In 1909, Charles B. Peoples took over the business and established a funeral home. Charles W. Peoples became a part of the business, and in 1948 he opened a funeral home in Falmouth. Today John W. Peoples and his sons, Jonathan and Christopher, operate the family businesses. The Peoples family has been serving the community for over 100 years. (Courtesy of Teresa Johnston.)

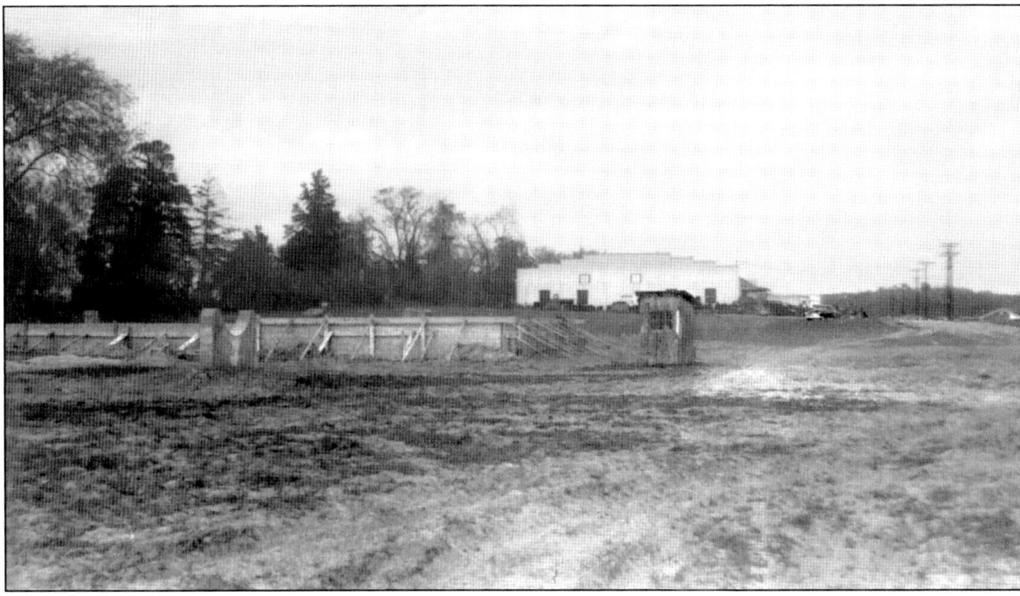

Fullers Manufacturing plant, seen in the background, began in the late 1940s as a company that remanufactured Ford engines. It continued this type of manufacturing until 1998, when it was sold to Vega. In the foreground, the newly poured foundations for the Midwest Bottle Gas Company's loading dock stand waiting for the building to be completed. (Courtesy of Paul Tuemler.)

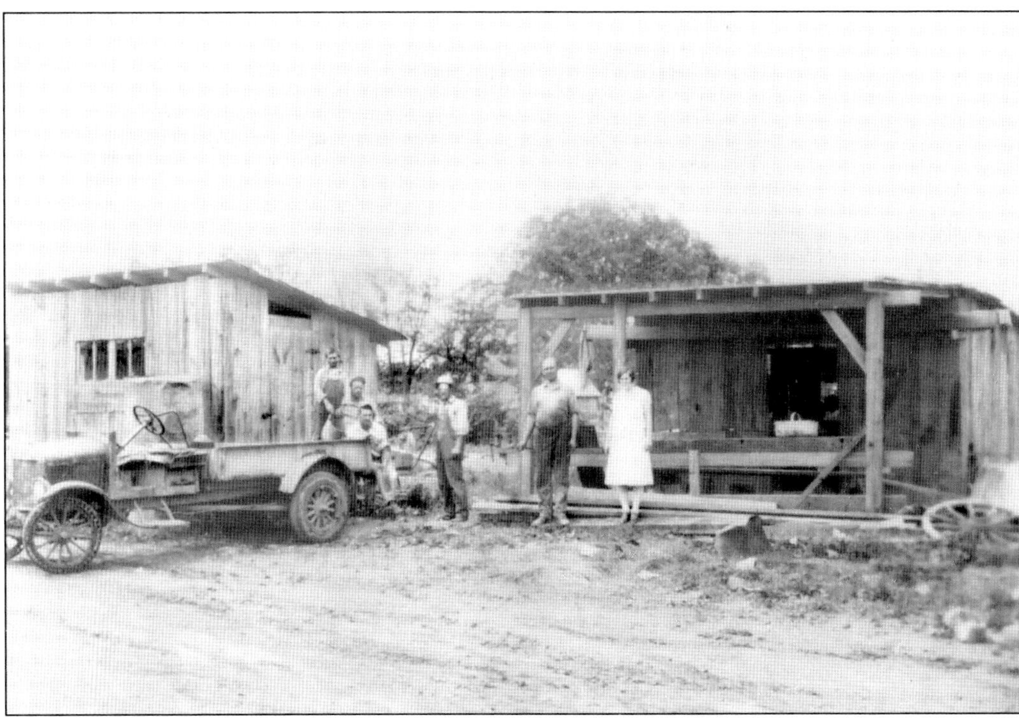

Taken between 1917 and 1920, this photograph shows a rural blacksmith's shop. In front of the work area are Charlie Ventler and his wife, Stella. The people around the truck are unidentified. (Courtesy of Billie Newman.)

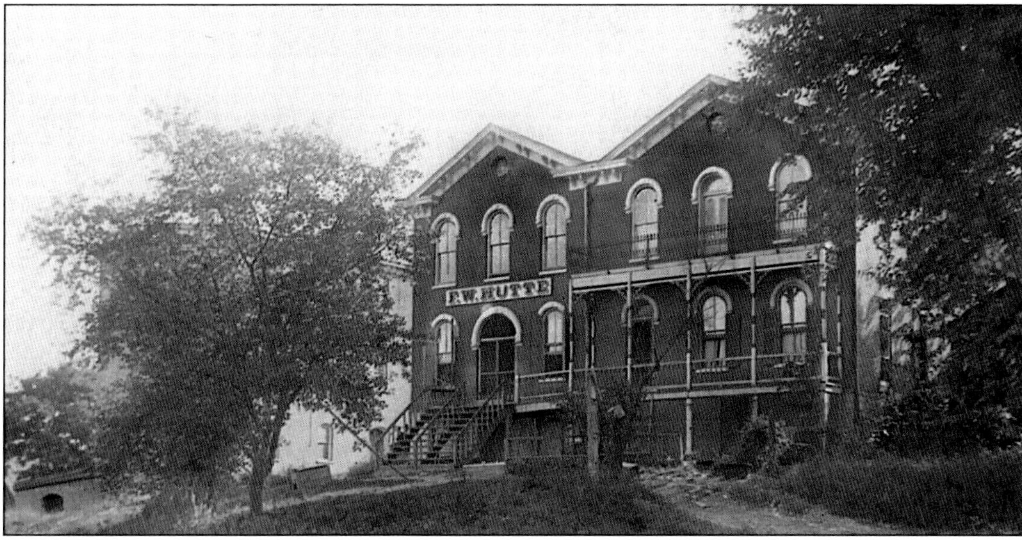

The F. W. Hutte general dry goods store and post office served the Carntown area for many years. The owners, Fred Hutte and his wife Pauline, came from Germany to begin a new life here. Hutte was a blacksmith and his wife ran the store. As the Huttes only spoke German, their daughters Henrietta and Freda assisted. Today the Black River Mining Company has its limestone mining operation in this area. (Courtesy of Chris Fossitt.)

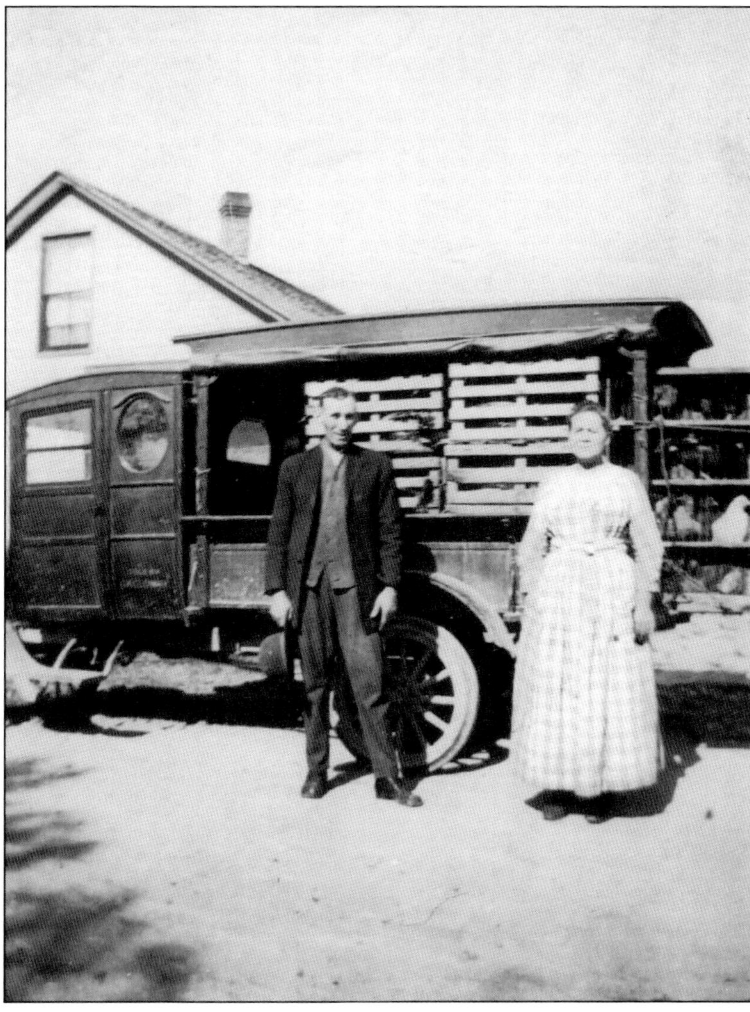

The couple posed beside their covered truck before heading out for delivery of fresh fowl to the local families and markets. (Courtesy of the Opal Jackson Family.)

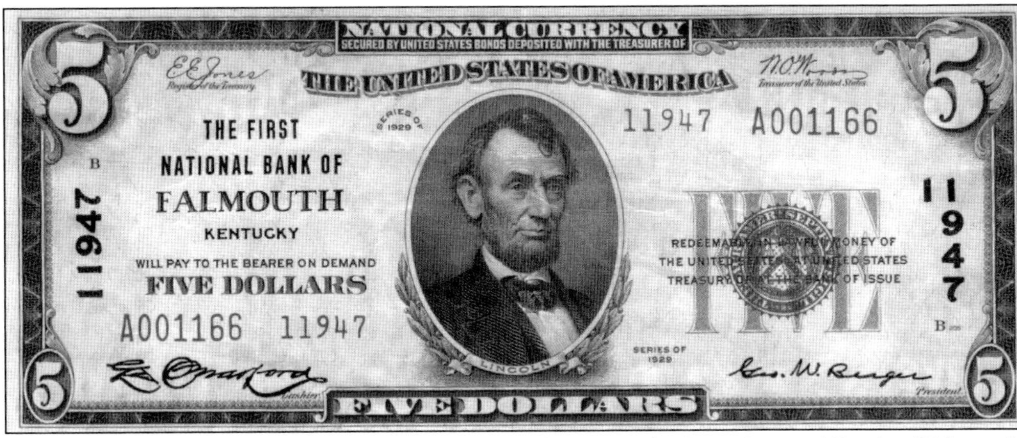

This is a facsimile of a $5 bill engraved with the bank name, The First National Bank of Falmouth, in 1929. The cashier, George C. Bradford, and the president, George W. Berger, signed the bills for printing. (Courtesy of Sherry DeWald.)

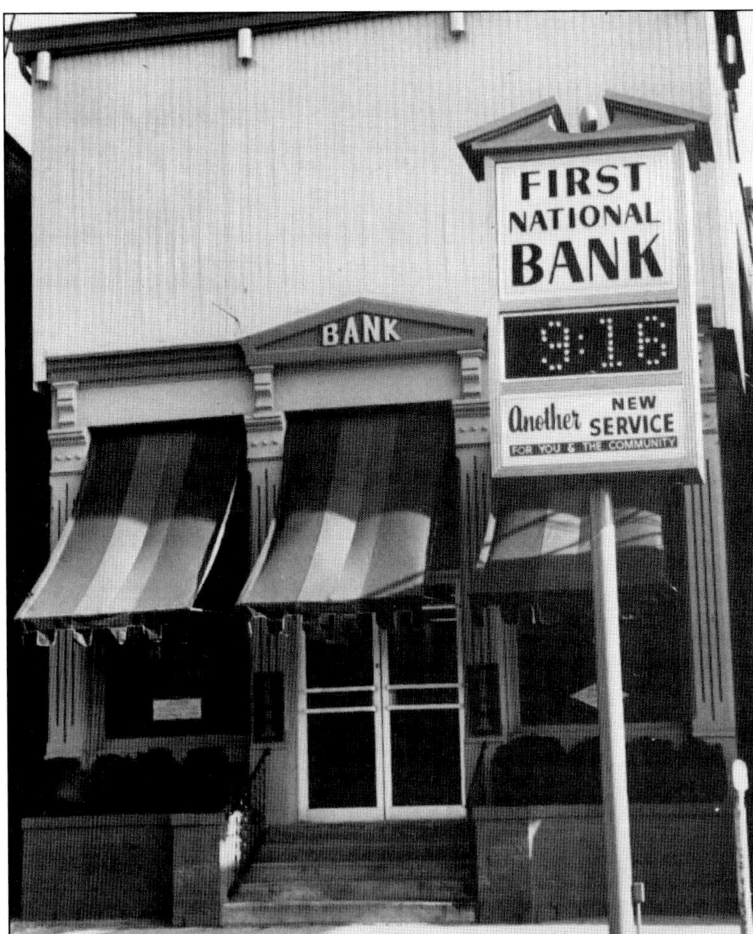

In 1921 the First National Bank of Falmouth opened its doors to the local community. The first president was George Berger; the vice president was Frank W. Conrad, and the cashier was George C. Bradford. The bank served the community until 1968, when controlling interest was sold. In 1971 the First National Bank once again became a locally-owned bank. In 1978 a rededication was held with a branch bank opening on US27 and Flour Creek Road. In 1983 a third branch on US27 in Falmouth was established. Today, none of these banks is in business. (Courtesy of Teresa Johnson.)

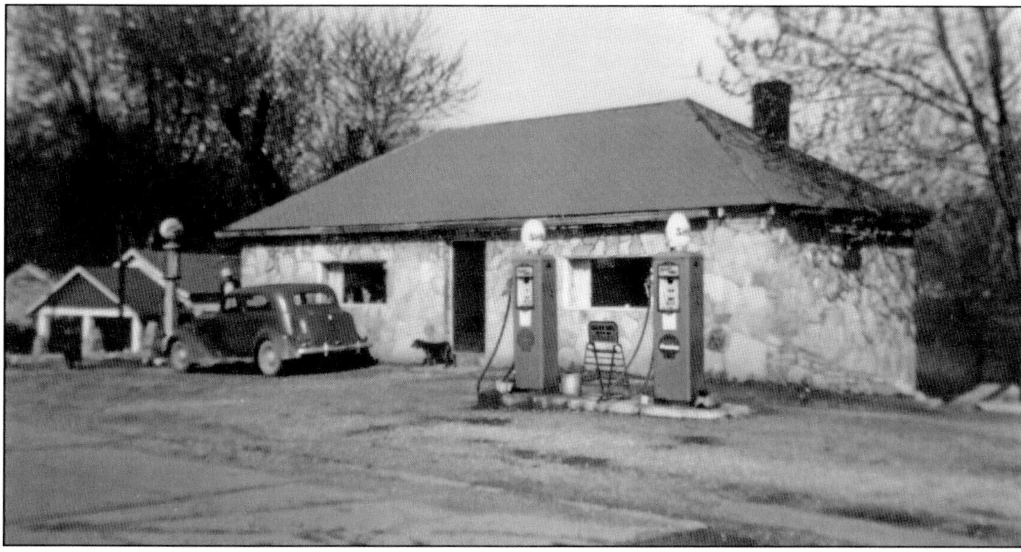

Crossing the bridge into Butler, this stone building stood on the right. Charles Henry and Mary Lancaster Stilwell owned the building, where they ran a gas station and restaurant business. They raised four children, Rhea, Jimmy, Lois, and Charles. The building was later remodeled to serve as a home. Even though the main building has been torn down for several years, a stone rest room building remains as a reminder of days gone by. (Courtesy of the Opal Jackson family.)

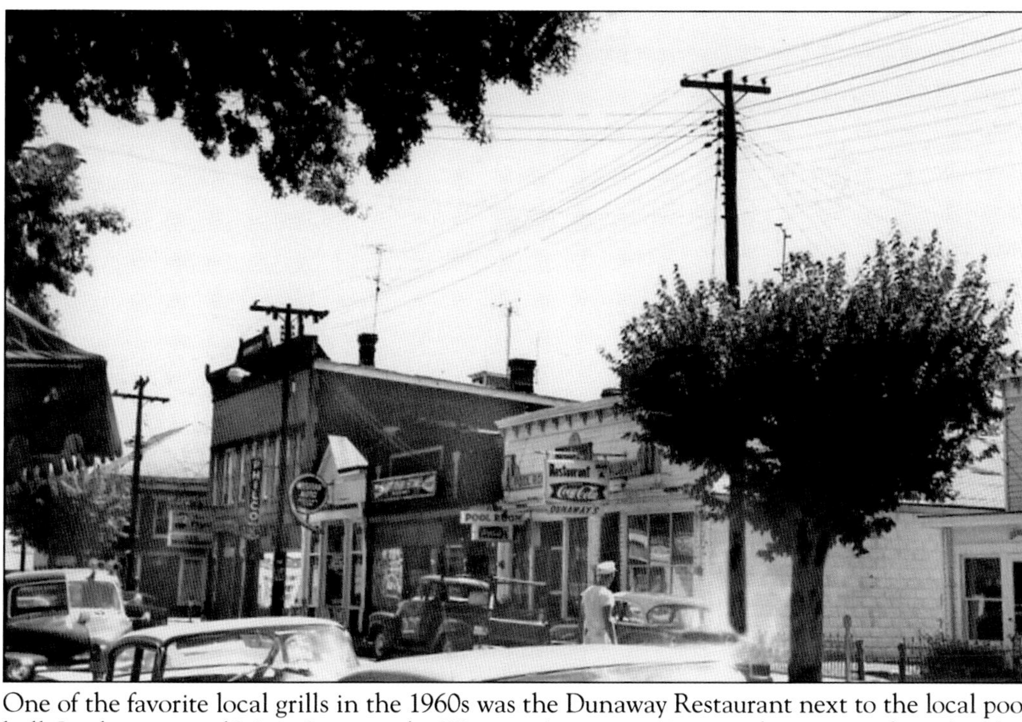

One of the favorite local grills in the 1960s was the Dunaway Restaurant next to the local pool hall. Looking toward Main Street is the Western Auto store. It carried a variety of supplies, but its best section was Christmas Toy Land. (Courtesy of Jerry Conrad.)

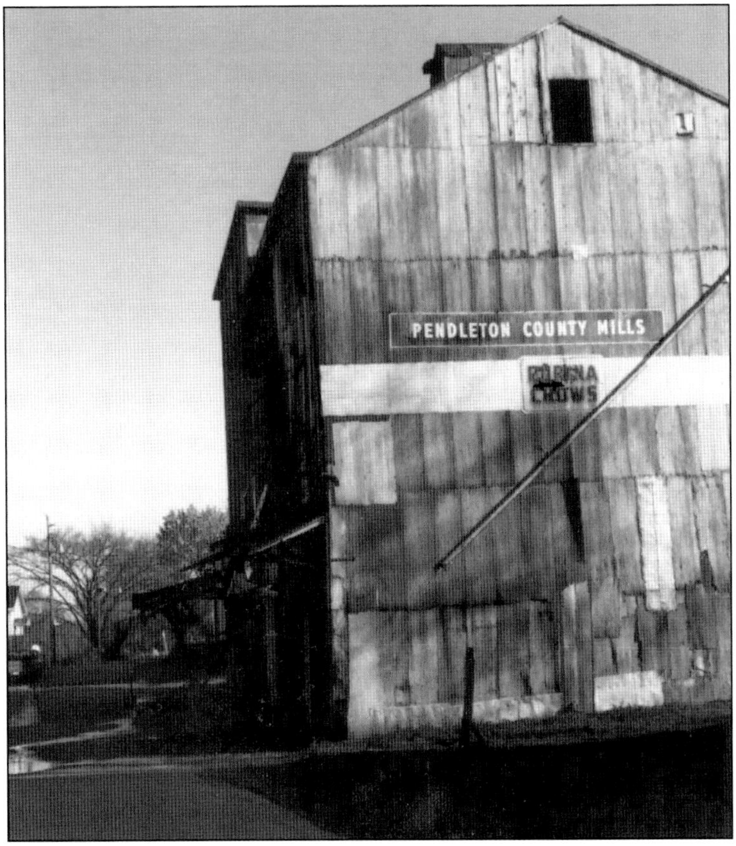

The Pendleton County Mills, formerly the Ideal Rolling Mills, was built about 1892 by R. B. McDonald. It was located on Second Street and operated by J. L. Galloway. The flour was made with rollers crushing the grain. It was owned by Donald Moore when it was dismantled in 1985. (Courtesy of George Lach.)

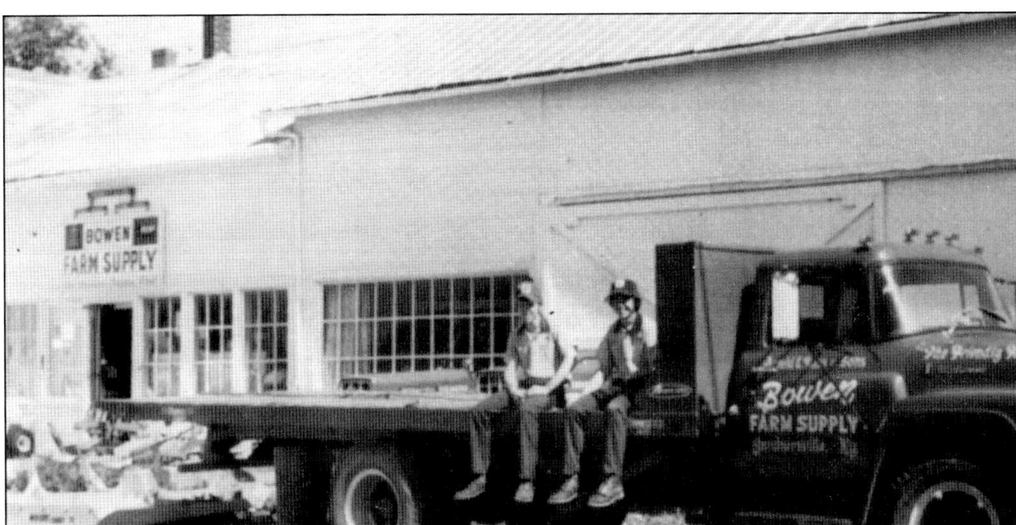

In 1927 L. E. Bowen operated the Gardnersville General Store and soon after became a dealer of International Harvester farm machinery. At this time, he opened the L. E. Bowen Farm Supply. In 1969 the name changed to Bowen Farm Supply after Bowen retired and his son-in-law, Arnold Ross, took over the business. It has continued to grow and has become a major dealer in John Deere machinery. (Courtesy of Teresa Johnston.)

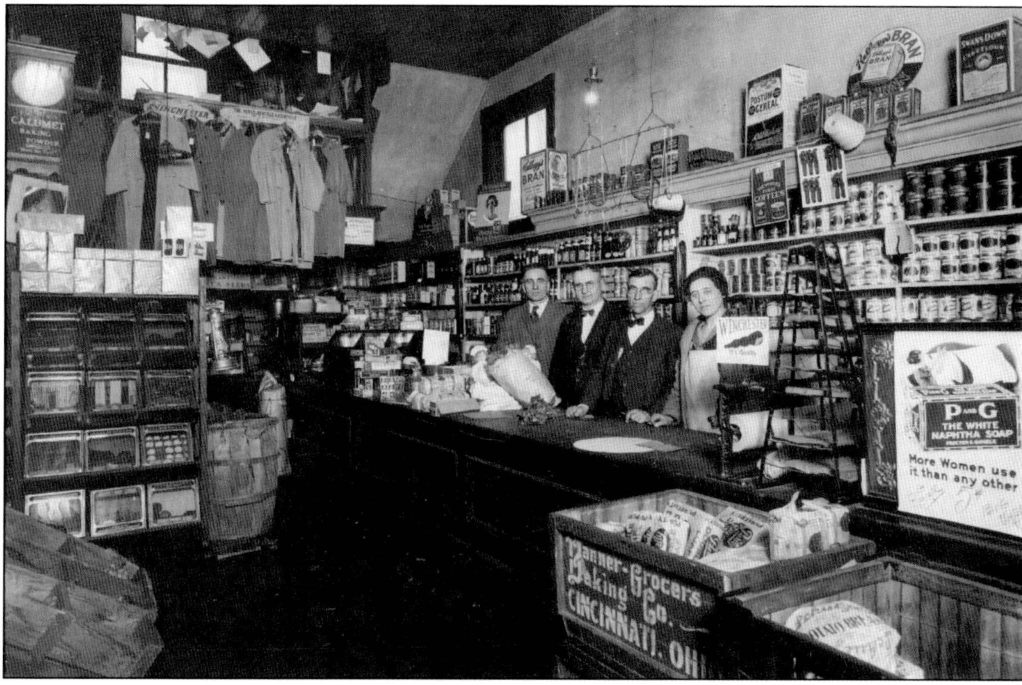

This picture shows the inside of a general store in Butler. The store carried most everything, including canned goods, Proctor and Gamble Naptha soap, cereal, and clothing. (Courtesy of the Opal Jackson family.)

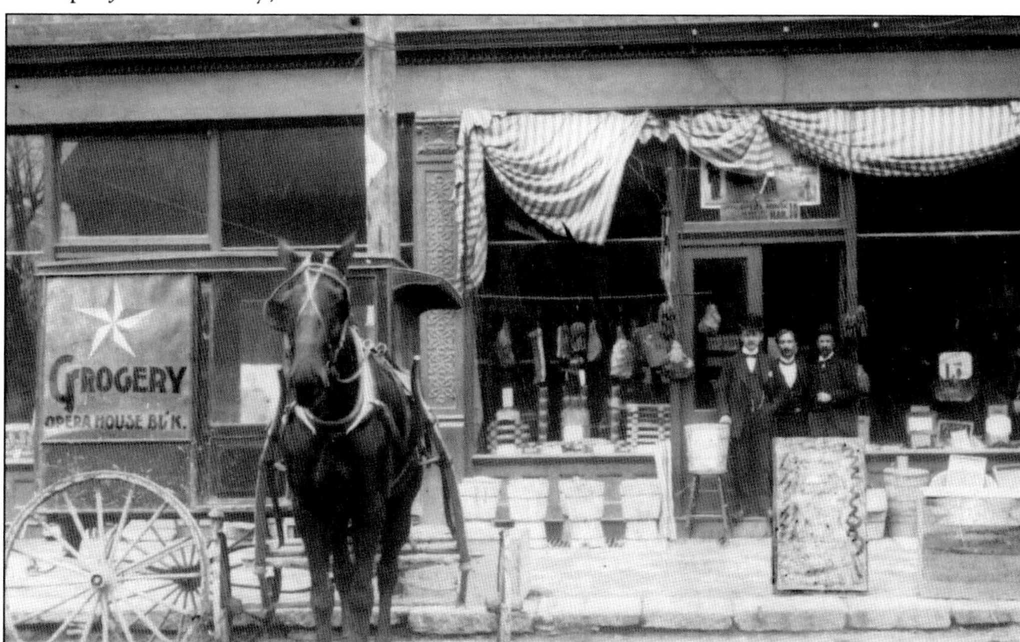

Standing on the Shelby Street side of the Assembly Building, three gentlemen stand in the doorway of the butcher and grocery shop while a horse waits with its wagon. Above the doorway is an advertisement for the "Opera," which was located on the second floor and used for theatrical or musical performances. At one time, silent movies were shown there. (Courtesy of Ron Moreland.)

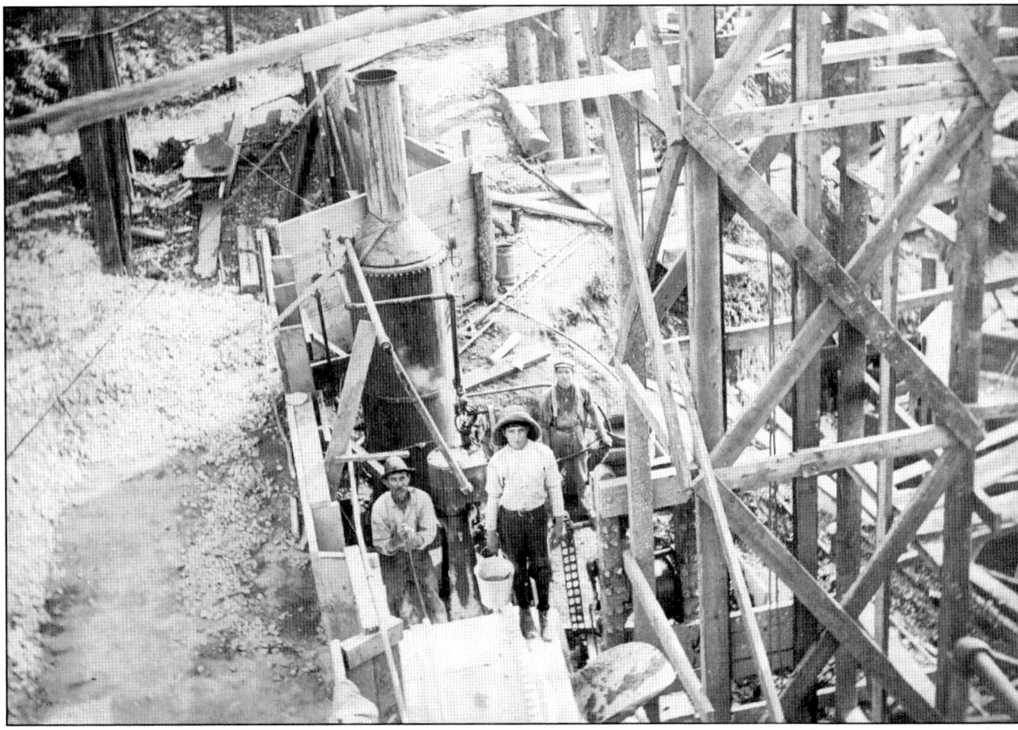

This unusual photograph shows two men working on a pier for one of the county's bridges. (Courtesy of Joyce Carson.)

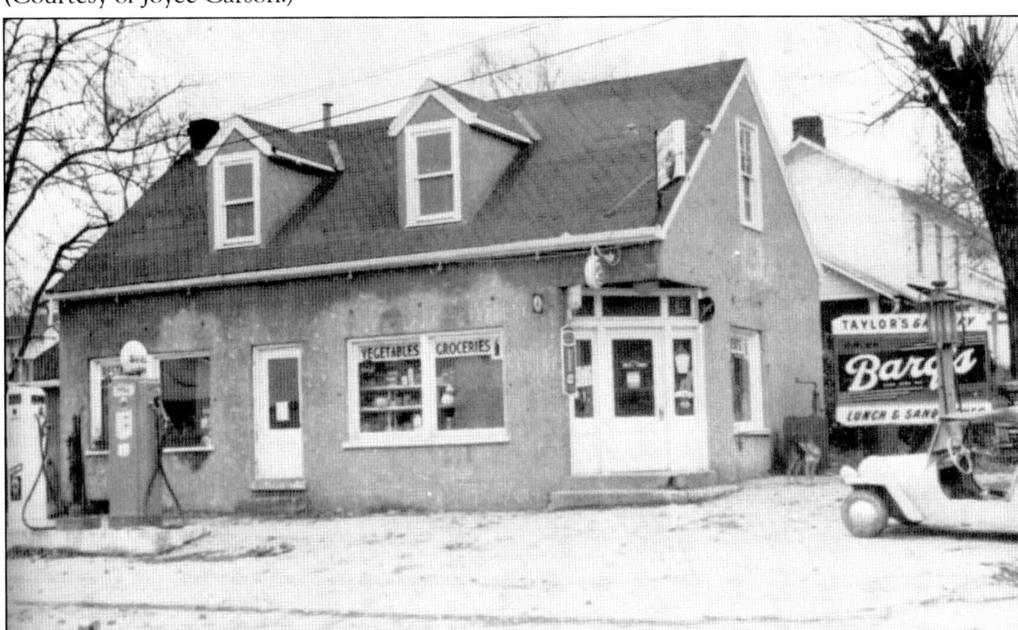

At the time this picture was taken, Taylor's Grocery was run by Alice Taylor. One could purchase a sandwich or lunch there also. This location and building have also been known as "Nellie's" and "Pam's Place." In the 1960s, Alice owned and ran the Kentucky Restaurant on US27 just south of Butler. (Courtesy of Velma Steele.)

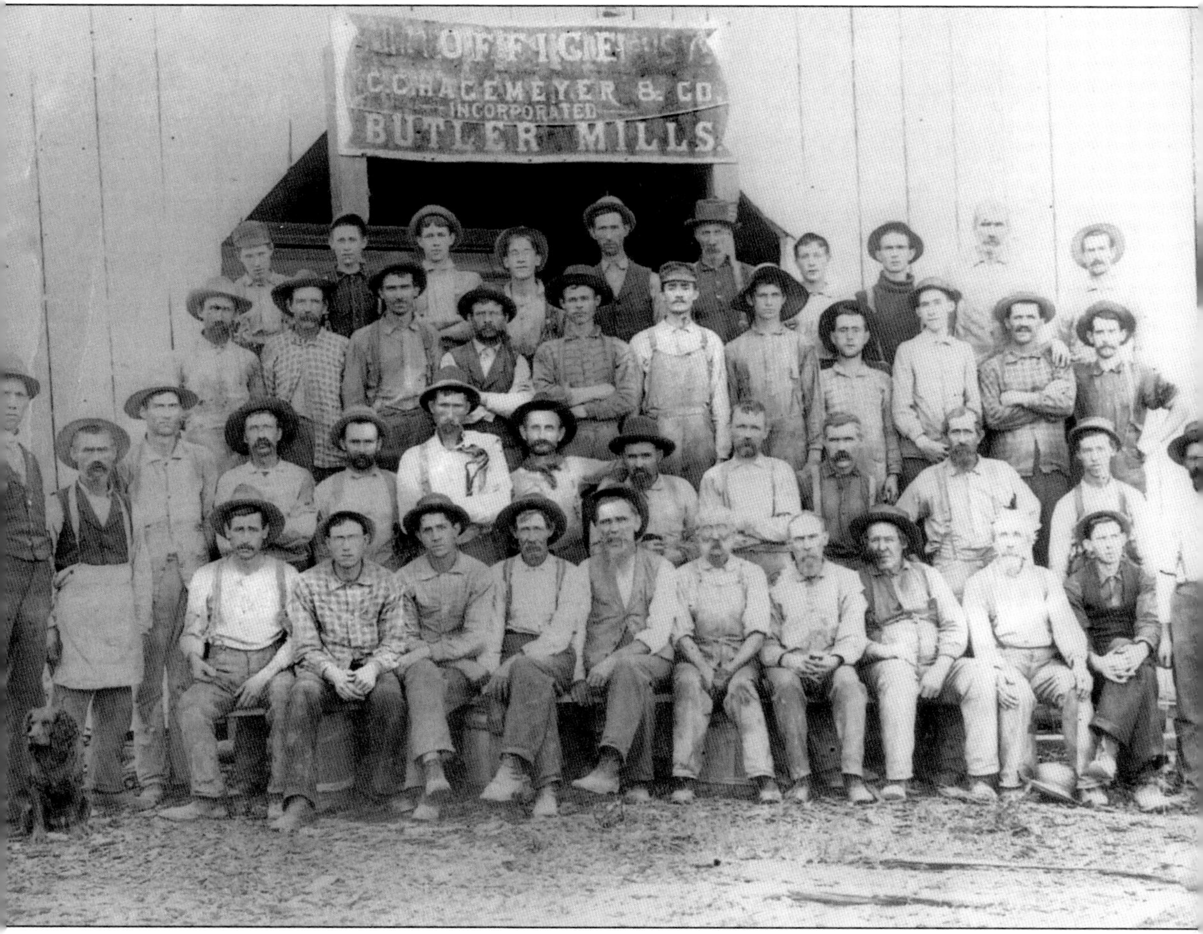

Seen here are the workmen of the Hagemeyer Mill in Butler about 1900. This mill was bought by Christian C. Hagemeyer in 1881 as a part of C. C. Hagemeyer and Company. Hagemeyer had previously run a mill for the L. L. Mining Company in Boston Station. He also owned the adjoining flour mill and several other businesses up and down Mill Street in Butler. These enterprises employed about 60 men. Some are seen here. From left to right they are (first row) unidentified, Walter Finley, Nuete Caldwell, stable boss John Hornbeek, Will Holmes, millwright Charles Dickerson, George Washington Nance, Steve Cundiff, ? Caldwell, and Harry T. Williams; (second row) bookkeeper Charlie Hagemeyer, Ike Moore, Ben Tarven, Tom Sorrel, Peter Howe, William Hornbeek, John Murphy, John Hargus, Theodore Hornbeek, mill engineer Paw Finley, Cliff Caldwell, Tom Cundiff, and Bud Ring; (third row) unidentified, Link Webster, Jake Skinner, unidentified, Lon Yelton, three unidentified, Mose Huff, Ralph R. Williams, Clab Piercy, and John Hargus Jr.; (fourth row) five unidentified, riverboat pilot G. Henderson, three unidentified, and Ben Huff. (Courtesy of the Opal Jackson family.)

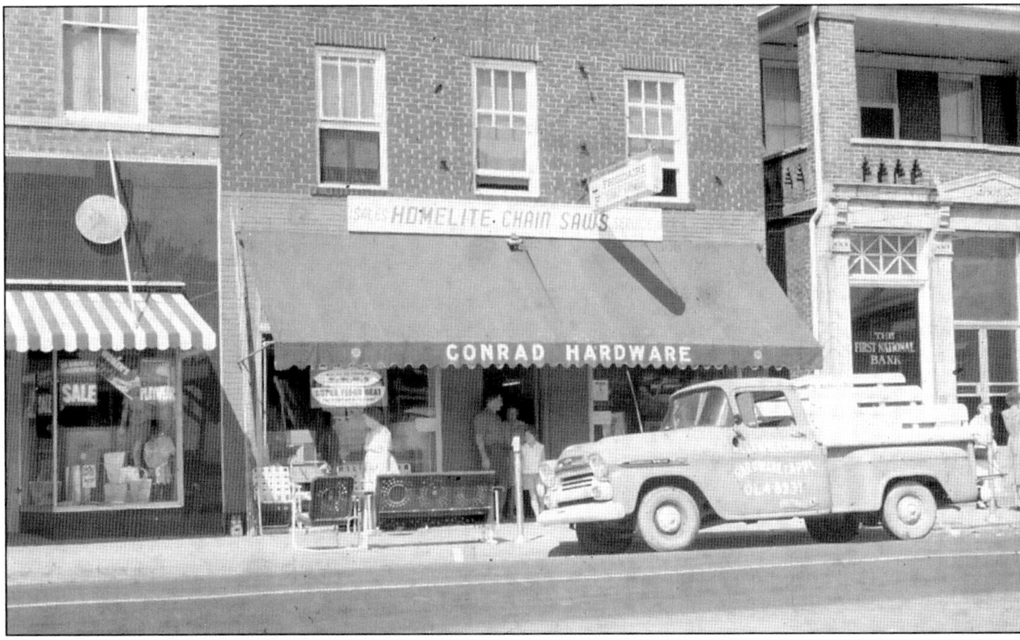

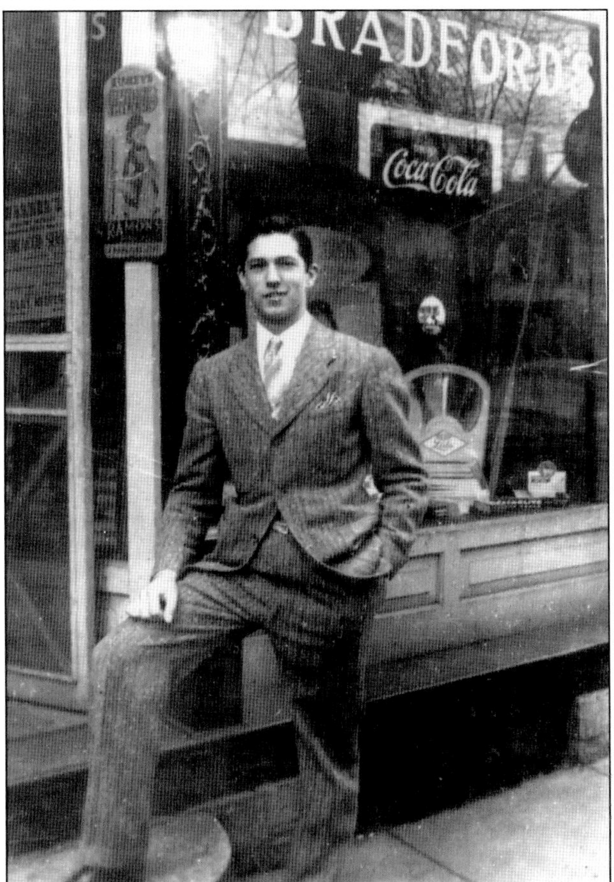

Conrad Hardware began in 1952 when former farmer Allen W. Conrad rented the building next to the First National Bank and opened a hardware store on Shelby Street. Business began with only hardware and related items, but by 1961 Allen rented a building down the street, adding furniture and giftware. In 1963 the furniture business was moved across the street to the first floor of what is now the Woodhead Mortuary. After the 1964 flood, the furniture store was moved to the second floor of the hardware building. In 1976 the Applegate building next door was purchased from R. Risk Arnold, and all the business moved there. (Courtesy of Jerry Conrad.)

The Bradford Cut Rate Store in Falmouth offered many items. There was a soda fountain, over-the-counter elixirs, sewing notions, and even a candy case full of penny candy. Standing on the steps is Bobby Belew, who worked at the soda fountain. (Courtesy of David Belew.)

The *Falmouth Democrat* was one of several newspapers in Pendleton County over the years. Adie O. Robertson was its editor and publisher. This newspaper was not in business for long, and from the note typed at the bottom, Robertson was in need of cash. This receipt was issued to A. Arnold on December 1, 1885, indicating that he had paid his subscription fees for the period from June 1884 to June 1886.

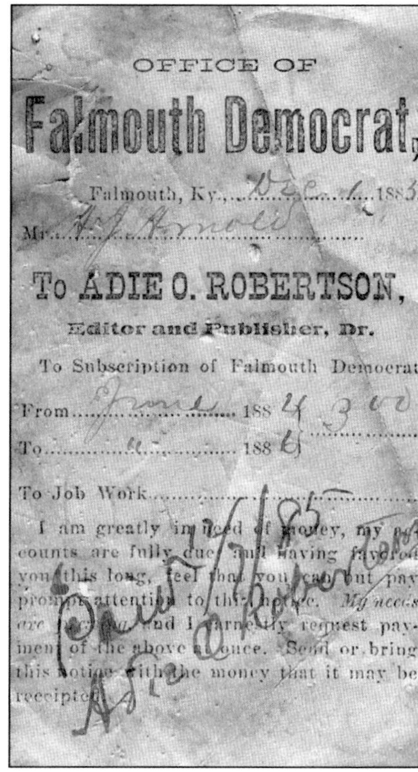
OFFICE OF

Falmouth Democrat,

Falmouth, Ky., ... 188

Mr. ....

To ADIE O. ROBERTSON,

Editor and Publisher, Dr.

To Subscription of Falmouth Democrat

From 188

To 188

To Job Work ....

I am greatly in need of money, my accounts are fully due, and having favored you this long, feel that you can but pay prompt attention to this notice. My needs are pressing, and I earnestly request payment of the above at once. Send or bring this notice with the money that it may be receipted.

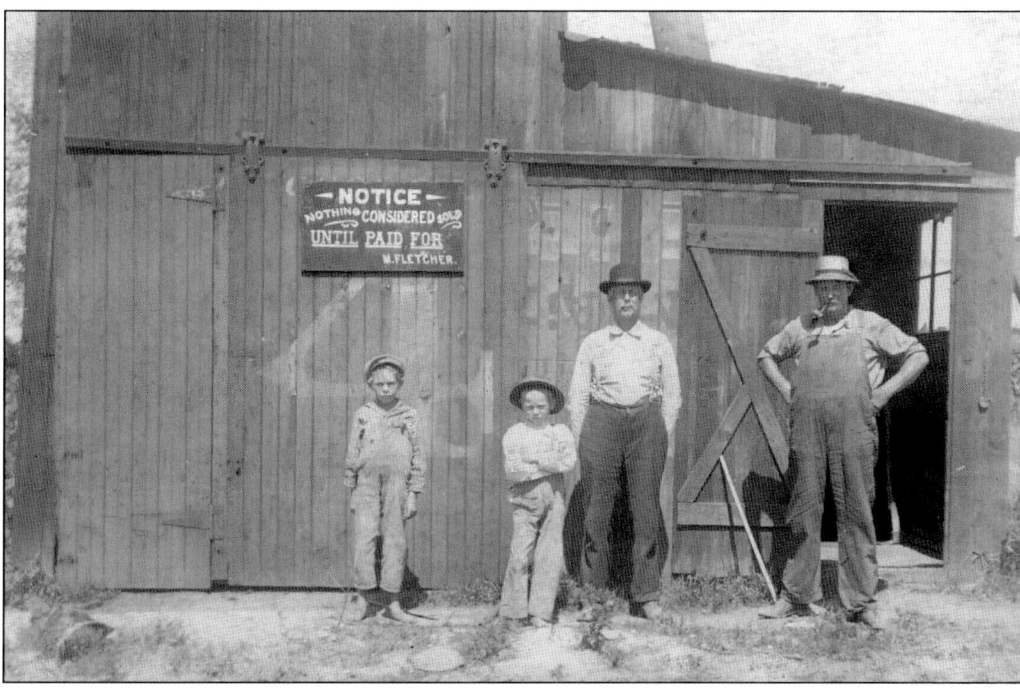

William Fletcher stands with his sons outside his farm supplies building. The notice on the side of the building reflects his terms of business. It states, "Nothing considered sold until paid for," and is signed by Fletcher. (Courtesy of Nancy Gulick Harville.)

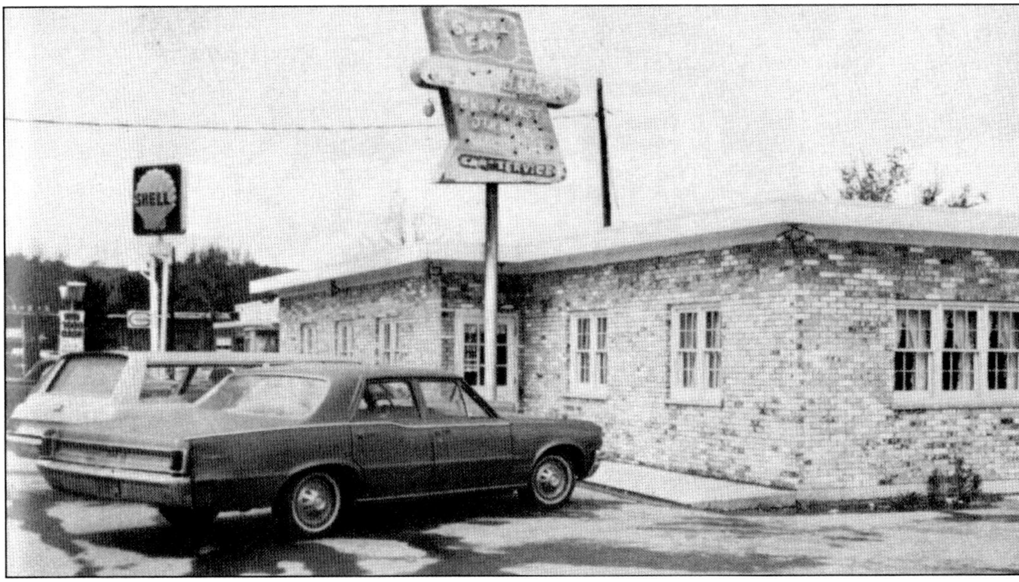

The Small Fry Drive-In Restaurant on US27 in Falmouth was operated similarly to chain restaurants with a car service. Imogene Jacobs and her husband owned this restaurant, which served the community between 1955 and the 1960s, offering home-cooked meals three times a day plus banquets for special meetings. Jacobs was famous for her cream pies. In 1964 she moved and opened a new restaurant at the south end of town under the name Stop and Tell.

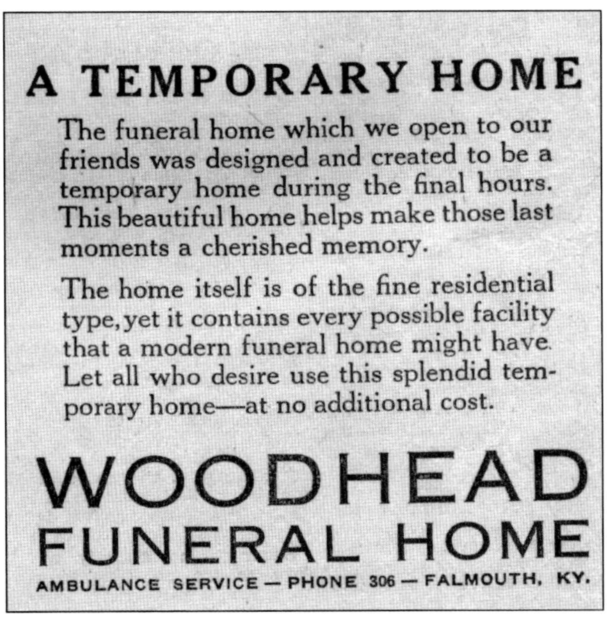

A TEMPORARY HOME

The funeral home which we open to our friends was designed and created to be a temporary home during the final hours. This beautiful home helps make those last moments a cherished memory.

The home itself is of the fine residential type, yet it contains every possible facility that a modern funeral home might have. Let all who desire use this splendid temporary home—at no additional cost.

WOODHEAD FUNERAL HOME

AMBULANCE SERVICE — PHONE 306 — FALMOUTH, KY.

This document was an advertisement placed in 1944. The Woodhead Funeral Home stands on property that was once pasture land. A home was built on the land by famed "Indian fighter" Reuben McCarty in 1865. After several changes in ownership over the years, John A. Woodhead purchased the home and all the land in 1937, remodeling the house to suit his needs for a home and business. Joseph Woodhead, son of John A. Woodhead, continued the business until his death in 1966. Today John Daniel Woodhead, grandson of John A. Woodhead, carries on the business with his wife and daughter. (Courtesy of Ray Chiles.)

Five

Recreational Activities

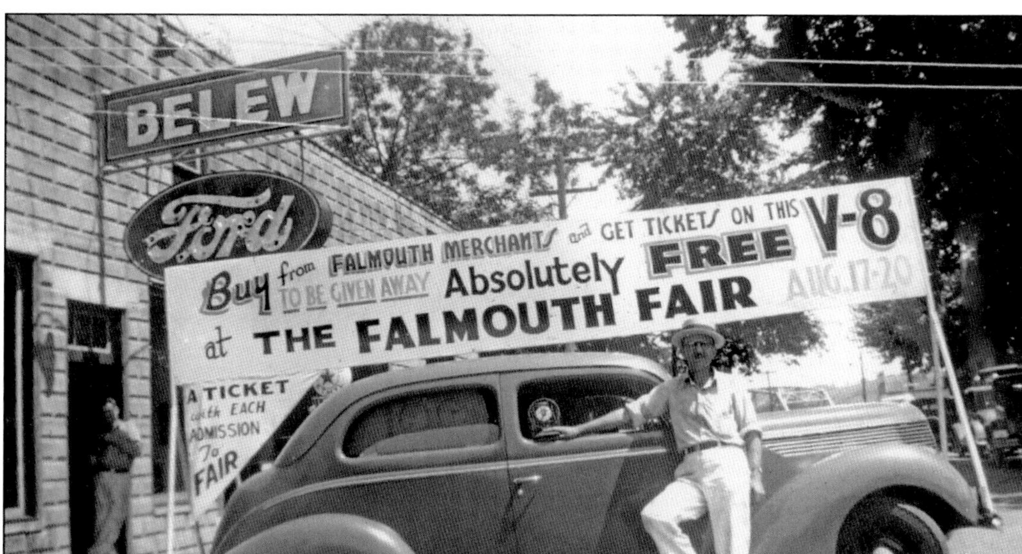

Merchants and event organizers worked to assist each other in this 1938 promotion for the Falmouth Fair and Pendleton County merchants. Leland Belew, seen here, was the owner of the Ford dealership on Second Street in the late 1930s. With his cooperation, a giveaway was organized. A ticket was given with each entry to the fair or with a purchase from a merchant. They were then placed in a drawing for the V-8 car in the photograph. (Courtesy of David Belew.)

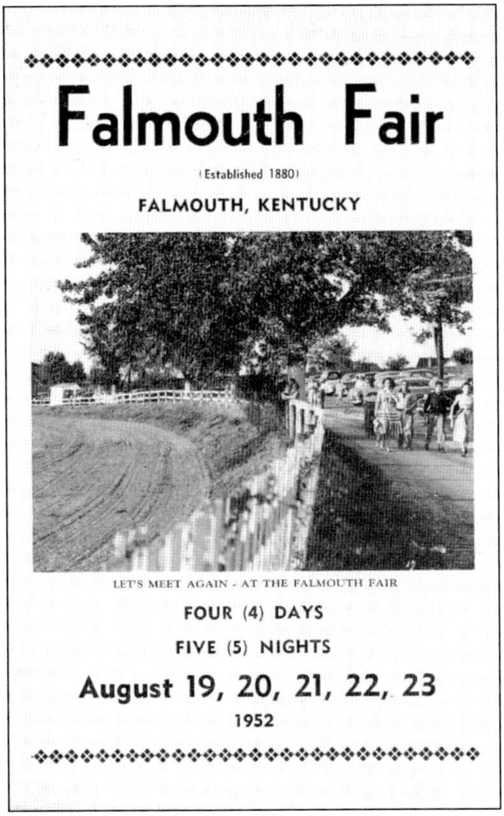

Falmouth Fair

(Established 1880)

FALMOUTH, KENTUCKY

LET'S MEET AGAIN - AT THE FALMOUTH FAIR

FOUR (4) DAYS

FIVE (5) NIGHTS

August 19, 20, 21, 22, 23

1952

Taken from the Falmouth Fair book in 1952, this page shows the entrance to the grounds. Parking is seen on the right, which was just below the roadway for US27. On the left of the patron walkway is the race track with the ticket booth sitting far back on the left. The fair ran for five nights and four days. (Courtesy of Cheryl York.)

The stands seen in this photograph are only a fading memory for many and a story of "the great fair" for others. The Falmouth Fair was established in 1879 in part as a means for local farmers to display their prized crops. It also filled the needs of local citizens to meet new people and renew friendships with others. As can be seen in this photograph of the grandstands, great numbers attended the fair. The "dinky" train passing through from Covington to Lexington made twice-daily stops for visitors arriving and departing the fairgrounds. (Courtesy of Robert Best.)

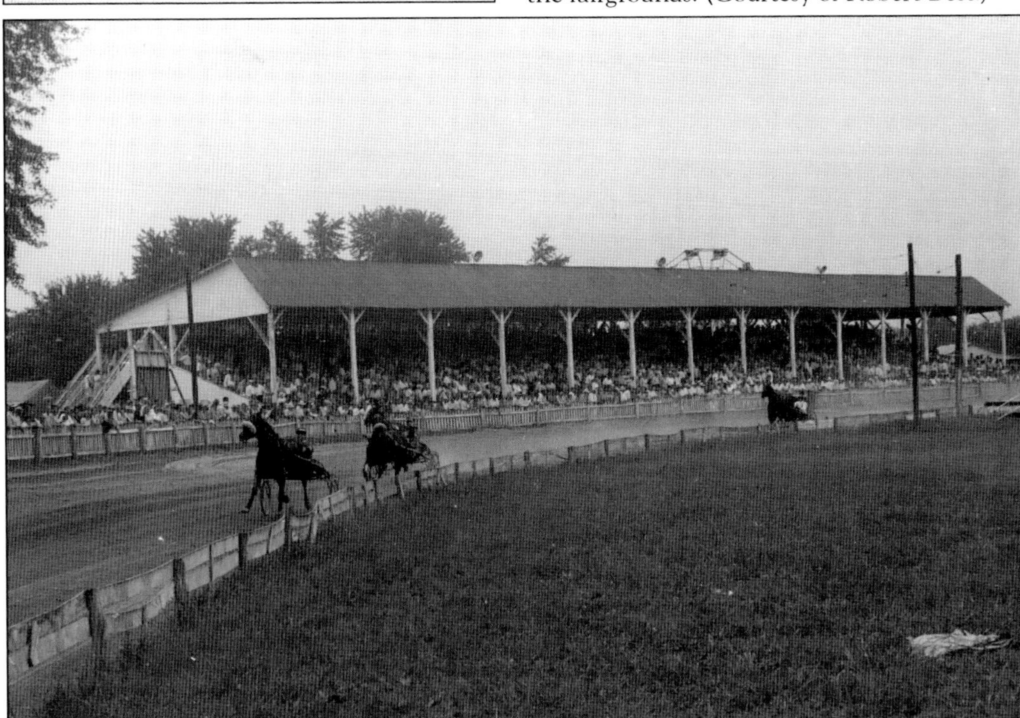

The Falmouth Fair made use of the trotting track for several other races. In this picture, fair patrons watch as a contender pushes his tractor to move as quickly as it can. From the dust being blown in front of him, it appears that he needs to move even faster. (Courtesy of Robert Best.)

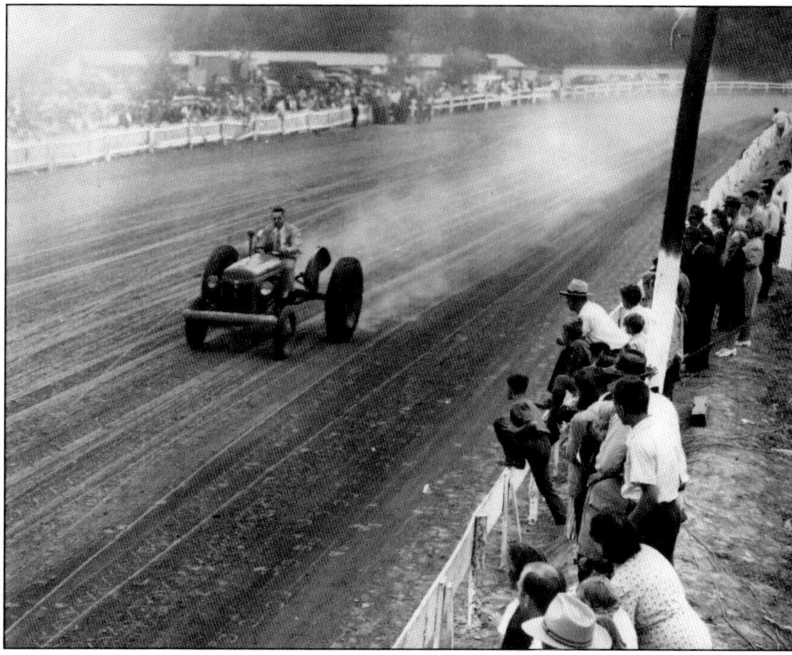

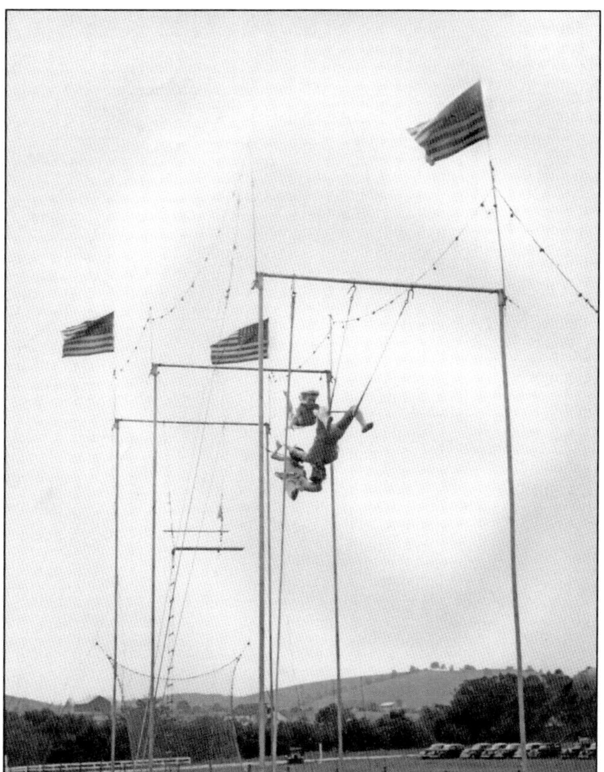

Not all of the excitement at the fair was on the race tracks. Nelson Breeze, who owned the Falmouth Fairgrounds from 1950 until his death in 1961, had spent 22 years in show business. He was especially known in the outdoor amusement area. Through his contacts and friends, the fair was an event of much excitement. This aerial show is an example. (Courtesy of Robert Best.)

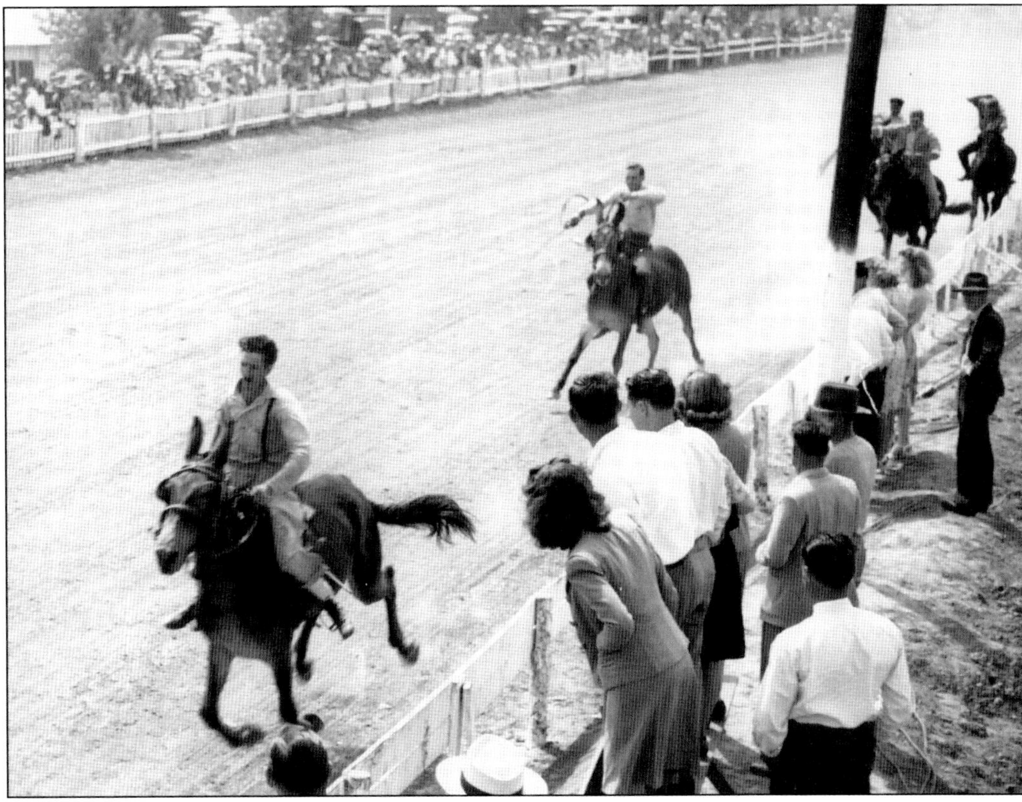

Crowds line the track to get a close view of the contestants in the donkey races held at the Falmouth Fair. While the various races are taking place, the midway offered rides and games to meet most every interest. The floral hall nearby gave the local gardeners, crafters, and farmers a chance to exhibit their best wares and a chance to win ribbons and premiums. Nelson Breeze was a part of the force that encouraged the state of Kentucky to promote agriculture by offering the premiums. (Courtesy of Robert Best.)

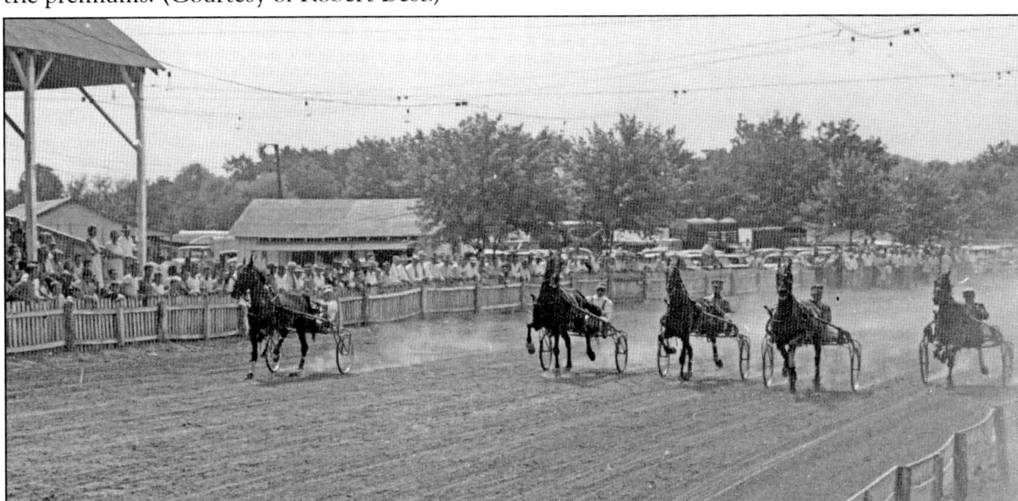

One of the biggest and most prestigious events held each year at the Falmouth Fair was the trotting races. This track was considered one of the best half-mile tracks of the time. (Courtesy of Robert Best.)

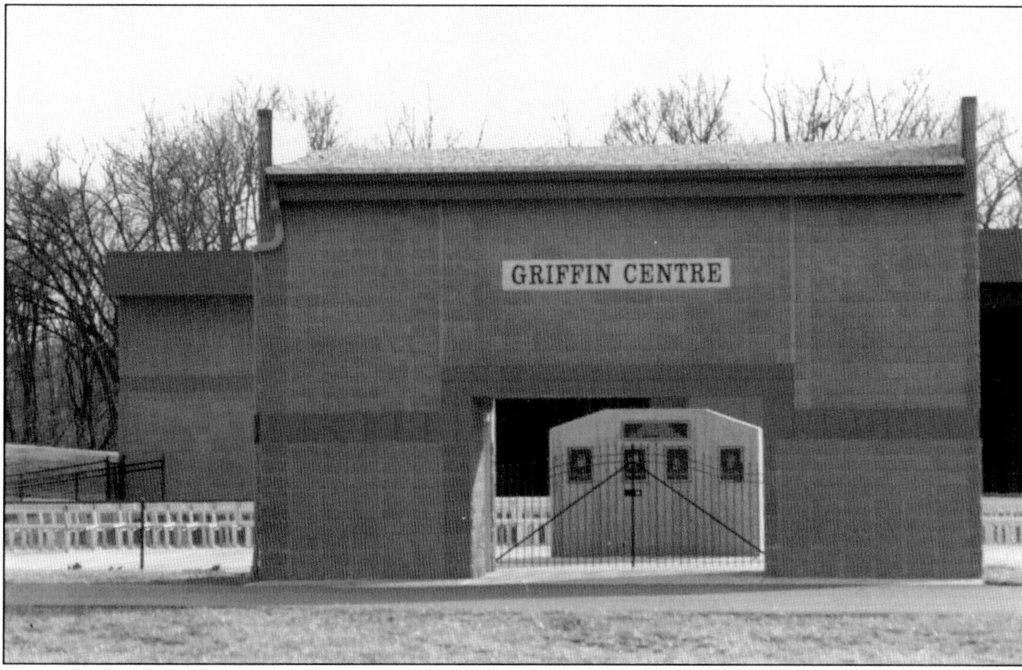

The Griffin Centre Amphitheater sits on grounds near Southern Elementary School. It was built for community use by the John L. Griffin family in honor of John L. Griffin and in memory of his wife, Rose, and sons, Ronald and James. The dedication of this structure was held July 3, 1993, during a celebration of the Griffin Industries' 50th anniversary. Gov. Brereton Jones, local school officials and board members, and the Griffin family all took part in the ceremony. Nick Clooney served as emcee with music artist Joy White opening for singer Lee Greenwood. (Above courtesy of Teresa Johnston, below courtesy of Paul Tuemler.)

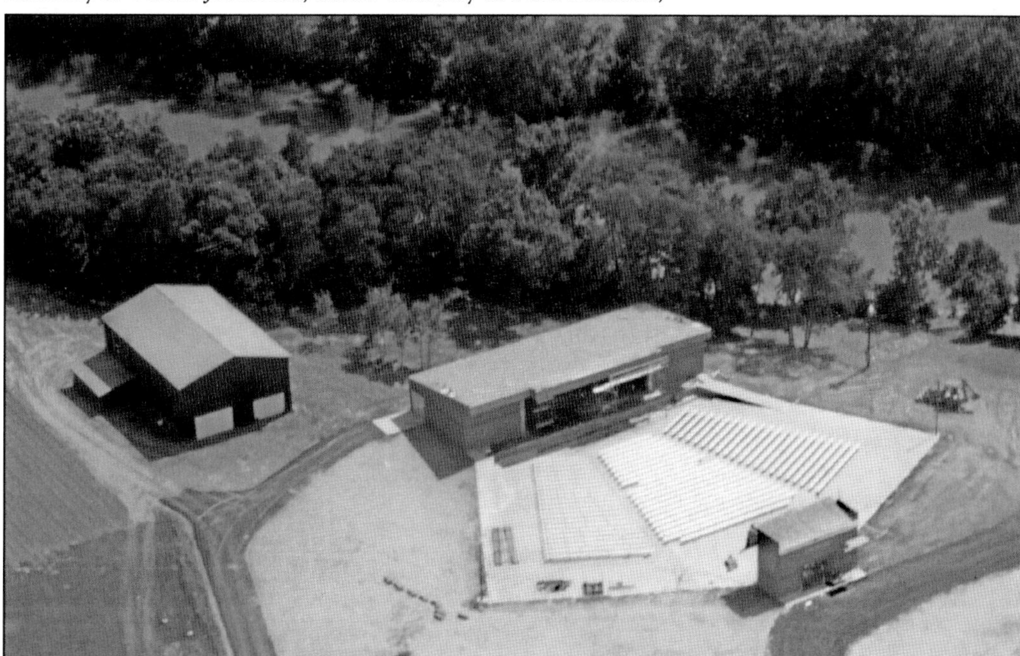

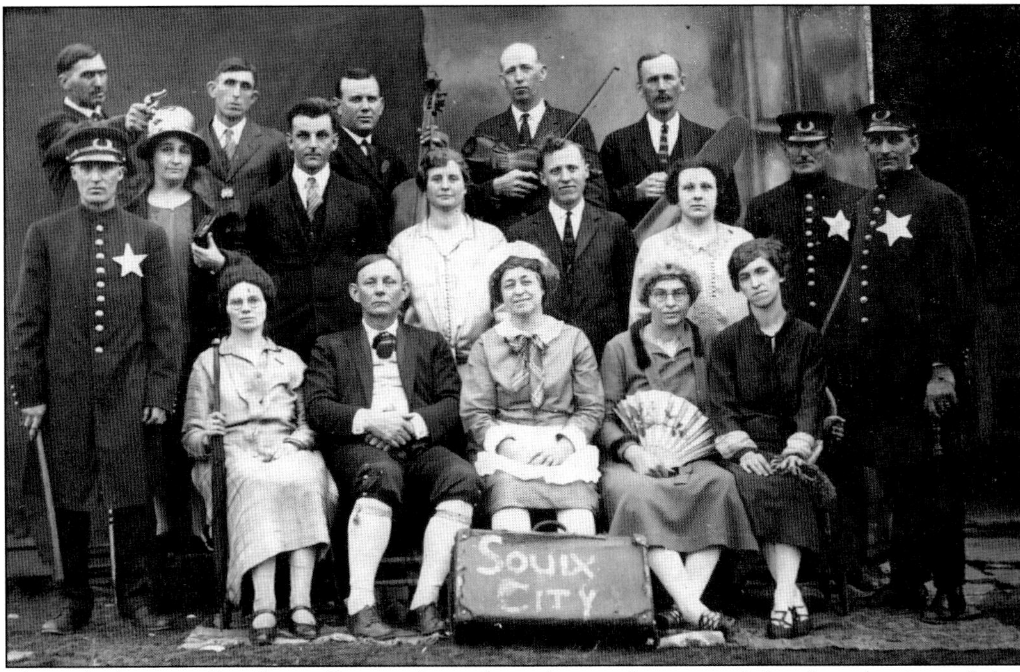

Through the years, Pendleton County showed its talent in the arts with local productions of plays and musicals given by churches and schools. In 1926 the play *Sioux City* was given by members of the Flour Creek Christian Church. From left to right, the cast shown here includes (first row) Ona Gosney, Claud Record, Artie Record, Lena Record, and Lilie Fryer; (second row) Howard Gosney, Edna Shoemaker, Henry Schalck, Edna Schalck, Raymond Montgomery, Alice Montgomery, Ila Record, and Frank Shoemaker; (third row) Will Hiteman, Percy Fryer, Spencer Dawson, Will Veirs, and Emmitt Record. (Courtesy of Mae Johnston.)

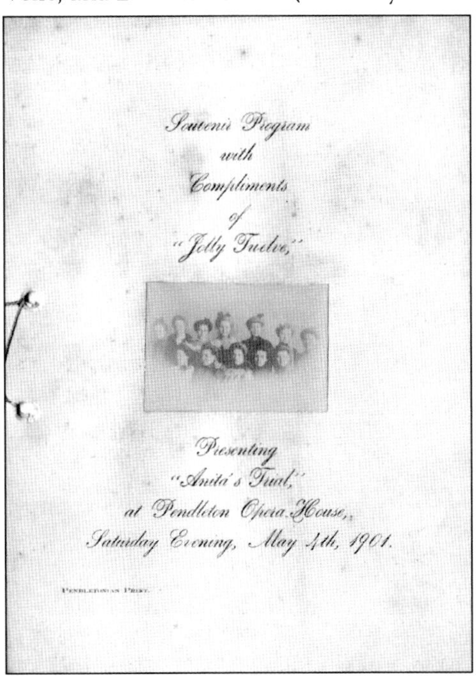

Souvenir Program
with
Compliments
of
"Jolly Twelve,"

Presenting
"Anita's Trial,"
at Pendleton Opera House,
Saturday Evening, May 4th, 1901.

The Pendleton County Opera House was located on the second floor of the Assembly Building, which was at the corner of Shelby and Main Streets. It served the community as a place for plays, graduations, and parties. One Saturday evening in 1901, the "Jolly Twelve" presented the play *Anita's Trial*. Pictured from left to right are (first row) Ella K. Wilson, Lou E. Redmon, Mary Holmes Stith, Alice Monroe Walton, and Blanche Galloway Woolery; (second row) Grace Applegate, Jessie V. Oldham, Lucy Browning, Mary Thompson Colvin, Francis Hall Grinnan, Frozie Dolphen, and Julia Dickerson Coppage. (Courtesy of Cheryl York.)

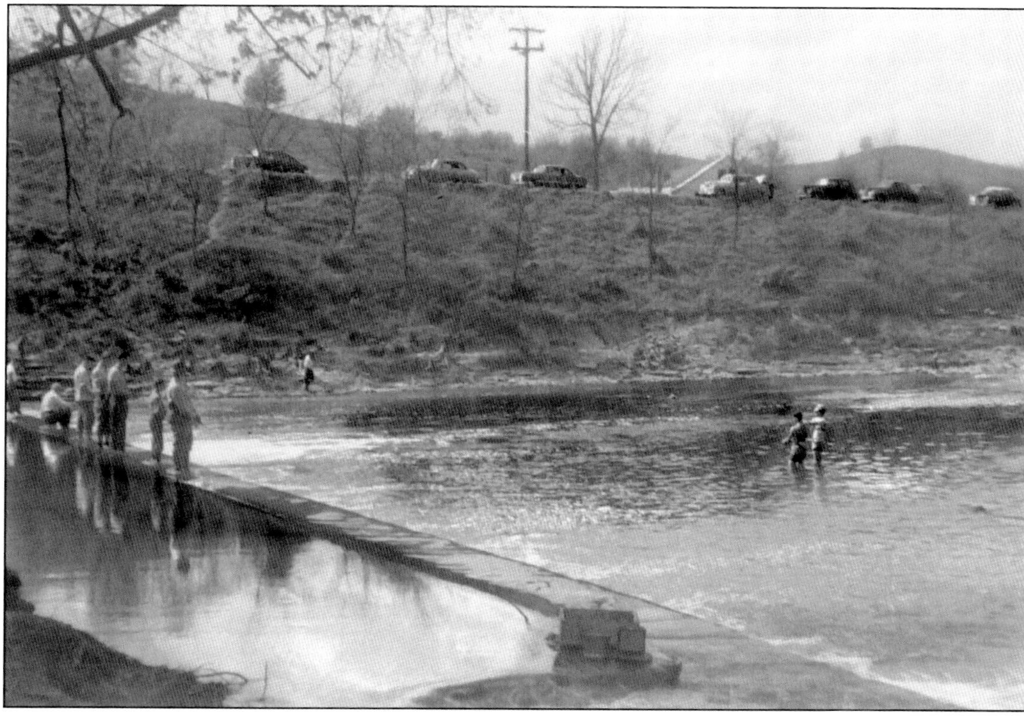

The Licking River served many purposes for the community, one of them being a place for fishing. Here in the early 1950s, several men are taking some time to catch supper or just a good story. (Courtesy of Shirley Tuemler.)

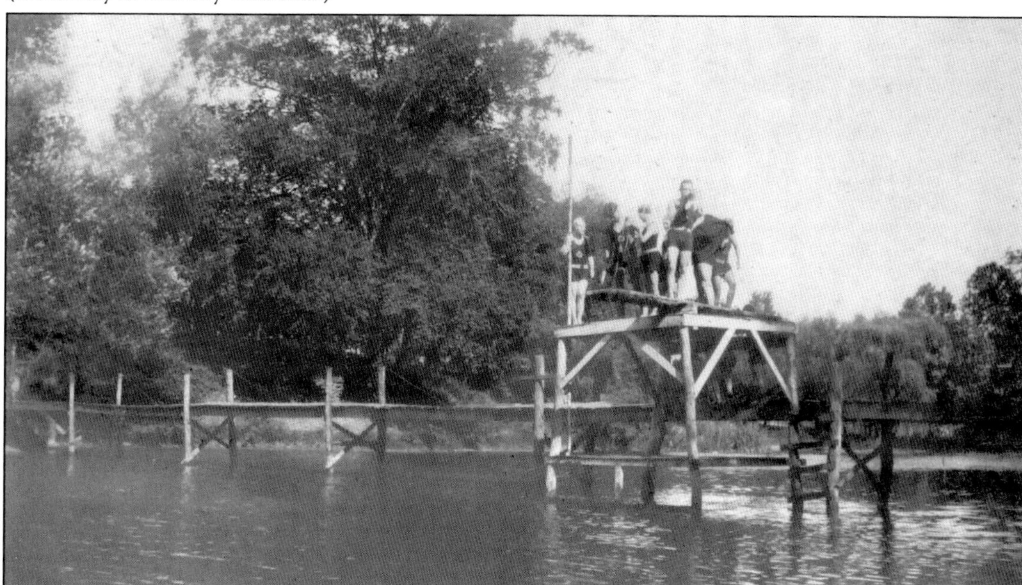

Grants Lake Resort was a popular spot for swimming on a hot summer day. Developed by Adoniran J. Grant and his wife, Nora Williams Grant, it began as a summer resort where guests could rent a cottage while enjoying delicious meals and the outdoors. Guests and citizens of the community made use of the facilities in the summer for fishing and swimming off of the footbridge. In the winter, when the lake froze over, it was a great place to ice skate. (Courtesy of Opal Jackson family.)

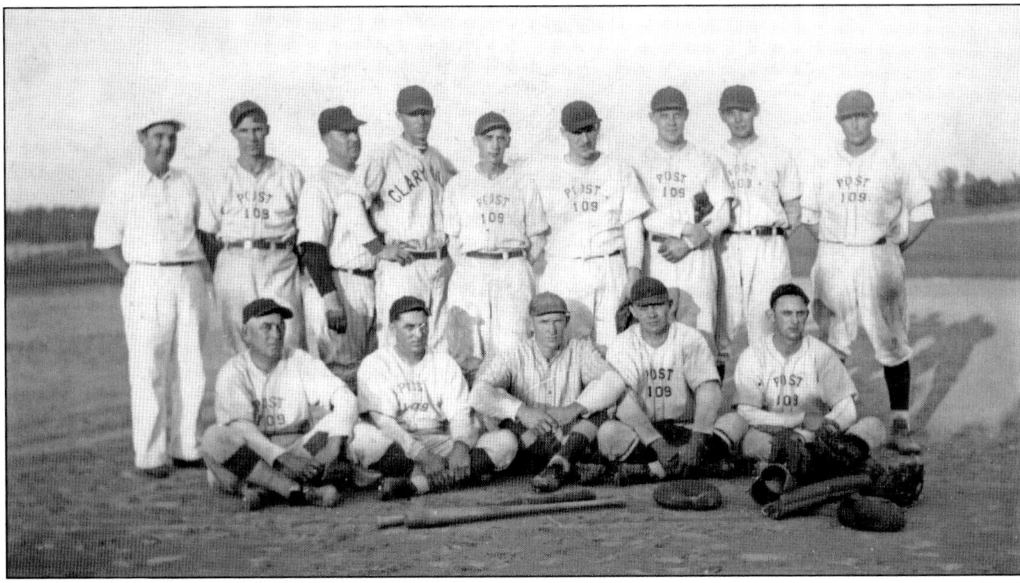

In the late 1930s and 1940s, the Ideal Field was located about a mile south of Falmouth on US27. Several local baseball teams used it for their league games. This photograph shows the Falmouth League, a semi-pro baseball team. Their sponsor was the *Post Times Star* newspaper of Northern Kentucky. The only member identified is Leo Conroy, who is standing second from the right. He played with the *Post* League before World War II as a pitcher. After the war, he was a member of the American Legion Team. (Courtesy of Pat Conroy.)

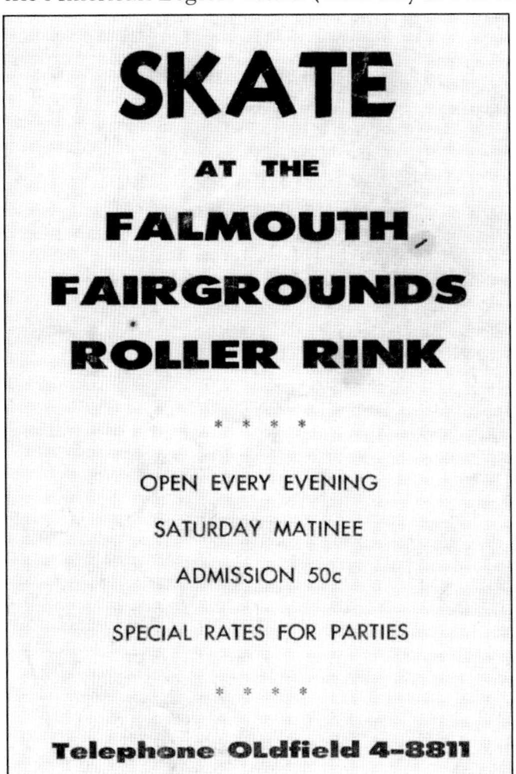

An early advertisement for roller skating is shown here. A fairground building contained the indoor year-round rink. Hosting parties and promoting good health and fun for all, it was the place to be.

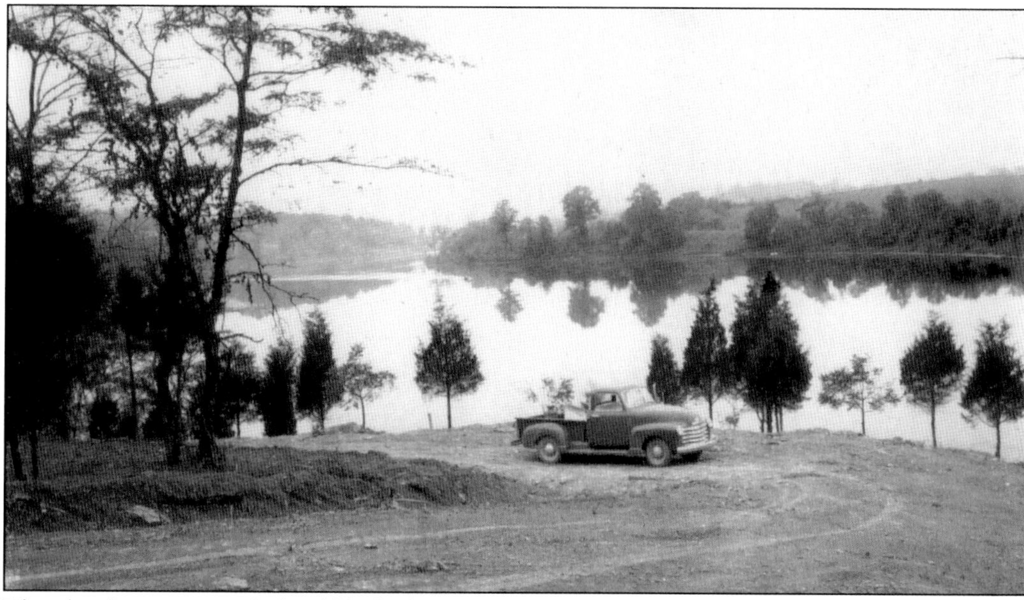

The idea that a state park should be built in Pendleton County was born in 1955, but it was not until 1957 that the Kincaid Park Development Association received directions to proceed with the purchase of land. J. Stark Davis, Charles Conrad, Earl Wallace, George Jacob, Robert White, Hoyt Best, Robert Best, and Ambrose Fields were some of the local men who succeeded in getting this accomplished. In 1958 a tract of land was deeded to the state for a lake and state park with money that had been raised from the local community. The Kincaid Creek area used to form this lake was home to the old Kincaid pioneer family and the George Cookendorfer family. The new park was opened in 1960 as Kincaid Lake State Park and soon after was named Falmouth Lake State Park. In 1989 an Olympic-sized pool was built, and swimming in the lake was discontinued. Fishing, camping, boating, tennis, hiking, and a nine-hole golf course entertain all who visit. The park name reverted back to Kincaid Lake State Park in 1970. (Above courtesy of Billie Newman, below courtesy of Teresa Johnston.)

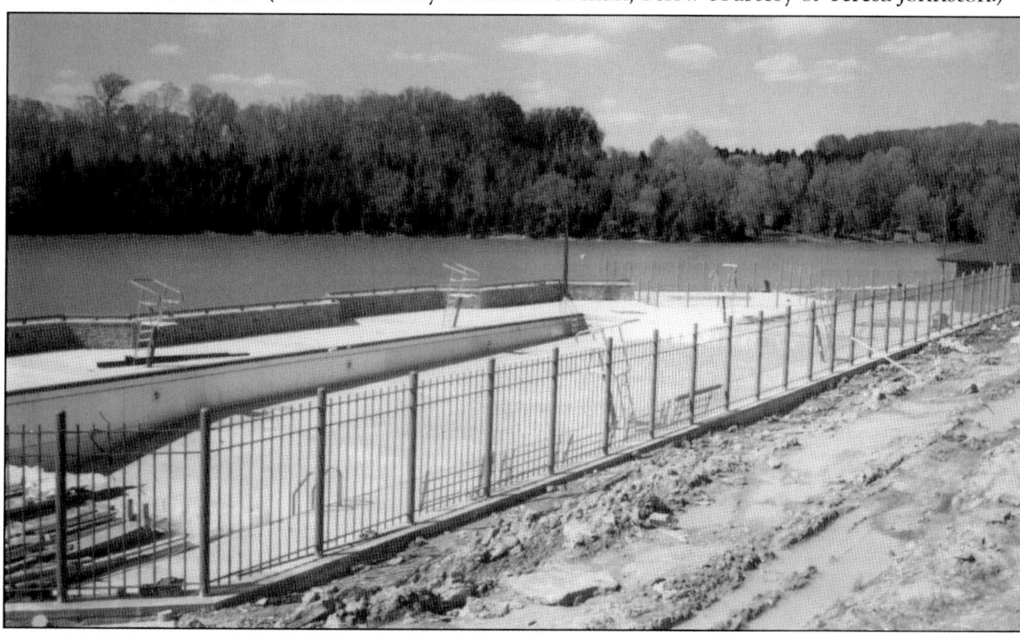

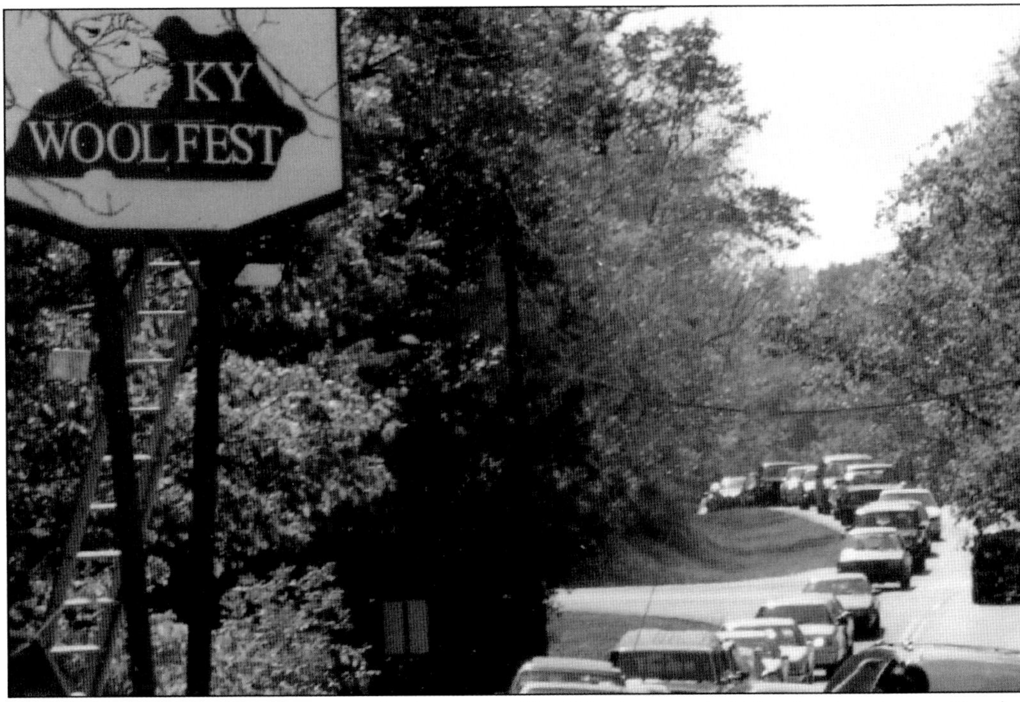

After many months of preparations, the Kentucky Wool Festival was held for the first time in October 1983. The committee looked to the past for a name and theme. It was found that at one time Kentucky was noted for its large sheep industry, and Pendleton County was among its leaders. After some discussion, it was decided to plan a festival around the woolen operations that flourished in Pendleton County. In just a few years, the Kentucky Wool Festival has become so widely known that upwards of 5,000 people have come to attend the three-day weekend event. (Courtesy of Velma Steele.)

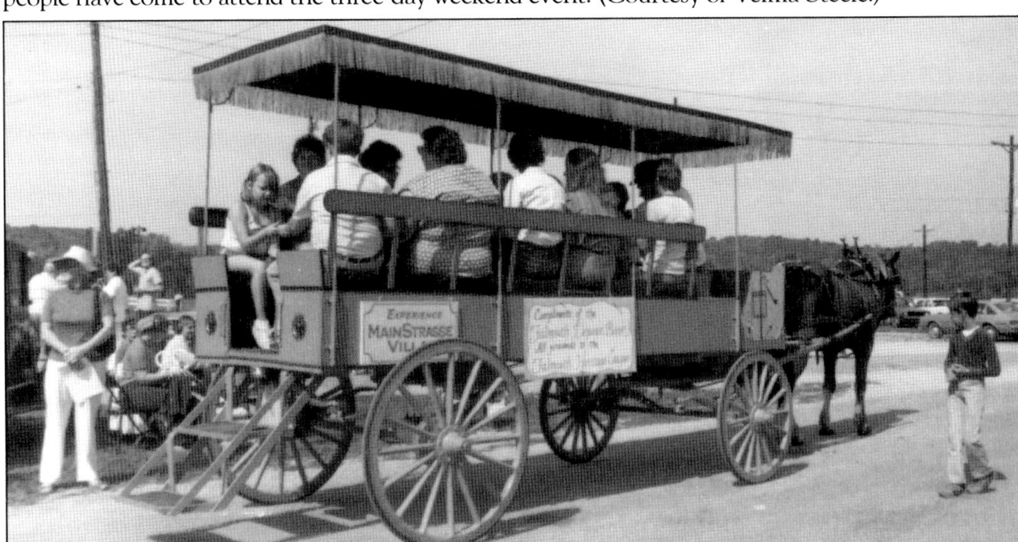

The Kentucky Wool Festival held its first event in October 1983 on the school grounds and former fairgrounds in Falmouth. As an added activity to promote the heritage of the community, a group researched and gathered information about the historical buildings and people of the town and wrote a commentary that was used on a wagon tour through Falmouth. (Courtesy of Shirley Tuemler.)

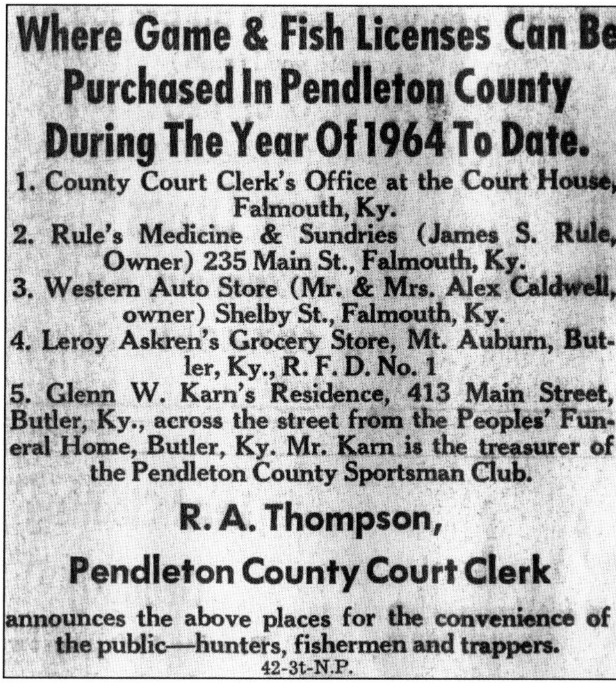

Where Game & Fish Licenses Can Be Purchased In Pendleton County During The Year Of 1964 To Date.

1. County Court Clerk's Office at the Court House, Falmouth, Ky.
2. Rule's Medicine & Sundries (James S. Rule, Owner) 235 Main St., Falmouth, Ky.
3. Western Auto Store (Mr. & Mrs. Alex Caldwell, owner) Shelby St., Falmouth, Ky.
4. Leroy Askren's Grocery Store, Mt. Auburn, Butler, Ky., R. F. D. No. 1
5. Glenn W. Karn's Residence, 413 Main Street, Butler, Ky., across the street from the Peoples' Funeral Home, Butler, Ky. Mr. Karn is the treasurer of the Pendleton County Sportsman Club.

R. A. Thompson,

Pendleton County Court Clerk

announces the above places for the convenience of the public—hunters, fishermen and trappers.

42-3t-N.P.

The county court clerk's office issued notices concerning places selling hunting and fishing licenses. This one for 1964 and later noted five businesses in Pendleton County that sold the licenses. (Courtesy of Teresa Johnston.)

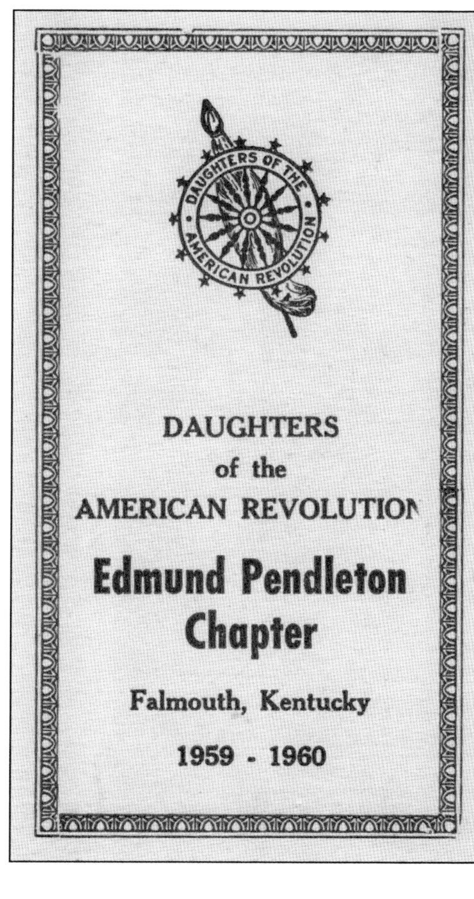

The Daughters of the American Revolution was first organized locally as the Edmund Pendleton Chapter on March 1, 1938, by Grace Ridgeway Shonert. She also served as the first regent. By 1960, there were 21 members on the roster. (Courtesy of Becky Byrd Giberto.)

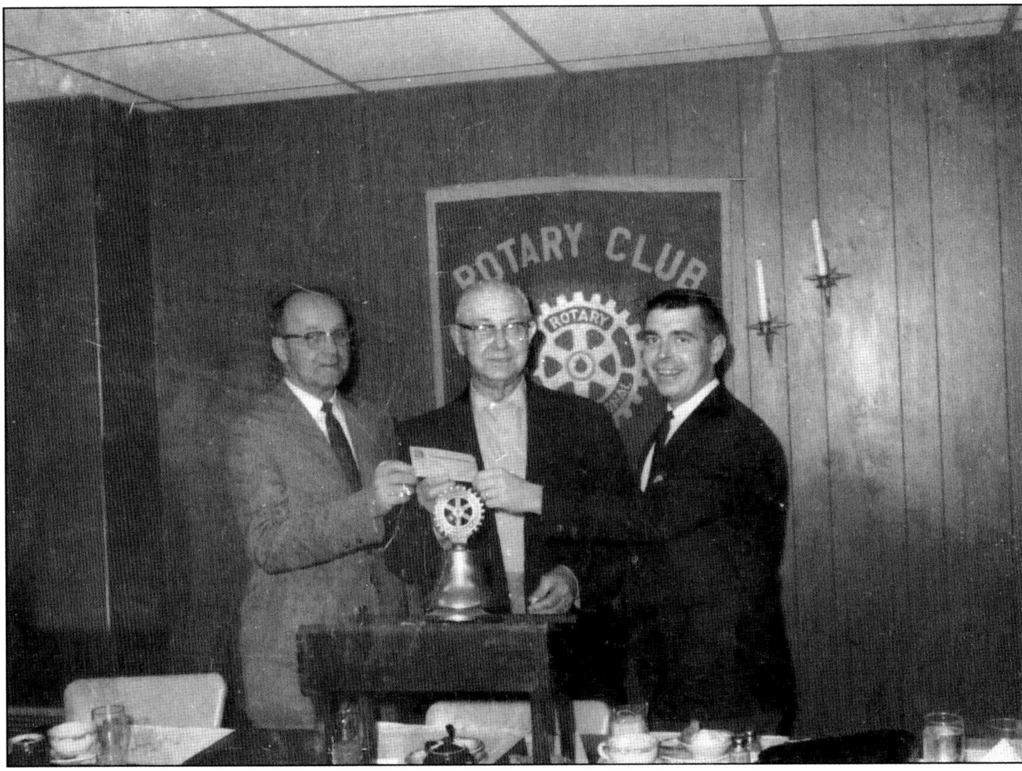

Receiving the Service Above Self award for his participation as a past president and charter member of the Falmouth Rotary Club is R. Risk Arnold. Bart Peak, district governor of Rotary Clubs, stands on the left, and Dan Woodhead is on the right. The Falmouth Rotary began as a part of the Cynthiana Rotary Club in 1924. (Courtesy of Becky Byrd Giberto.)

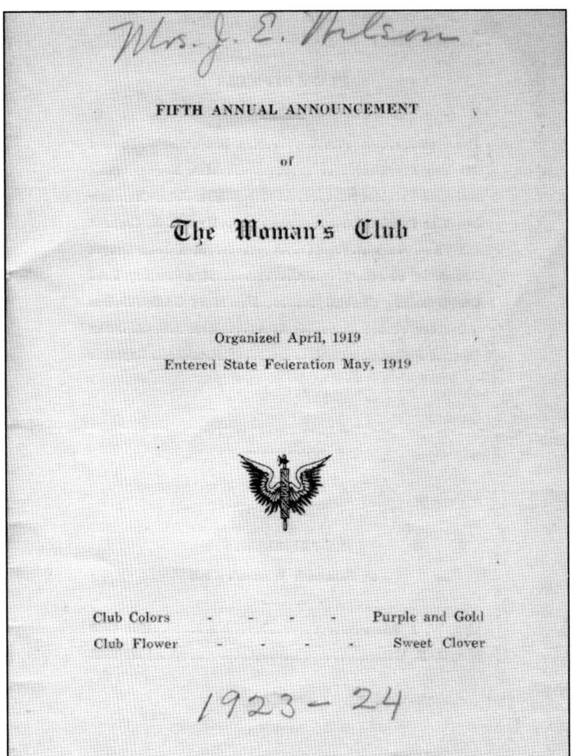

Mrs. J. E. Wilson

FIFTH ANNUAL ANNOUNCEMENT

of

The Woman's Club

Organized April, 1919

Entered State Federation May, 1919

Club Colors - - - - Purple and Gold

Club Flower - - - - - Sweet Clover

1923-24

Falmouth and Butler both had a Woman's Club. The Falmouth Woman's Club was organized in 1919 with Grace Ridgeway Shonert as the first president. The Butler Woman's Club began as a book club in 1927 before organizing and becoming federated in 1937. Anna Mae Blades was the Butler club's first president and served as such until 1938. (Courtesy of the Falmouth Woman's Club.)

Six

Trials and Tribulations

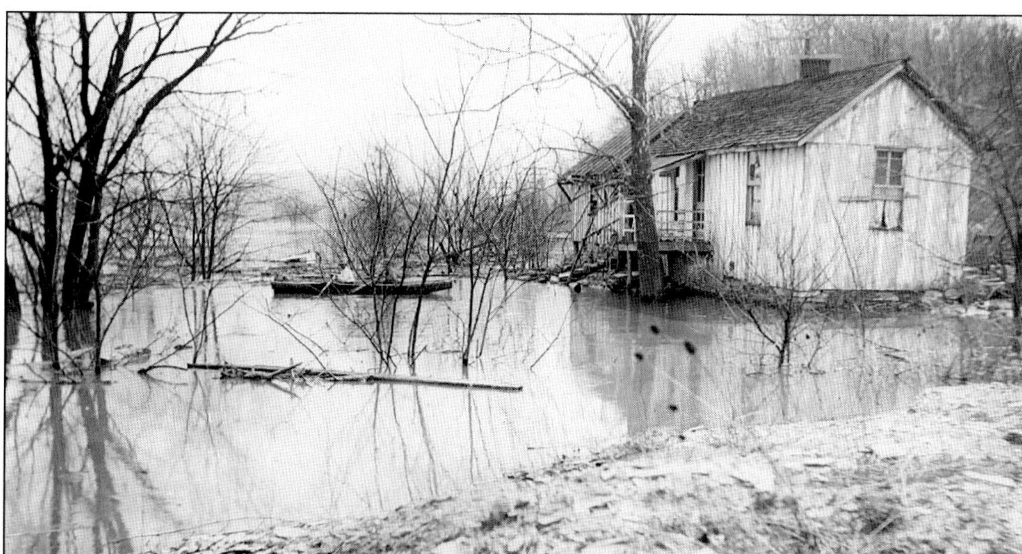

On a cold winter day in January 1937, the Ohio River inundated Carntown as it rose to its highest flood levels to that date. The small town sat along a narrow area of land in Pendleton County bordering the Ohio River. Residents had to be evacuated by boats to the hills surrounding their homes and businesses. (Courtesy of Chris Fossitt.)

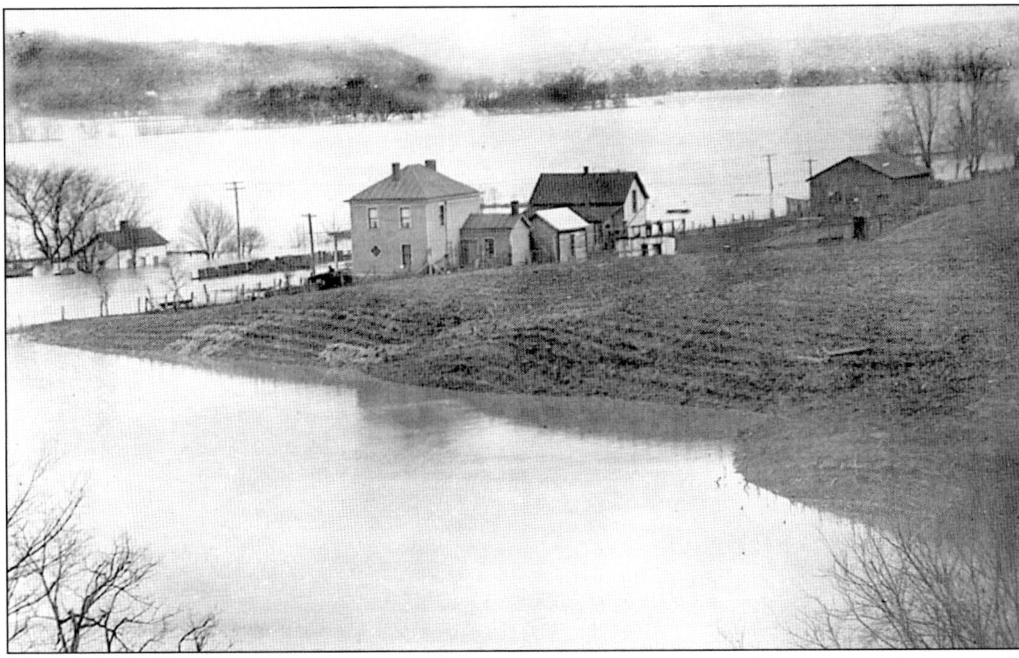

In 1937, the Ohio River at Carntown pushed creeks that flowed into the river out of their banks and into the lowlands. Cresting at about 80 feet, the Ohio covered the roadways and railways that ran along the river's edge and separated homes. The Licking River at Falmouth crested on January 23 at just above 41 feet (flood stage is considered 28 feet). This was the highest the river had been in the town's history. Fighting snow and the cold temperatures, men rescued people and their belongings. Cars and trucks lined East Shelby Street at the intersection of Broad Street, assisting the evacuations. (Above courtesy of Chris Fossitt.)

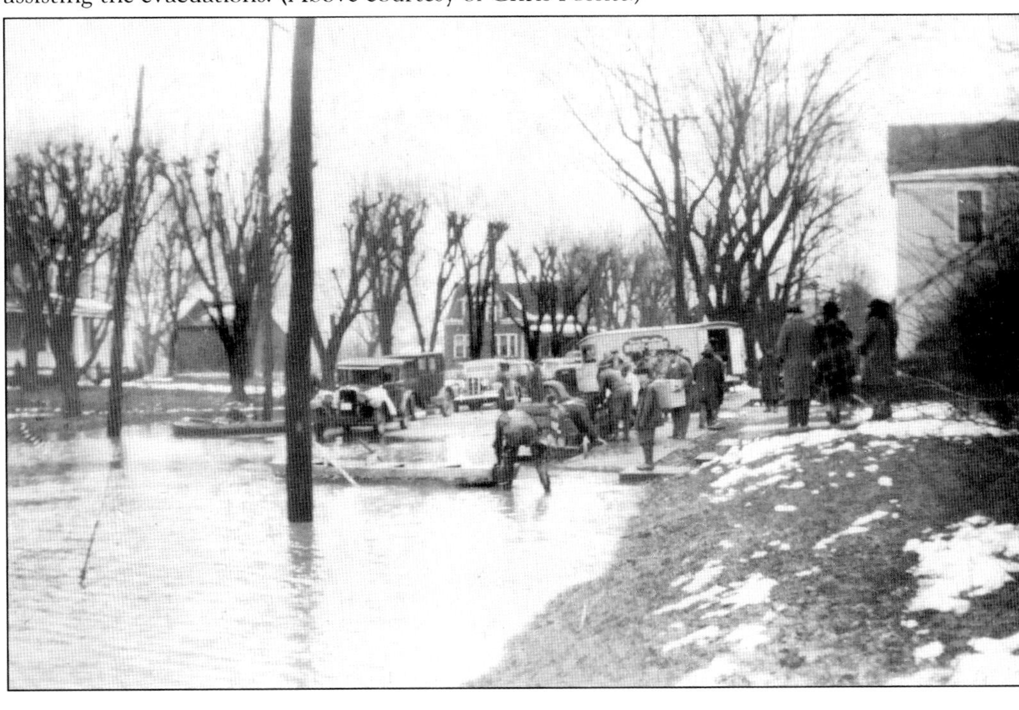

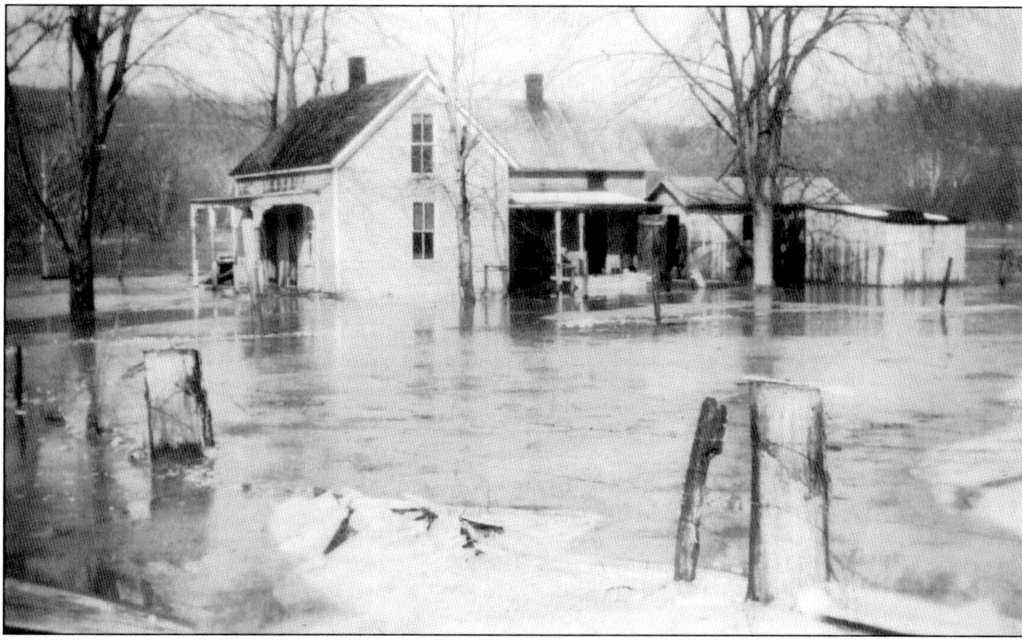

Butler also felt the effects of the 1937 flood. Most of the flooding struck in the area along Mill Street, damaging homes and businesses. The major disaster was when ice flowing down the Licking River collected against the piers of the old covered bridge. The ice tore at the base of the wooden structure, damaging it beyond repair. (Courtesy of the Opal Jackson family.)

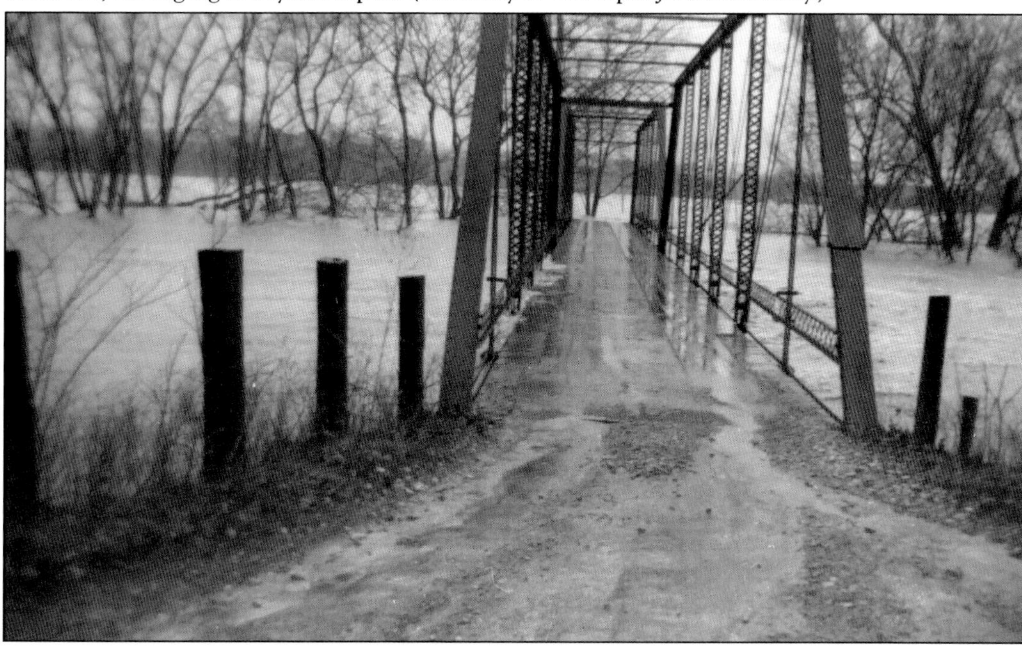

The 1964 flood was a disastrous problem for the towns of Falmouth and Butler, but it was also a problem for other county residents. Travel was inhibited by the floodwaters that covered county bridges, low roadways, and railway crossings. The passage across the old one-lane bridge at Hayes Station was threatened by the rising Licking River. This picture looks east toward Falmouth. (Courtesy of Stanley Bishop.)

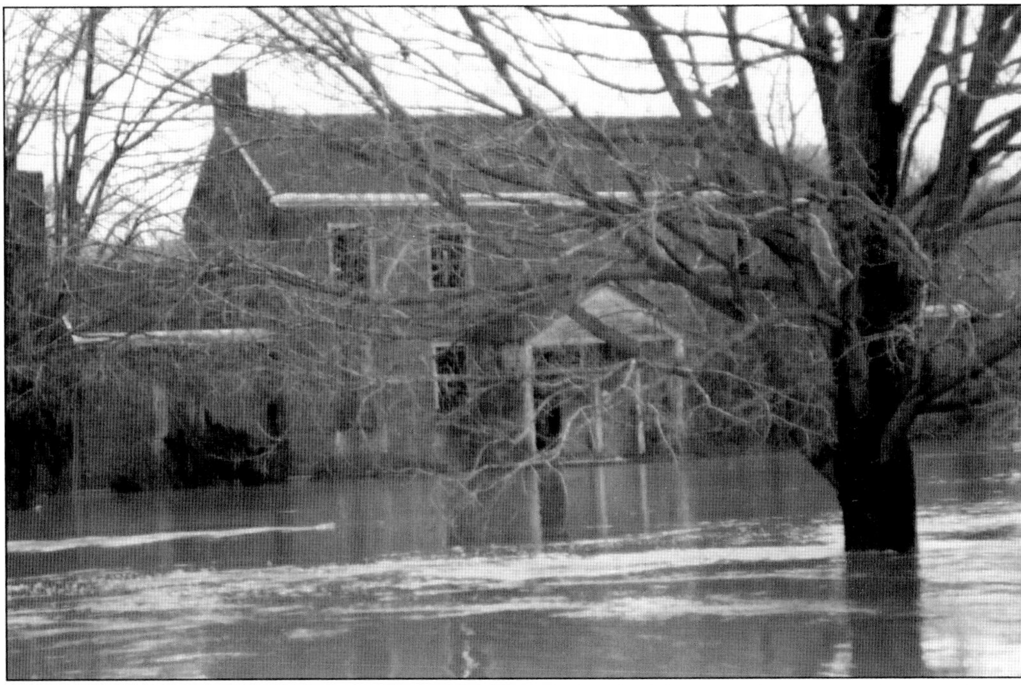

Shoemakertown, just outside Falmouth, was frequently flooded due to its location at the confluence of the two Licking Rivers. The waters had gotten into the Oldham house on only one previous occasion due to its location on a small rise in the land. In 1964 the vacant home was flooded when the rivers rose to a crest of 47 feet, above the 1937 height, setting a new record.

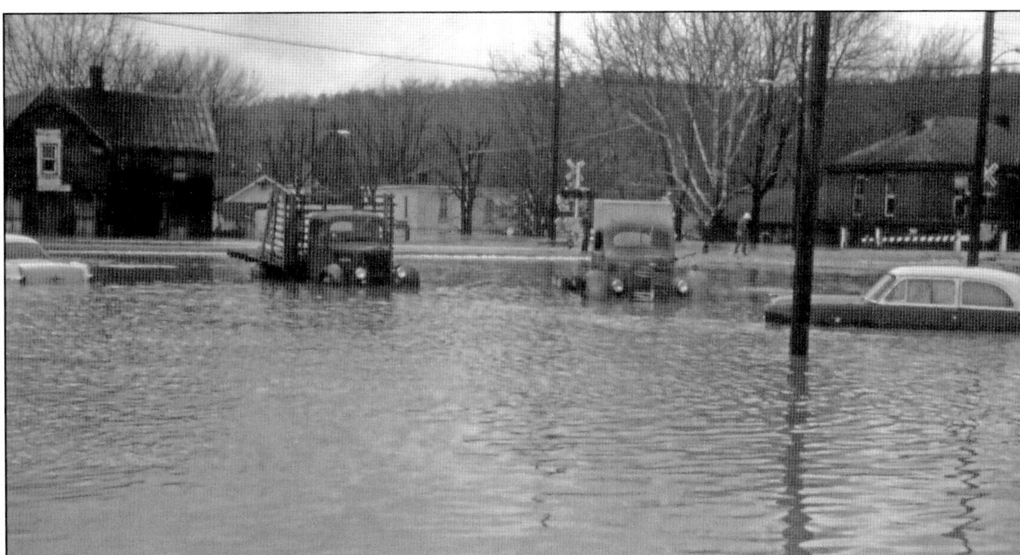

When the Licking Rivers rose to 47 feet in 1964, water covered more of Falmouth than ever before. The vehicles parked at the Railroad Depot area were thought to be safe from any rising water as this part of the downtown had never experienced flooding. Over 400 homes in the area were damaged or destroyed. At this time, flood insurance was not available for assistance in the rebuilding process. (Courtesy of George Lach.)

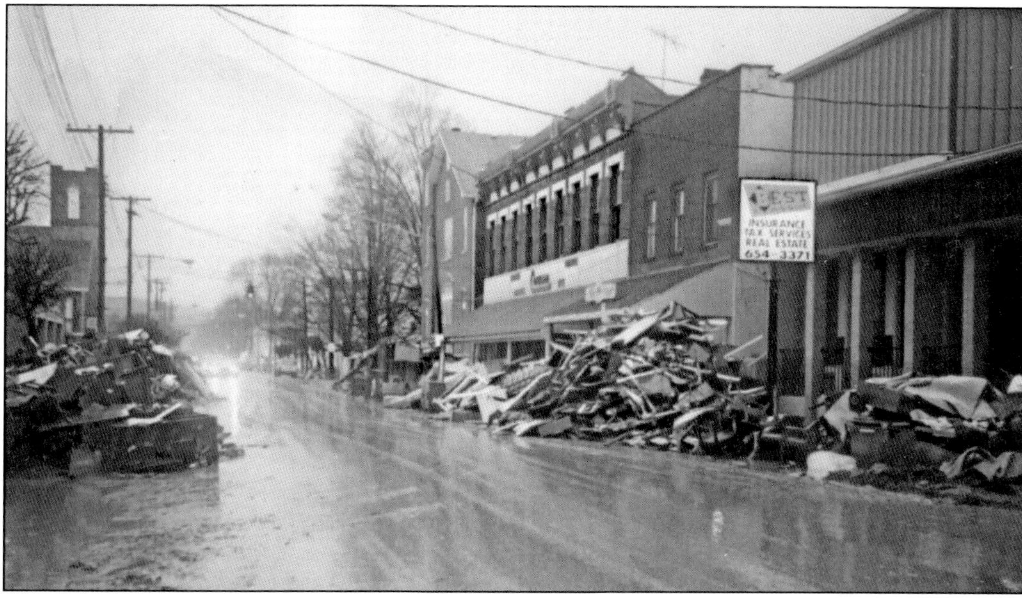

The downtown West Shelby Street business district suffered severe damage in March 1997 as the two Licking Rivers rose to heights that remain documented as a 100-year-high. River waters rose over 50 feet in 24 hours, covering 80 percent of the town. Looking toward the railroad, this photograph documents the piles of debris left on the streets. This debris contained both damaged inventory of the businesses and portions of walls, floors, and display structures. The streets were kept wet in order to lessen the effects of the mud as it dried to dust to protect the volunteers and residents. Five people perished in this disaster. (Courtesy of Russ Conrad.)

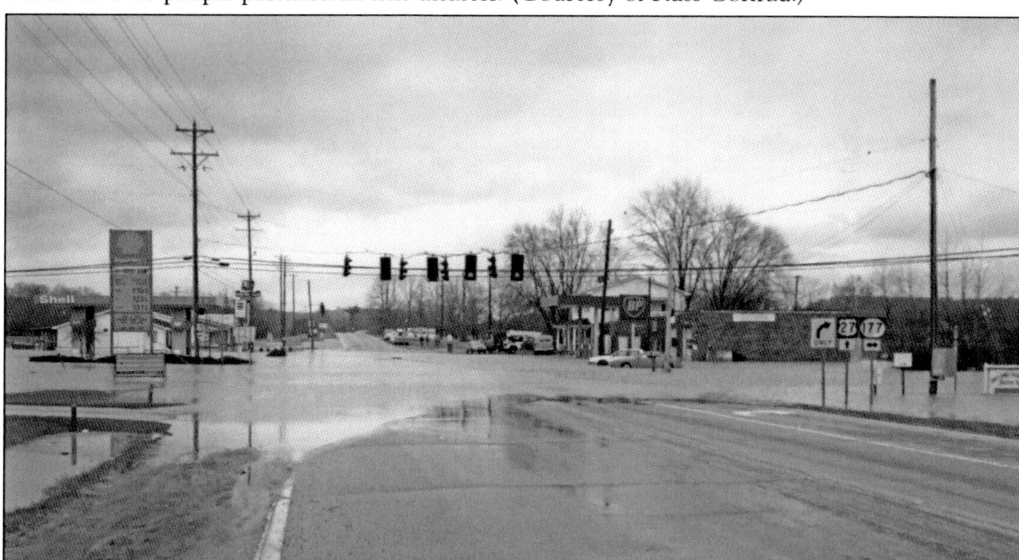

The Licking River at Butler crested several hours after it did in Falmouth. In this photograph, the intersection of US27 and KY177 shows the height it reached in this area. The low areas of KY177 going into Butler were flooded while the homes and businesses along Mill Street saw the waters reach 17 feet inside. Other parts of Butler and other areas throughout the county were also cut off and damaged by the rising water. The lives of the entire community of Pendleton County were forever changed. (Courtesy of Billie Newman.)

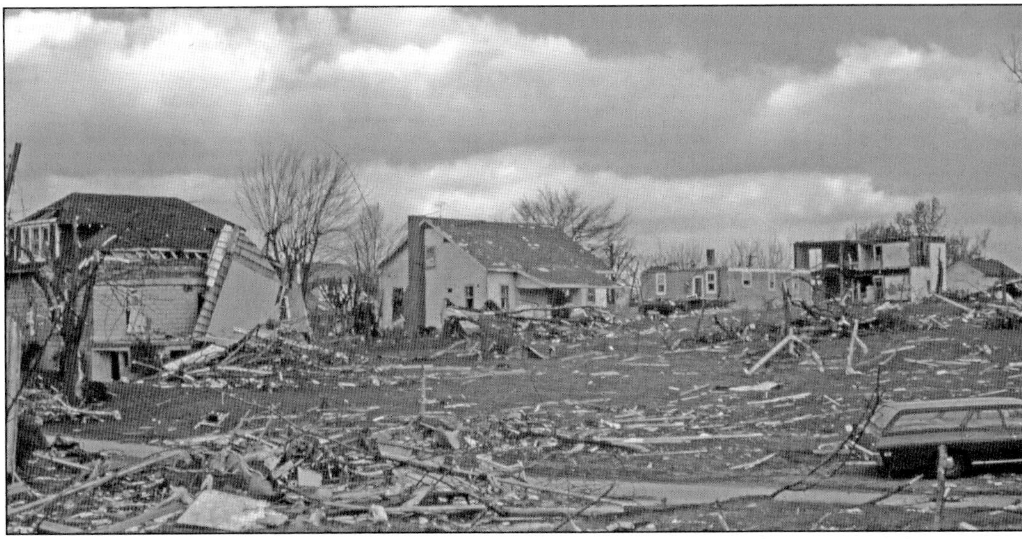

It happened on April 23, 1968, and lasted about 20 minutes. Falmouth was struck by a vicious tornado. Approximately one-third of the homes in Falmouth were destroyed or severely damaged, and four people were killed. Masonry and frame homes were equally damaged. The tornado traveled from the western part of the county, damaging several farms as it headed into town. It approached Falmouth from the area of Riverside Cemetery and continued down Maple Avenue, past the Falmouth School, and through the newly built housing area. The massive destruction can be seen here. The above photograph is a view from Robbins Avenue of the backs of the homes that sat on Broad Street. The image below shows the damage done to the housing section. On the left corner of the street sat John Hinton's television repair shop and his home. This location is now the home of the First Baptist Church. (Above courtesy of George Lach, below courtesy of Teresa Johnston.)

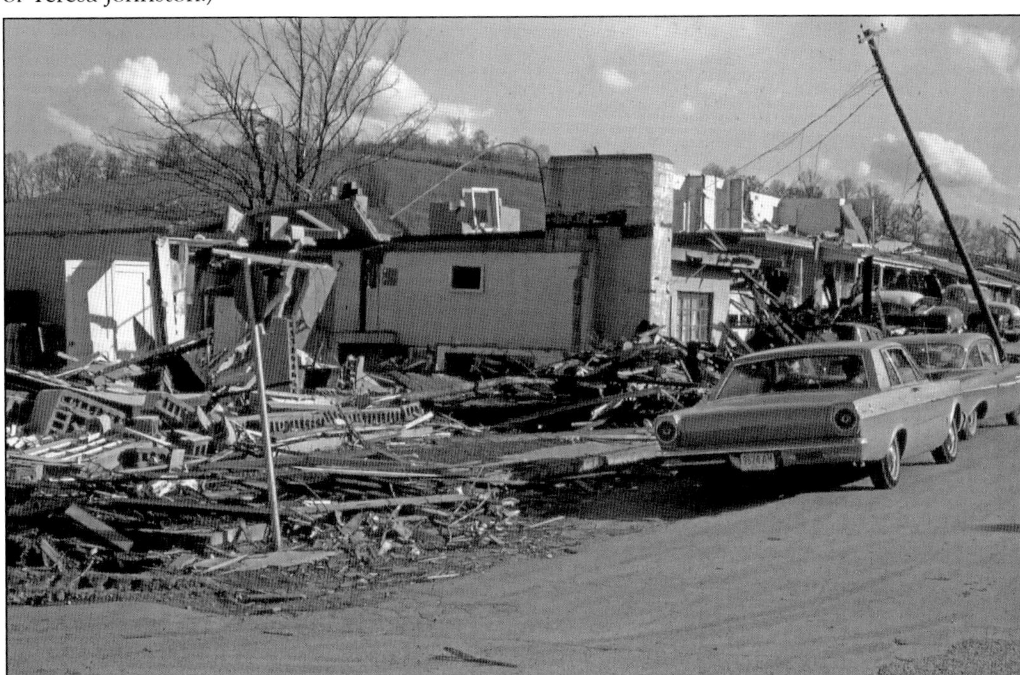

Seven

Pendleton County Historical and Genealogical Society

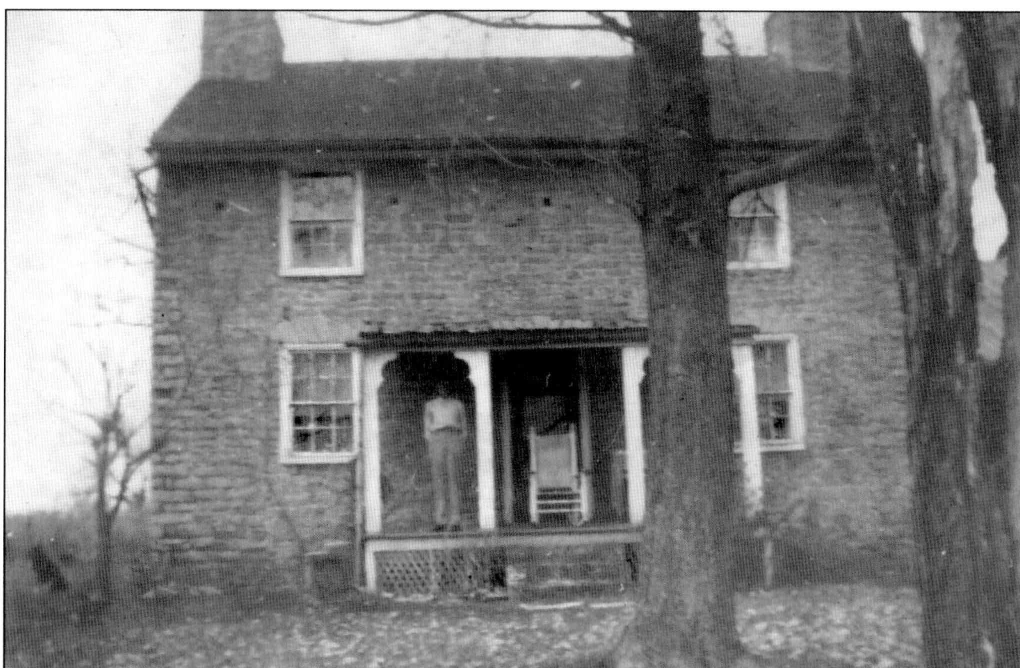

The Fryer stone house stands near Butler, Kentucky. Built by Walter Fryer, construction was started in 1811 and completed in 1813. It was occupied by six generations of the Fryer family until it was sold in 1999. Pendleton County surveyor Howard Johnston and his wife, Alta Mae Fryer Johnston, were the last occupants. (Courtesy of Teresa Johnston.)

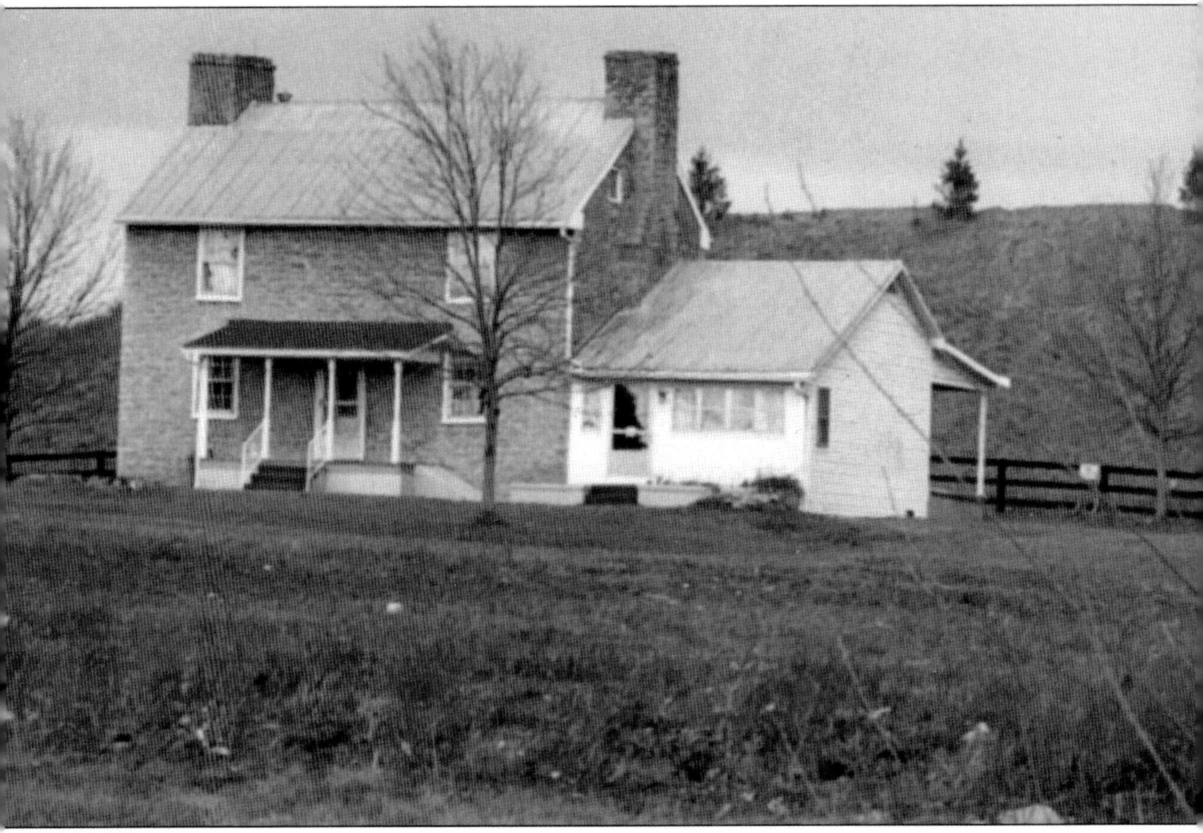

The Fryer stone house, seen here as it looks today, is currently being remodeled by the Pendleton County Historical and Genealogical Society. It has been leased for 100 years from Hilltop Stone, LLC and is serving as the society's home. The building will also house the future Pendleton County Historical Museum, with research materials including copies of the Barton Papers. (Courtesy of Teresa Johnston.)

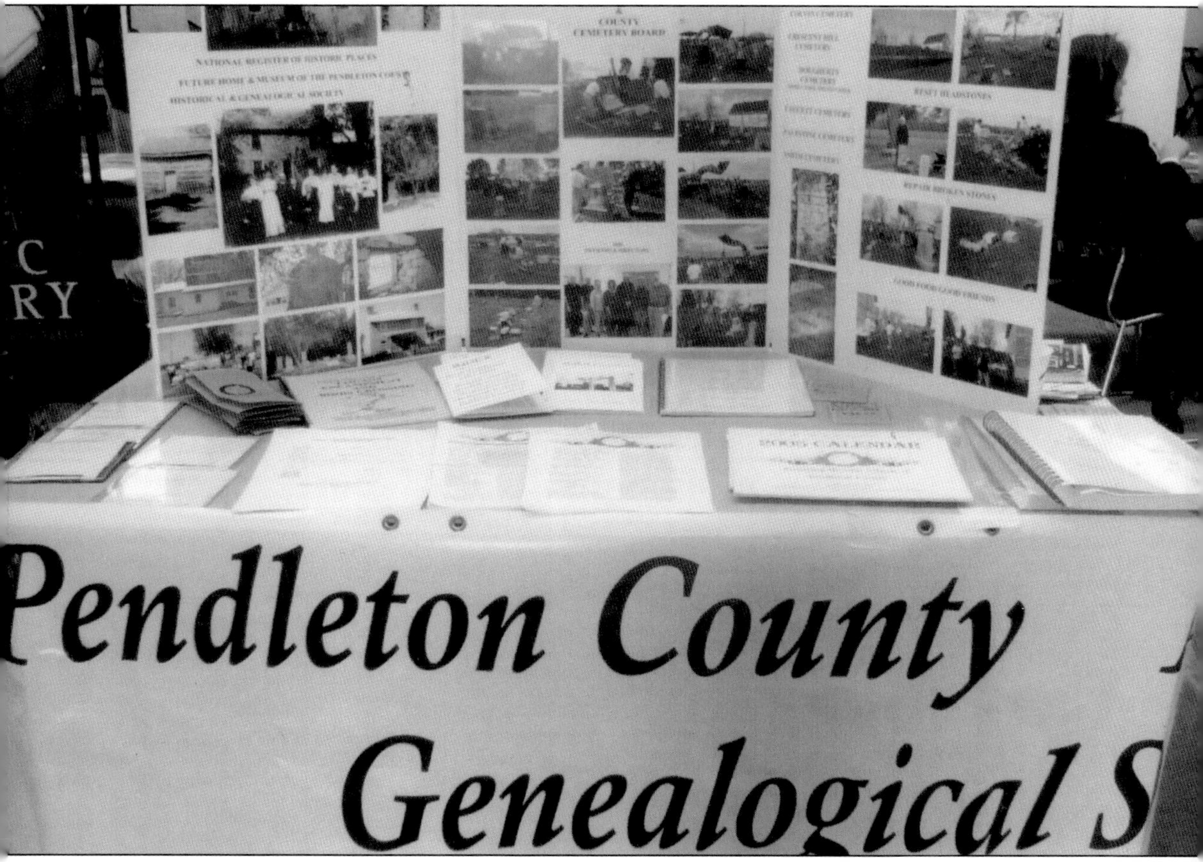

The Pendleton County Historical and Genealogical Society was organized in October 1993 with Larry Ford as the first president. Eric Nagel was the vice-president, Clarita Stephens was secretary-treasurer, and Mildred Belew was the newsletter editor. The current officers are Penny Conrad,president; Henry Aulick,vice-president; Frank Hussung, second vice-president; Mildred Belew,secretary; Ron Moreland,treasurer;and Charlie Pyles, Teresa Johnston,and Sandy Craddock,directors. (Courtesy of Charlie Pyles.)

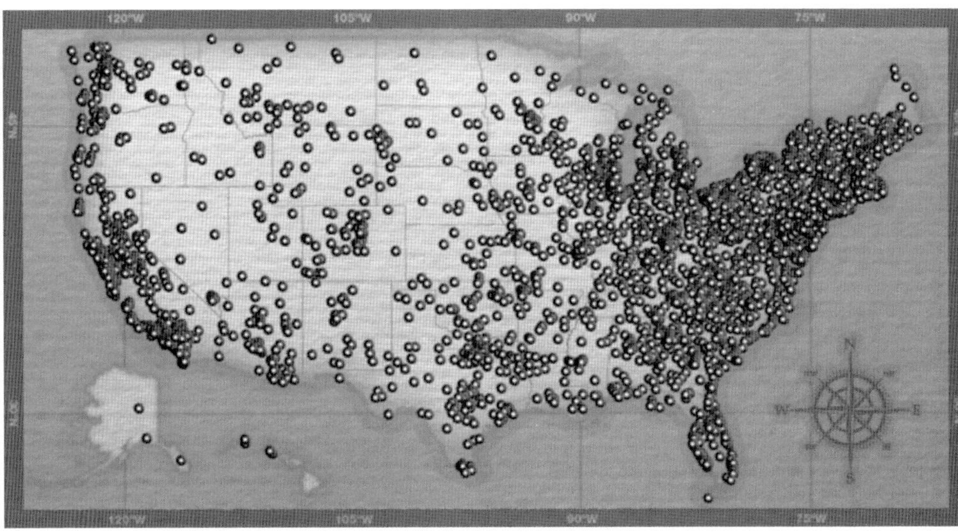

Consistent with our mission to preserve history on a local level, this book was printed in South Carolina on American-made paper and manufactured entirely in the United States. Products carrying the accredited Forest Stewardship Council (FSC) label are printed on 100 percent FSC-certified paper.

MADE IN THE USA